CRITIQUES OF
EVERYDAY LIFE

Everyday life is fast becoming a key concept within the social sciences
and humanities. In this contemporary and highly relevant new book,
Michael E. Gardiner proposes that there exists a counter-tradition
within everyday life theorizing. This counter-tradition has sought
not merely to describe lived experience, but to transform it by
elevating our understanding of the everyday to the status of a critical
knowledge.

In his analysis Gardiner engages with the work of a number of significant theorists and approaches, including:

- The French tradition of everyday life theorizing, from the Sur-
  realists to Henri Lefebvre, and from the Situationist International
  to Michel de Certeau
- Agnes Heller and the relationship between the everyday, ration-
  ality and ethics
- Carnival, prosaics and intersubjectivity in the work of Mikhail
  Bakhtin
- Dorothy E. Smith's feminist perspective on everyday life.

Critiques of Everyday Life demonstrates the importance of an alternative, multidisciplinary everyday life paradigm and offers a myriad
of new possibilities for critical social and cultural theorizing and
empirical research.

Michael E. Gardiner is Associate Professor of Sociology at the
University of Western Ontario.

CRITIQUES OF EVERYDAY LIFE

Michael E. Gardiner

London and New York

First published 2000
by Routledge
11 New Fetter Lane, London EC4P 4EE

Simultaneously published in the USA and Canada
by Routledge
29 West 35th Street, New York, NY 10001

Routledge is an imprint of the Taylor & Francis Group

© 2000 Michael E. Gardiner

Typeset in Garamond by
Exe Valley Dataset Ltd, Exeter
Printed and bound in Great Britain by
TJ International Ltd, Padstow, Cornwall

British Library Cataloguing in Publication Data
A catalogue record for this book is available
from the British Library

Library of Congress Cataloging in Publication Data
Gardiner, Michael, 1961–
Critiques of everyday life/Michael Gardiner.
p. cm.
Includes bibliographical references and index.
1. Life. 2. Social history–Philosophy. 3. Sociology–Philosophy.
4. Lefebvre, Henri, 1905–. 5. Bakhtin, M. M. (Mikhail Mikhaælovich),
1895–1975. 6. Heller, Agnes. I. Title.

BD435. G34 2000
302′/1–dc21   00–020671

ISBN 0–415–11314–8 (hbk)
ISBN 0–415–11315–6 (pbk)

FOR RITA

CONTENTS

ACKNOWLEDGEMENTS

This book has been the product of a rather long period of gestation, interrupted at various points by factors bodily and psychological, as well as numerous changes in institutional affiliation. I would like to thank a number of people at several institutions, not so much for their specific input into this project, but for their unstinting goodwill and moral and intellectual support at various junctures in my career over the last ten years or so: Barry Sandywell, the late Arthur Brittan and Phil Stanworth at the University of York; Arthur W. Frank and Tom Langford at the University of Calgary; Peter Baehr, Volker Meja and Ron Schwartz at Memorial University of Newfoundland; and finally Bob Barsky, Danièle Bélanger, Lori Davies, Julie McMullin, Mireya Folch-Serra, Clive Thomson and especially Chuck Levine at my present home, the University of Western Ontario. I would also like to thank my wonderful parents, George and Mary Gardiner, and express my love and gratitude to my wife and partner, Rita, to whom this book is dedicated and without whom it would never have been completed. I would like to credit Chris Rojek with helping to formulate the specific framework of this project, and to thank Mari Shullaw, the current Sociology editor at Routledge, for her remarkable patience and timely advice. I also thank the anonymous reviewers for their useful comments and constructive criticisms regarding an earlier draft manuscript. Finally, I acknowledge with gratefulness the funding of a Social Science and Humanities Council of Canada post-doctoral grant, which facilitated the research and writing of a number of core chapters in this book.

It is time to wake up, to revive the slogan which, a quarter of a century ago, in May 1968, echoed through the streets of Paris, time to be realistic enough to ask for the impossible, for what our system, its high priests and pundits, its propaganda machine and its mass media have as their task to describe as impossible or, if you prefer, dangerously utopian.

Daniel Singer

Only he who, by decision, has made his dialectical peace with the world can grasp the concrete.

Walter Benjamin

1

INTRODUCTION

The everyday is platitude (what lags and falls back, the residual life with which our trash cans and cemeteries are filled: scrap and refuse); but this banality is also what is most important, if it brings us back to existence in its very spontaneity and as it is lived – in the moment when, lived, it escapes every speculative formulation, perhaps all coherence, all regularity. Now we evoke the poetry of Chekhov or even Kafka, and affirm the depth of the superficial, the tragedy of nullity. Always the two sides meet (the amorphous, the stagnant) and the inexhaustible, irrecusable, always unfinished daily that which escapes forms or structures (particularly those of political society: bureaucracy, the wheels of government, parties). And that there may be a certain relation of identity between these two opposites is shown by the slight displacement of emphasis that permits passage from one to the other, as when the spontaneous, the informal – that is, what escapes forms – becomes the amorphous and when, perhaps, the stagnant merges with the current of life, which is also the movement of society.

Maurice Blanchot

When referring to the phenomenon of everyday life, the great French sociologist and philosopher Henri Lefebvre was fond of mentioning G. W. F. Hegel's maxim 'The familiar is not necessarily the known'. By invoking this cryptic phrase, Lefebvre was striving to put his finger on something that, partly by virtue of its very pervasiveness in our lives, remains one of the most overlooked and misunderstood aspects of social existence. Although he was convinced that critical sociological analysis could shed considerable light on the nature of the everyday and highlight the central role it plays in the social world, Lefebvre was equally certain that there would always remain something fundamentally mysterious and obscure about its workings. Mysterious, yet at the same time substantial and fecund, everyday life is the crucial foundation upon which the so-called 'higher' activities of human beings, including abstract cognition and practical objectifications, are necessarily premised. Accordingly, we must be concerned with redeeming its hidden and oft-suppressed potentials. Rather than compare moments of human creativity to lofty mountain-tops and equate everyday life with plains or marshes, Lefebvre submits that a far better metaphor is to construe the everyday as fertile humus, which is a source of life-enhancing power as we walk over it unnoticed. 'A landscape without flowers or magnificent woods may be depressing for the passer-by', he writes, 'but flowers and trees should not make us forget the earth beneath, which has a secret life and a richness of its own' (1991a: 87).

This is a book about theories of everyday life, the largely taken-for-granted world that remains clandestine, yet constitutes what Lefebvre calls the 'common ground' or 'connective tissue' of all conceivable human thoughts and activities. It is the crucial medium through which we enter into a transformative praxis with nature, learn about comradeship and love, acquire and develop communicative competence, formulate and realize pragmatically normative conceptions, feel myriad desires, pains and exaltations, and eventually expire. In short, the everyday is where we develop our manifold capacities, both in an individual and collective sense, and become fully integrated and truly *human* persons. However, I should make it clear that this is not another primer on mainstream sociologies of everyday life, of which there are many (Douglas *et al.* 1980; Karp and Yoels 1986). Nor is it a substantive study of particular aspects of daily life in contemporary society. Rather, my goal is different, and perhaps more theoretically ambitious: to uncover and explicate a 'subterranean' tradition – or better, a counter-tradition – of thinking about everyday life, one that has been largely ignored or marginalized in the social science literature, at least within the Anglo-American academic world.

It is apparent that the last couple of decades have witnessed a burgeoning interest in the sphere of everyday life, as marked by numerous lines of inquiry established by cultural studies, feminism, media studies and postmodernism. Indeed, we can talk about something of an epistemic shift in this area. Yet there have been few concerted attempts to survey, in a systematic and synoptical fashion, the theories that have underpinned such developments. In general terms, such a counter-tradition evinces a pronounced hostility towards abstract social theorizing (ranging from Saussurean-inspired structuralism to economistic Marxism and Parsonian-style functionalism), and a concomitant stress on the quotidian or non-formalized aspects of social interaction, what Michel Maffesoli (1990) has termed 'sociality'.[1] As such, the theorists and approaches discussed here are concerned with a number of interlocking phenomena that have generally been sidelined within mainstream twentieth-century social theory, such as human affect and emotions, bodily experience and practical knowledges, the role played by 'lived' time and space in the constitution of social experience, language and intersubjectivity, and interpersonal ethics. Such theories have also, as Kaplan and Ross characterize it, been preoccupied with elevating 'lived experience to the status of a critical concept – not merely in order to describe lived experience, but in order to change it' (1987: 1). The perspectives examined here lie on the cusp between a phenomenology that takes the 'fine grain' of everyday life seriously as an integral starting-point of inquiry, and an analysis of wider social and historical developments motivated ultimately by what Jürgen Habermas calls an 'emancipatory interest'.[2] Such a critical approach to the theorization of everyday life strives to overcome the pervasive dichotomy in social science between the objectivism of structuralist approaches and the subjectivistic tendencies of more conventional interpretive theories. Within the context of the present study, I have chosen to focus on the following thinkers and traditions, which I have organized as discrete chapters in roughly chronological order: Dada and Surrealism, Mikhail Bakhtin, Henri Lefebvre, the Situationist International (concentrating on Guy Debord and Raoul Vaneigem), Agnes Heller, Michel de Certeau, and Dorothy E. Smith.[3]

In this introduction, I wish to pursue two major objectives: first, to distinguish the counter-tradition discussed here from such established approaches as ethnomethodology or phenomenology, as well as those more recent theories that gesture towards the problematic of everyday life, especially cultural studies and postmodernism; and secondly, to tease out some of the common threads that link each of the thinkers and traditions outlined in particular chapters. As to the first of these objectives, we can say that, historically speaking, there have been two central impulses within modernist sociology, stretching from its roots in eighteenth-century social philosophy through the classical period of the nineteenth-century to the post war era: the 'system' perspective on the one hand, and a 'micro'-oriented, interpretive approach on the other (Swingewood 1991). For many decades, the system perspective held sway: the central idea here is that culture and society operate as overarching, objective systems that function to integrate the individual into the whole, a perspective exemplified by Comte, Durkheim, Parsons, and orthodox Marxism. According to this view, social actors are effectively 'cultural dopes', to use Harold Garfinkel's term, who internalize passively extant social roles and behavioural norms (whether consensual or a reflection of class-specific interests), thus acting to reproduce, in a largely automatic and unwitting fashion, social structures and institutions. By the end of the nineteenth century, however, a reaction against the system perspective began to gather force, and with it the realization that the human sciences could not be satisfied with the construction of abstract, general principles about how social structures functioned to maintain society as a quasi-organic whole. Accordingly, European *Geistewissenschaften* thinkers like Wilhelm Dilthey, Heinrich Rickert and Max Weber, as well as American pragmatists like George Herbert Mead, claimed that it was not enough simply to describe the functioning of a structure, system or institution. One must also have an interpretive under-standing of the latter's *uses*, of how human beings develop an 'insider's knowledge' of particular social processes and utilize this understanding so as to act in a voluntaristic and creative fashion. The symbolic and intersubjective meanings that people utilize reflexively to comprehend themselves and their world cannot be brushed aside in the quest for a scientific sociology. As such, the social sciences had to come to grips with the contextual aspects of everyday experience *vis-à-vis* the actor's own subjective viewpoint.

In the postwar period, the impact of this interpretive turn was reflected in the emergence of a wide variety of microsociologies, including ethnomethodology, symbolic interactionism, the pheno-menology of Alfred Schütz and Berger and Luckmann, and Erving Goffman's 'dramaturgy'. All of these are, without a doubt, import-ant contributions to the study of everyday life, and their influence remains palpable (Adler and Adler 1987). However, from the perspective of the present study, they are deficient in several crucial respects. First, such approaches can be located firmly within the familiar metatheoretical and epistemological assumptions of academic social science. Although they rail against macrosociology for ignoring the specificities of everyday life and the complex meanings that adhere to the most apparently 'trivial' of human activities, none of them really seek to abandon the pretence to objectivity, scholarly detachment and non-partisanship that has served to legitimate the social sciences for the last 150 years. Although they do focus on the practical accomplishments of skilled social actors in the course of their day-to-day lives, these perspectives tend to reinforce, rather than subvert, the pervasive dichotomy between specialized and non-specialized knowledges, thereby bolstering the authorial power of what André Gorz (1993) calls the 'expertocracy'.[4] Secondly, although such approaches assert that the starting-point of valid sociological knowledge must begin with daily life and its contextual or 'indexical' meanings, the everyday is generally perceived as a relatively homogeneous and undifferentiated set of attitudes, practices and cognitive structures. For Schütz et al., everyday life exists as a 'paramount reality', a pre-constituted world that is necessarily taken-for-granted and viewed as a quasi-natural, unalterable horizon of action by lay members. Everyday life, in this view, corresponds to a stable order that gives social actors what Anthony Giddens (1984) has termed 'ontological security', through the provision of appropriate roles and typified behaviour patterns. Although it is possible to step back from the everyday lifeworld and describe it in more precise, scientific terms, what Schütz refers to as 'second-order' accounts, this level of analysis remains the prerogative of trained social scientists, involving the transcription of mundane practices and knowledges into a more organized, systematic and implicitly superior discursive form (Smith 1987). Hence, the everyday world constitutes an overarching, conformist reality that is transmitted to succeeding generations via the acquisition of language-skills and behavioural norms. The concept of 'everyday life' remains a purely descriptive or analytical concept. Questions about intersubjective ethics or the ideological structuring of everyday consciousness, for instance, do not figure prominently, insofar as actors are held simply to engage in routines and justify them performatively in an *a posteriori* manner.

The formalistic character of this viewpoint is somewhat ironic, given that interpretive sociologies have tried to claim a fidelity to the concrete particularities of social situations and practices. As Alvin Gouldner (1975) has observed, these approaches have generally been ethnographic, empiricist, and covertly positivist in their orientation, despite frequent protestations to the contrary. They do not view the everyday lifeworld as a particularly 'deep' or complex phenomenon in an ontological or hermeneutical sense. Thus, everyday life is construed as an eternal and unsurpassable feature of the social world. Although there might be minor role confusions or value-conflicts, it remains a non-contradictory and essentially unproblematical component of social existence. By contrast, for the theorists discussed in this book, everyday life *does* have a history, one that is intimately bound up with the dynamics of modernity (and, some would argue, postmodernity). Hence, it is riven with numerous contradictions and marked by a considerable degree of internal complexity (Crook 1998). It must be acknowledged that everyday life incorporates a form of 'depth' reflexivity, which is necessary if we are to account for the remarkable ability that human beings display in adapting to new situations and coping with ongoing existential challenges, as well as to explain the enormous cross-cultural and historical variability that daily life manifests. This reflexivity displays both discursive and pre-discursive, embodied qualities, as well as unconscious elements, as Pierre Bourdieu, Anthony Giddens and others have pointed out. Although everyday life can display routinized, static and unreflexive character-istics, it is also capable of a surprising dynamism and moments of penetrating insight and boundless creativity. The everyday is, as Maffesoli puts it, 'polydimensional': fluid, ambivalent and labile. Perhaps we could say that one of the primary goals of the theorists discussed here is to *problematize* everyday life, to expose its contradictions and tease out its hidden potentialities, and to raise our understanding of the prosaic to the level of critical knowledge. Whereas for mainstream interpretive approaches the everyday is the realm of the ordinary, the alternative pursued here is to treat it as a domain that is potentially *extra*ordinary.[5] The ordinary can become extraordinary not by eclipsing the everyday, or imagining we can arbitrarily leap beyond it to some 'higher' level of cognition or action, but by fully appropriating and activating the possibilities that lie hidden, and typically repressed, within it. That everyday life is not as impoverished or habit-bound as conventional social science (of both a macro- and microsociological persuasion) usually assumes is a point that is made forcefully in the following passage from John O'Neill's *The Poverty of Postmodernism*:

> It cannot be sufficiently stressed that *the common-sense world is not a reified and unreflexive praxis*. It is full of art and humour, it is explored in literature, art, song, film and comic strips. Common-sense knowledge is far from being a poor version of science. It is self-critical and, above all,

capable of dealing with the contradictions and paradoxes of social life that otherwise drive sociologists off into utopias, anachronisms, and nostalgias that make ordinary people suspicious of the intellectual's grasp of reality. We ought to reject the social science stereotype of the rigidity of custom, habit and instinct in human affairs.

(1995: 172)

This brings me to my final point regarding mainstream interpretive sociology: that in developing a critical knowledge of everyday life, we must go beyond merely describing the pragmatic activities of social agents within particular social settings. Everyday life cannot be understood in a *sui generis* sense, because we are compelled to relate it analytically to wider sociohistorical developments. We cannot be satisfied with a surface account of ordinary social practices and modes of consciousness, because to do so would remain at the level of what Karel Kosík (1976) calls the 'pseudo-concrete'. That is, we must also be concerned to analyse the asymmetrical *power relations* that exist between a given bureaucratic or institutional system and its users (Warf 1986). The key argument here is that, as Jürgen Habermas (1983, 1987) has frequently pointed out, in the context of modernity systems are dominated by a technocratic or productivist logic. The overriding criterion of success within such systems is their efficient, utilitarian operation, rather than the satisfaction of non-instrumentalized needs as expressed by particular individuals and communities. It is to this technocratic rationality that the 'non-logical logics' of everyday life are generally contrasted and opposed by the theorists examined in this book. Such a focus on ingrained power imbalances also raises the possibility that ideological factors can play a significant role in structuring our 'common-sense' view of the world, and that lay members' accounts of their situation are often partial and circumscribed, if not 'false' in some narrowly epistemological sense, as implied by certain Marxian theories of ideology.[6] Social agents are not 'cultural dopes', but nor are their thoughts and actions fully transparent to them. As Bourdieu cogently notes, whilst people's everyday interpretation of their social world has considerable validity that must be recognized and accorded legitimacy, at the same time we should not succumb to 'the illusion of immediate knowledge' (Bourdieu *et al.* 1991: 250; also Watier 1989). Critical reason and structural analysis therefore have a crucial role to play in exposing such patterns of ideological determination and enhancing what Melvin Pollner (1991) has called a 'radical reflexivity', whereby people can develop a heightened understanding of their circumstances and use this comprehension as the basis of conscious action designed to alter repressive social conditions.

Thus far, I have been concerned to contrast the critical approach to the study of everyday life with mainstream microsociological theories. The differences are, I think, fairly straightforward. However, the situation becomes somewhat more complex if we consider two more recent approaches that, in certain respects, also set out to challenge the received epistemological assumptions and rigid disciplinary boundaries enforced by modernist social science: namely, cultural studies and postmodernism. With respect to the former, it is clear that some notion of 'everyday life' has been a central, even foundational concept in its development, from its origins in the work of Richard Hoggart, E. P. Thompson and Raymond Williams in the 1950s, to the more formal establishment of British cultural studies (the so-called 'Birmingham School') in the 1970s and its more recent extension to Australia, North America, and beyond (Johnson 1986/7). Indeed, many of the figures discussed in this are often cited as key theoretical influences within cultural studies. However, Laurie Langbauer (1992: 47) makes the valuable point that although crucial to the vocabulary and general sensibility of the cultural studies paradigm, everyday life is 'so taken for granted by it, that it is almost never defined', much less examined systematically. Cultural studies has, moreover, become increasingly amorphous and diffuse in recent years, and has lost much of the critical and politically engaged character that it displayed in its original incarnation. The result is a distressing tendency that Meagan Morris (1988) has described as the 'banalization' of cultural studies, whereby the critique of consumer capitalism and socioeconomic inequities has been supplanted by a vague, depoliticized populism. Increasingly, the 'everyday' is evoked in a gestural sense as a bulwark of creativity and resistance, regardless of the question of asymmetries of power, class relations, or increasingly globalized market forces (McChesney 1996; McRobbie 1991).

This brings me to the relationship between critical theories of everyday life and postmodernism, which is a complex issue. Admittedly, there are many similarities: both camps excoriate abstract reason, and acknowledge that human life exhibits many non-rational tendencies, embodied desires and poetical qualities that cannot be captured in the reductive explanatory models favoured by positivist social science; they equally privilege marginalized, 'unofficial' and de-centred spaces and practices over centralized, bureaucratic systems, and seek to give a voice to the silenced; both are critical of the myriad dualisms (mind/matter, nature/culture, masculine/feminine), aporias and blindspots of modernity; and, finally, they both evince an overriding preoccupation with such phenomena as culture, intersubjectivity and language. But there remain crucial differences. The theorists discussed in this study are thoroughly critical of modernity, but in an eminently *dialectical* fashion, acknowledging both its negative and positive qualities. All the thinkers discussed here reject the sort of Cartesian, abstract reason and mind/body dualism that has been the hallmark of instrumental rationality, but without wholly abandoning critical inquiry and sociopolitical analysis. Each asserts the need to engage in *ideologiekritik*, in order to forgo a lapse into a postmodernist relativism.[7] In this, they consistently reject what Alex Callinicos (1985) calls 'textualism', by which he means a reduction of complex social practices to the workings of language or discourse, and they repudiate a politics of the sign, or transgression for its own sake, so long as these are detached from a wider vision of social transform-ation and the full realization of human possibilities. Lefebvre, in particular, was alert to the dangers and limitations of this sort of purely symbolic politics, as expressed through modes of ironization and satirical distanciation endorsed by many contemporary postmodernists:

> Symptomatically, any transgression which ceases to be an act and becomes a state is in fact no more than a flight (needless to say, a flight backwards). Transgression turns into retrogression. It is a prayer in the void, and in spite of substituting an immanence – life, immediate enjoyment – for a dead transcendence, it never gets beyond nihilism; it is a relapse into adolescence, manufactured by and accept-ing oppression – even a relapse into the infantile condition, with its discursive babelism.
>
> (1976: 40–1)

Adherents of the critical approach to the study of everyday life therefore take an explicit ethico-political stance, and place consider-able stress on the potential for individual and collective agency to transform existing social conditions, a strategy that is anathema to practitioners of mainstream social science no less than the more co-opted and compromised versions of postmodernism.[8] The question

9

then arises: what are the central themes that run through the writings of the seemingly disparate thinkers and traditions I have chosen to focus on in this study? First, as intimated above, there is general agreement that everyday life is not a fixed or eternal feature of social life, but that it has a discernable history, and has to be understood in relation to the central experiences and dynamics of Western modernity. Premodern societies formed a relatively coherent, organic totality, and different activities and knowledges were more fully integrated into everyday life (Bauman 1994). Lefebvre (1991a) suggests, for instance, that although everyday life in earlier times did have repetitive elements, these mirrored the rhythms and cycles of nature, and so existence was relatively less alienated than in contemporary society. Similarly, Bakhtin (1984a) and Heller (1978) argue that in late medieval and Renaissance society, the boundaries between high and low culture, and between official and unofficial spheres of activity, were much more fluid and permeable, and daily life was not as rigidly compartmentalized as it is today. Furthermore, as Michel Foucault points out in *Discipline and Punish* (1977), the operation of power in premodern societies was a relatively straightforward and rudimentary affair, one that was transparent to most observers. Bodies were punished in a flagrantly violent and highly visible fashion, but there was little attempt to win over the hearts and minds of the common people to the legitimacy of a particular regime. As such, the broad masses were left to their own devices in most aspects of their daily lives, once a nominal allegiance to the *status quo* was secured. Even the Catholic Church, the most monolithic and pervasive institution in medieval and early modern Europe, had only a minimal influence over the lives of peasants and artisans, and many localized and essentially still pagan customs and rituals continued to persist just beneath the surface of social life (Abercrombie *et al.* 1980; Zijderveld 1982). With the consolidation of modernity, however, the scope of the mechanisms of social control have broadened, encroaching on more and more areas of life. This development has been parallelled by a process of structural differentiation, in which, as Mike Featherstone puts it, 'science, art, philosophy and other forms of theoretical knowledge originally embedded within everyday life become progressively separated and subjected to specialist development, followed by a further phase whereby this knowledge is fed back in order to rationalize, colonize and homogenize everyday life' (1992: 162). Differentiation has promoted what the writer and poet T. S. Eliot called a 'dissociation of sensibilities', and the establishment of a series of pervasive dualisms (nature vs. culture, mind vs. matter) that have served to valorize an abstract idealism at the expense of an embodied, practical rationality. With the transition to modernity, and the fracturing of the social world into a multiplicity of specialized practices, everyday life emerges as something that is 'left over', and hence of little consequence in relation to such 'superior' pursuits as politics, the arts, or science.[9] Nonetheless, we continue to dwell within everyday life in contemporary society; it is the place where routine praxis occurs and concrete bodily and intersubjective needs are formulated and met. It cannot be simply transcended by ideological fiat. But the cycle of daily life is severed progressively from the more 'advanced' sectors of modernity, including technological innovation, industrial production and mass communications. Once established and accorded institutional and ideological support, as Lefebvre notes, it is difficult to circumvent the abstract, formal reason that increasingly dominates our lives and to breach the myriad dualisms that have splintered lived experience. The abstractions of modernity become a kind of substitute for real life, a vicarious existence that is equally a denial and negation of essential, corporeal human powers and potentialities. 'For us', suggests Lefebvre, 'the *dualities* of mind and matter, the ideal and the real, the absolute and the relative, the metaphysical and the tangible, the supernatural and the natural, have become a living duplicity, a lining, a facade, a fake, just impotence and lies lived out under the pretence of thought, poetry and art' (1991a: 123).

The domination of metaphysical reason under the regime of modernity is reflected in the orientation of mainstream social science as well, which typically views society as a set of 'structures' or 'institutions', wherein social actors are motivated solely by a narrow, purposive rationality. Hence, another key argument that runs through the work of all the thinkers discussed here, but particularly in the writings of Certeau, Heller and Smith, is the notion that social science as it has been traditionally practised – and more broadly, the knowledge-forms that are congruent with the rationalized requirements of modernity – is itself a hegemonic enterprise that seeks to impose itself on competing, non-official knowledges. Regardless of the political or ethical sympathies of individual social scientists, the disciplines of sociology, psychology or political studies have been organized in such a way as to participate in the operation of what Michel Foucault has called 'power/knowledge'. This usurpation and devaluation of 'minor', non-specialized knowledges is accomplished by isolating practices from their everyday, intersubjective context and treating them as pure 'facts' or 'datum'. These are formulated as law-like, objective principles and thereby subordinated to the power of the sociological gaze.[10] In embracing the criterion of scientific objectivity, which represents a blatant imposition of power that mainstream interpretive approaches do not substantially reverse, the social sciences have effectively bypassed any engagement with the ethico-political qualities of social relationships, and have instead devoted themselves to the 'construction of representations into laws imposed by the states of things' (Certeau 1986: 200). Bourdieu (1998), for instance, has argued persuasively that abstract, theoretical reason cannot hope to capture all the nuances of everyday practice and the forms of mundane rationality that inform them. The former thereby perpetrates a kind of 'symbolic violence' upon the latter, which serves to bolster the elitism and hyper-specialization and the prevailing patterns of the accumulation of symbolic and cultural capital that have characterized late capitalist societies. Notwithstanding this, a particular form of abstract rationality, one that has come into being within particular sociohistorical circumstances, does not exhaust the possibilities of human experience and consciousness (Benjamin 1983/4). There are other viable manifestations of thought and action that lie outside the formalized knowledges of establishment science and which are not so overtly hostile to the subterranean tempos and qualities of everyday life. Mundane practices are not entirely reducible to 'higher', more scientific descriptions; to suppose this is to adhere to what Wald Godzich calls the 'gnostic conception of rationality', which is symptomatic of 'the sense of loss of historical agency that accompanies the fragmentation of the self characteristic of social abstraction' (1986: xx–xxi). Some aspects of daily life remain hidden and obscure, beyond the understanding of the fully legible 'Cartesian space' that scientific rationalism strives to construct and enforce. 'The everyday escapes', Blanchot reminds us. We must recognize that what is promoted as objective science is merely the 'commonsense' of a narrow and impoverished technocratic rationality. Accordingly, as Queroz usefully puts it, the history of the social sciences

> merges with the permanent production of a cleavage
> between the artificial and transparent languages of science
> and the obscurity of ordinary language. Thus science,
> allegedly neutral and value-free, displays all the character-
> istics of a strategy: it creates institutions which are subject

to standards of productivity and to a hierarchy of experts. The limited space of the institution is a site of power from which the outer world – that is, the object – is analysed, made visible and transparent.

(1989: 36)

The manner in which the processes of modernity and mainstream approaches to social inquiry have affected everyday life serves to highlight another shared theme: the contradictory and fractured, even schizophrenic nature of lived experience in the contemporary era.[11] Everyday life is vulnerable to the effects of commodification and bureaucratic structuring, and exhibits tendencies towards passive consumerism and an inward-looking, unreflective and routinized form. Late capitalism seems especially prone to such phenomena as social atomism, moral nihilism and possessive individualism, wherein personal identity is constructed increasingly through patterns of consumption rather than forms of communal and interpersonal dialogue (Bauman 1992; Shields 1992). Modernity promotes a thorough-going process of *reification* – the transformation of living, dynamic relations between people into static connections between things. Hence, the everyday lifeworld has acquired an artificial triviality and repetitiveness because it is progressively under the thumb of a bureaucratic, functionalist logic. The result is a homogenization of the concrete particularities of everyday lifeworld, an 'emptying out' of the richness and complexity of daily experience – a 'night in which all cows are black', to paraphrase Hegel. This prevents us from grasping the qualitative features of the real; we remain blind to the nature of 'difference' or 'otherness'. What is repressed in modernity, as Michael André Bernstein characterizes it, is precisely 'the force of the prosaic, the counter-authenticity, if you will, of the texture and rhythm of our daily lives and decisions, the myriad of minute and careful adjustments that we are ready to offer in the interests of a habitable world' (1992: 182). Agnes Heller (1984a), for instance, argues that daily life in Western societies is dominated by habit, custom and mechanical routinization, all geared towards an unreflective activity of self-preservation. Likewise, Raoul Vaneigem (1983), one of the main theorists of the Situationist International, asserts that late capitalism is pervaded by a vulgar ethos of 'survivalism' at any cost. The metaphorical richness of language-use in everyday contexts, for example, is replaced by a debased sign-system of increasing rigidity and monological authorial force. Indigenous languages and local

13

dialects are disappearing rapidly under the weight of mass-mediated signifying systems; corporate symbols are becoming omnipresent and visually more streamlined and simplified, an archetypal example being the Nike 'swoosh'. The qualitative meanings that we normally attach to lived space are under assault by innumerable strip-malls, advertising billboards, and the like, which colonize and commodify every nook and cranny of the urban landscape. Time is equally vulnerable to technocratic structuring, as communications and computer technologies have proven remarkably successful in condensing and 'domesticating' time (Simpson 1995). We are filled with horror at the prospect of 'wasted time'. Leisure is no real escape, as Debord and Lefebvre knew well, because it is a highly structured and manipulated experience, the site of pseudo-enjoyment rather than genuine dis-alienation. Everyday life often takes on the form of an 'organized passivity'; it has become alienated and degraded to such an extent that we dream of escaping it in myriad day-dreams, fantasies of metaphysical transcendence, and religious chimeras of every kind (Cohen and Taylor 1976). As Gambacorta cogently summarizes, the 'sense of alienation that pervades this daily life experience [means that] daily gestures establish relationships not with "others" but with "the other" – that is, with the perennial degeneration of every activity into something objectified and divided, with what is perennially remote, inaccessible and a constant source of threat to one's integrity' (1989: 131).

The overarching theme of reification and alienation is something that is common to all the thinkers and traditions discussed in the present study. It is usually identified with Western Marxism, although can also be found in the work of Georg Simmel and other non-Marxist social theorists. Since many of the thinkers I examine here take their cue from a critical Marxist tradition, this is not surprising, but there are certain differences between the theorists under discussion and other, perhaps better-known currents within Western Marxism, particularly the Frankfurt School. Unarguably, the original members of the Frankfurt School, especially Theodor Adorno, Max Horkheimer and Herbert Marcuse, were keenly interested in rescuing and preserving the concrete and the particular from the homogenizing effects of the commodity-form and capitalist social relations. Adorno, for one, was intensely concerned about what he called the 'withering away of experience' in his masterful work *Minima Moralia* (1974), which he believed to be a consequence of 'identity-thinking', the tendency under modernity to conflate the real with a totalizing, abstract system of static concepts. However, the Frankfurt School pursued this line of thinking only in a speculative and philosophical rather than pragmatic, sociopolitical sense; the result, as Ben Agger puts it, is that they viewed the everyday as 'irredeemably pedestrian and commodified' (1998: 142). In the perspective of Adorno *et al.*, techniques of social control had become perfected to such an extent, and 'false consciousness' so pervasive, that moments of non-alienated or emancipated experience could only be glimpsed furtively in the most avant-garde of artworks and forms of theoretical production, in aesthetic and intellectual experiences which, by virtue of their very complexity and symbolic opacity, resisted absorption into what they termed the 'culture industry'. In abandoning the search for tendencies towards progressive social change within the terrain of everyday life itself, the central thinkers of the Frankfurt School could only fall back onto a kind of Weberian pessimism and baroque *kulturkritik* that displayed many elitist and anti-populist tendencies (Anderson 1976; Baugh 1990).[12] For the thinkers discussed in this book, by contrast, *it is the everyday world itself* that is open to redemption, to positive and empowering transformation, although they would not dispute the notion that art, culture or intellectual inquiry are integral to a fully lived human existence. The everyday exhibits a certain strength and resilience that enables it to resist domination by identity-thinking. Despite the best efforts of technocrats, intellectuals and urban planners, beneath the reified ideas and domineering practices of objectivistic social science and bureaucratic reason individuals and communities retain a remarkable ability to combat the drift towards what the Frankfurt School called a 'totally administered world'. So although modernity is marked by a logic of control and domination, the Orwellian nightmare of a thoroughly bureaucratized social existence is always deferred, partly because perfectly controllable systems are simply not possible (as chaos theorists are fond of reminding us), but also because we subvert the total commodification and homogenization of experience through myriad (if sometimes fleeting) expressions of passion, non-logicality and the imaginary. These emancipatory moments are endemic in the everyday, and remain opposed to the utilitarian greyness of official society, overshadowed as it is by the logic of the commodity-form and an ethos of productivism. In the minutiae of everyday life, therefore, we find a polysemy of gestures and symbols the very 'banality' of which is worth savouring. Daily life, as Gambacorta observes, represents 'the most obstinate channel of the emergence of resistance, the perception of possibilities, and the reawakening of the conscience' (1989: 130).[13]

To a certain extent, the everyday has this resistant quality simply because its very presence is not always registered by the panoptic gaze of bureaucratic power; it remains an inchoate and heterodox mix of fluid, multiple and symbolically dense practices and thoughts, a 'black rock that resists assimilation' (Certeau 1984: 60). Everyday life is the realm of the 'messy', the impure, a 'conjunction of habit, desire and accident' (Kaplan and Ross 1987: 3). Pina Lalli (1989) asserts that contemporary Western societies are caught between a 'Faustian' logic of technologically driven control and epistemic certitude on the one hand, and a 'Franciscan' one of community, care, ecological concerns and intimacy on the other. These logics are inextricably intertwined in the contradictory, fractured space of everyday life. And because the Franciscan logic can never be fully contained by the Faustian, everyday activities always express transcendental elements of the imaginary and the utopian, and conform to what the philosopher of utopia Ernst Bloch has called the 'principle of hope'.[14] So everyday life evinces an irreducibly imaginative and symbolic dimension, and it cannot simply be written off as the realm of the trivial and inconsequential. It is the very 'messiness' of daily life, its unsystematized and unpredictable quality, that helps it escape the reifying grip of nomothetic social science and technocratic planning. As Blanchot suggests, the everyday constitutes 'a utopia, and an Idea, without which one would not know how to get at either the hidden present, or the discoverable future of manifest beings' (1987: 13). Further- more, for the thinkers discussed here, especially Lefebvre and Bakhtin, the human body constitutes a focal point of resistance, because it has an organic vitality that cannot be easily suppressed. Whereas for Foucault the body is best understood as an 'empty signifier' that can be reconstructed *ad infinitum* through the operation of external discourses of power, according to Lefebvre *et al.* the body manifests sensuous, inarticulate desires and impulses that cannot be fully colonized by rationalized systems. Human embodiment retains the trace of a longing for communal solidarity, of intense collective experience and action, and of the need for physical proximity and intimacy with concrete others: 'the *body* makes its reappearance as one of the elements and foundations of subversion, rather than some "knowledge" or other' (Lefebvre 1976: 74). So it is in the apparently ordinary gestures of the everyday, the unspoken desires of the body and 'microscopic' expressions of care

16

and solidarity, where the redemptive promise of everyday life continues to persist, in the interstices of more formalized social relations and organizational structures. The everyday 'marks the site not only where people are determined in ways they cannot see, but where they project and imagine utopically how to think outside and elude what determines thought and imagination' (Langbauer 1992: 51).

To recapitulate the central argument thus far: although the possibility remains that the complexity, depth of experience, and intensity of interpersonal relationships located within everyday life will be impoverished, this sphere also contains resistant or counter-hegemonic qualities that point towards the possibility of a radical dis-alienation and full 'humanization' of social life. Estrangement, though highly ingrained and reflected in the more routinized and manipulated qualities of daily existence, is not a permanent feature of the human condition, as existentialists like Heidegger and Sartre generally assumed. This lamentable state of affairs can be super-seded through acts of individual and collective self-realization. The everyday must therefore be understood dialectically; it is simul-taneously an alienated and potentially liberated state (Gottdiener 1996). 'Even at its most degraded, the everyday harbors the possibility of its own transformation; it gives rise, in other words, to desires which cannot be satisfied within the weekly cycle of production/consumption', assert Kaplan and Ross. 'It is in the midst of the utterly ordinary, in the space where the dominant relations of production are tirelessly and relentlessly reproduced, that we must look for utopian and political aspirations to crystallize' (1987: 3). This emphasis on the vitality of the utopian impulse as it is located within everyday life constitutes another significant feature that tends to characterize all the theorists discussed in this book. However, this is not what is generally identified with utopianism – that is, an abstract model of social perfection articulated by intellectuals and social elites, projected into an unknowable future, and imposed on a recalcitrant reality. This 'blueprint' paradigm of utopianism, which is a salient feature of modernity that has been excoriated (not without some justification) by conservatives and postmodernists alike, is not espoused by Lefebvre, Certeau *et al.* Rather, the utopian moment is emblematic of a longing for a different, and better way of living, a reconciliation of thought and life, desire and the real, in a manner that critiques the *status quo* without projecting a full-blown image of what a future society should look like. In this sense, utopianism is a sensibility that is oriented towards futurity and cognizant of the possibilities of social change as these are inscribed within the fabric of daily life: '*we are all utopians*', as Lefebvre asserts, 'as soon as we wish for something different' (1984: 75; also Gardiner 1995; Levitas 1993).[15]

This emphasis on utopianism raises, in turn, the issue of ontology. Although it would seem axiomatic to claim that the social world is constructed actively by human beings (albeit under specific conditions inherited from the past, as Marx pointed out, and within certain natural constraints), in the context of modernity our world generally appears, not as an ever-developing process, but as a reified, thing-like entity. Kosík (1976: 24) argues convincingly that the identification of what is immediately present to consciousness as the alpha and omega of reality is symptomatic of what he calls the 'atomist-rationalist' conception of the world. This refers to a worldview in which reality is held to be coterminous with simple elements and empirical facts, a perspective that has dominated Western philosophy from Descartes and Leibnitz to the twentieth century. The reduction of the world to that which is directly observable and quantifiable represents for Kosík and other critics a simplification and impoverishment of reality, one that dovetails historically with the economic imperatives of capitalism and the technological domination of nature (Leiss 1972; Sohn-Rethel 1978). In isolating elements from the complex, dialectical whole that conjoins nature and society, we fail to see the inherent tendencies towards change and transformation in our world. This static, atomistic cosmology – which simultaneously reflects and legitimates the *status quo* – therefore represents the fetishization of an alienated experience, what Kosík describes as 'the projection of certain *petrified* historical conditions into the consciousness of the subject' (1976: 5). How, then, are the effects of reification to be understood critically and resisted? Put differently, how do we encourage the realization that the social and natural worlds are *processual* in character, complex amalgams of positive and negative forces that resist any tendency towards stasis and fixity?

In the everyday life perspective examined here, reification is generally subverted in two ways. The first strategy concerns the development of what Kosík calls the 'dialectical-critical' method, which, unlike the atomistic-rationalist conception, sensitizes us to the mediatedness of things, their complex interconnections, and their relation to the whole. It is a form of knowledge that is ultimately rooted in sensuous human activity, or praxis, within the terrain of daily life, but that also incorporates a broader, more synoptic sociohistorical perspective as well. Lefebvre, for instance, advocated a 'return to the concrete', but he realized that the only way to consummate this project was to study the everyday in a critical, sociological sense, to expose its mystified character and to grasp its inherent contradictions, ambivalences and emancipatory tendencies. This, in turn, relied on a conception of what he called the 'total man' (sic, and passim) – that is, some notion of the totality of human qualities, experiences and potentialities, some of which are repressed or distorted under capitalist social relations, but which must remain a distant horizon, a heuristic that can only be approximated, and never fully realized.[16] The critique of everyday life, in other words, must be attuned to all facets of human existence: the poetic, irrational, corporeal, ethical and affective. Hence, we can locate in this tradition a 'passionate critique', one that parallels Ernst Bloch's argument that critical thought must incorporate, in addition to the 'cold stream' of logical sociological investigation and analytical rigour, a 'warm stream' of impassioned and creative speculation that strives to transcend the conceptual closure effected by dominant ideological discourses. Only then will we be able to recognize a 'difference in what is possible which will allow us to stand back from this greyness of the "already there" in order, precisely, to criticize it' (Trebitsch 1991a: xvii).

Secondly, and less abstractly, we are admonished to circumvent reification by locating embryonic forms of transformative social change within the hidden recesses of everyday life itself, particularly in those moments when the ossified and reified structures of modern society are defamiliarized and exposed to critical consciousness. 'Everyday life harbors the texture of social change', write Kaplan and Ross, and 'to perceive it at all is to recognize the necessity of its conscious transformation' (1987: 4). So critique is not a purely intellectual process; it must be in synchronicity with the actual sociohistorical process itself and the 'base-line' of everyday life. Only then, as Lefebvre suggests, can we transform abstract thought into a 'dialectical consciousness of life, in life: unity of the mediate and immediate, of the abstract and concrete, of culture and natural spontaneity' (1991a: 76). Whereas dominant ideologies define and sanction certain patterns of life as 'natural' or 'inevitable' – which helps to give the everyday the unreflexive and taken-for-granted quality that such phenomenologists as Berger and Luckmann or Schütz allude to – such transgressive moments problematize, 'make strange', and thereby subvert the ideological and bureaucratic structuring of everyday life. In Eugene Lunn's words, these moments

19

operate to 'freshen perceptions and cleanse the senses and language of routine, habitual, and automatic responses, to "defamiliarize" expected and ordinary connections between things in favour of new, and deeper ones' (1982: 34). When such disruptions of daily routines occur, and actors can no longer rely on commonsensical notions and typified behavioural responses, we are able to examine critically prevailing traditions and received ideas, and our receptivity to alternative modes of being, what Bakhtin called the 'buds and shoots of new potentialities', is heightened dramatically. Different thinkers examined in this book refer to divergent types of such phenomena: the Surrealists, for instance, looked at the 'marvellous', poetic flashes that irrupted into everyday life in the most unexpected situations and defied our habitualized expectations. Lefebvre, for his part, evoked the 'festival' as an example of a spontaneous, ecstatic and collective affirmation of transfigured social relationships, in a manner that both transcended and enriched everyday life, as did the Situationists, who also referred to such premodern forms of celebratory sociality as the potlatch. Bakhtin, likewise, found succour in the 'carnivalesque', which for him revealed the arbitrariness of not only established linguistic or literary conventions, but also a whole range of institutional arrangements and social roles right down to our conceptions of history, of individuality and sexuality, and even of time, space and nature. Carnival, writes Bakhtin, 'discloses the potentiality of an entirely different world, of another order, another way of life [which] is lived by the whole man, in thought and body' (1984a: 48). All such forms of defamiliarization encourage the conceptualization of existing modes of experience and perception from a different point of view, allowing us to grasp the reification of social relations under capitalism and bureaucratic socialism, and demonstrate that other, less hierarchical and exploitative social relations are possible. They are all examples of what Bloch called the *novum*, by which he meant the periodic introjection of the radically new into the apparently stable, and which makes its appearance in different forms and unexpected historical junctures.

A final theme is a concern with ethics and intersubjectivity, which is especially pronounced in the writings of the early Bakhtin, Certeau and Heller. In challenging what Robert Stam (1989) calls the 'hermeneutical nihilism' that marks both postmodernism and scientistic positivism, we must affirm that human rationality is, as Certeau contends, 'in its fundamental workings, *ethical*' (1986: 220). Under modernity, our behaviour becomes increasingly 'automatic' and self-interested. By living according to pre-scripted narratives and rigid behavioural schemas, our moral sense is atrophied. We know 'how' to do things, in a purely technical or pragmatic capacity, but we no longer know 'why' we do them, because of the schism between purposive and substantive rationality that Max Weber was concerned to analyse. This 'ethical passivity' must be overcome: each person has to make meaningful their own immediate space of existence and relate to others dialogically, rather than mono-logically, to use Bakhtin's terminology. In Heller's view, for instance, individuals in the context of modern social relations find it extremely difficult to realize themselves as fulfilled, creative and non-alienated creatures. The result is that people fixate obsessively on the minutiae of their daily lives, and what is socially 'generic' – that is, the gamut of species-specific powers and potentialities – are repressed, and remain unappropriated. For Heller, everyday life under modernity (as opposed to the Renaissance, for example) is an alienated form of existence, because instrumental thinking and acting dominate our lives, and the concrete 'other' disappears as a genuine dialogical partner. Revelling in a kind of solipsistic particularism gives us the illusion of autonomous freedom, but a genuine moral attitude must be attuned to the demands of more universalistic notions of human responsibility and freedom, based on such overarching considerations as mutual recognition, inter-personal dialogue, and what she calls 'radical tolerance'. In taking this stance, we must go beyond the subject–object paradigm charac-teristic of modernity, and opt instead for a 'subject–subject' per-spective, one that is marked by the interaction of 'a plurality of authors and contracting parties', whereby a 'hierarchy of know-ledges is replaced by a mutual differentiation of subjects' (Certeau 1986: 217). We are all participants, whether 'specialists' or not, in the construction of a shared discourse, a ceaseless dialogue through which we should aim at a continuous reinterpretation and revitaliz-ation of meaning and value within the horizon of our everyday lives.

By way of a concluding remark, I do not want to give the impression that the work of the particular thinkers and traditions discussed in this study is marked by some sort of overarching, totalizing unity. To imply this would be to obscure the differences between them and impart to the reader a distorted and misleading picture. For instance, whilst there is a clear intellectual lineage that runs throughout the French tradition, from Dada and Surrealism though Lefebvre and the Situationists to Certeau, this development is marked by significant conceptual, epistemological and sociopolitical divergences. As an example, whereas the Surrealists were enamoured with Freudian notions of the poetic qualities of dreams and the unconscious and preoccupied with essentially aesthetic questions, Lefebvre and the Situationists found little of value in psychoanalytic concepts and moved the focus from art *per se* to a broader sociocultural perspective. (And although Debord was one of his students, Lefebvre found Debord's notion of the construction of alternative 'situations' too abstract and overly intellectualized.) Certeau, however, was influenced strongly by one of Freud's most prominent disciples, the French psychoanalyst Jacques Lacan. Moreover, whereas Lefebvre and the Situationists felt that human alienation and reification were so deeply rooted that a supersession of consumer capitalism and a complete transformation of society was required – although even Lefebvre found Situationist politics too ultra-leftist for his tastes – Certeau was more concerned with the exploration of transient moments of creativity and subversive tactics within the parameters of the existing system. By contrast, Agnes Heller's work on everyday life develops out of Georg Lukàcs's version of Hegelian Marxism, especially his notion of *Alltäglichkeit* (the 'ordinariness' of everyday life), and she tends to concentrate more on questions of an ethical or existentialist sort. For her part, Dorothy Smith's approach has multiple influences, ranging from Marxian political economy to critical phenomenology (especially Merleau-Ponty) and various microsociologies, but her writings are most distinctive in that they strive to incorporate recent advances in feminist theory in order to explain how gender-inflected social practices and modes of consciousness impact on everyday life.[17] Finally, Bakhtin's early writings on 'prosaic' forms of intersubjectivity are derived mainly from the neo-Kantian and phenomenological traditions; his later encounter with Marxism was mediated by the more straightforwardly Marxist writings of certain members of the so-called 'Bakhtin Circle', especially Pavel Medvedev and V. N. Voloshinov. Bakhtin's relationship to Marxism is by no means clear-cut, and continues to be a source of intense scholarly controversy; however, it is clear that the sociological and Marxian influences in his writings tended to increase over time, reaching their apotheosis with his most overtly utopian and politicized work, *Rabelais and His World*.

Such differences are, however, more a matter of emphasis than substance. As such, I remain confident that the reader will discover enough congruities in the various approaches I discuss here to give this book a continuity and thematic coherence. It is therefore to be hoped that this study will constitute a useful resource for further investigations into the theory and practical transformation of everyday life. I conclude with the following words from John O'Neill, whose work stands as something of a testament to the importance of the critical everyday life perspective and the potentially innovative role it can play in reorienting and reinvigorating the project of emancipatory social theory. 'The sociologist who neglects the claims of everyday life', writes O'Neill,

> promotes the realm of crisis. Forgetful of one's attachment to everyday life, he or she then speaks of 'discovering' social reality. This way of talking, however, overlooks the massive fact of the *already known* everyday world. [The] alternative to this attention to the commonplace is to treat people as things, which is to ally sociology with the forces that already seek to dominate them or to bring about their compliant subjection. Much of the 'scientificity' of the study of humans is already in the paid service of this project of political control. [The] defence of everyday life, of common-sense knowledge and values constitutes the radical task of interpretive sociology. It requires that sociologists be prepared to set aside their narcissism in order to work as the underlabourers in the world of everyday life with which in all other respects they retain kinship.
>
> (1995: 174)

2

DADA AND SURREALISM: POETICS OF EVERYDAY LIFE

Dada is the only savings bank that pays interest in eternity.
Richard Huelsenbeck

Surrealism appears to me in its essentials as a sort of rage, a
rage against the existing state of things.
Georges Bataille

INTRODUCTION

Dada and Surrealism are widely regarded as two of the most
significant and influential avant-garde cultural movements of the
twentieth century. Today, when many original Surrealist images
adorn everything from advertising billboards to compact discs, it is
perhaps all too easy to overlook both the radicalism of the original
Dada and Surrealist traditions and the depth of the sociocultural
critique of modern civilization they articulated. Specifically, Dadaists
and Surrealists identified *everyday life* under modernity as the central
locus of sociocultural inquiry, and they felt strongly that any viable
politics of liberation would have to be fought on this terrain. Daily
life under capitalism, they believed, was becoming increasingly
degraded, routinized and 'cretinized', in that the individual's
capacity for autonomous action and creative self-expression was
being squandered in the pursuit of material wealth and social status.
Above all, bourgeois morality demanded the *sacrifice* of personal
happiness and well-being to a series of rarefied abstractions –
honour, discipline, family, country and capital. As Tristan Tzara,
one of the original founders of Dada, observed: 'all these notions had
once answered to human needs, now nothing remained of them but
a skeleton of conventions' (cited in Lewis 1990: 3). The successful

24

pursuit of these goals required a blind adherence to rigid, constraining social roles and a narrow utilitarian rationalism that robbed people of their individuality and their ability to realize their true desires – a dehumanizing situation that the early twentieth-century Viennese novelist Robert Müsil summed up in the haunting phrase 'men without qualities'.

Many of these sceptical attitudes had existed for some time in European intellectual circles – for example, in the various Romantic reactions to industrialization and Enlightenment thought (Sayre and Löwy 1984). However, Dada and Surrealism evinced an uncompromising and iconoclastic character that represented a 'total' critique of Western civilization, one that was often allied with radical or revolutionary politics and that went far beyond the nostalgic musings of the Romantics. For instance, rather than adopt the Romanticist practice of treating the aesthetic or poetic realm as a kind of idealized refuge from the spiritual and moral blight of modernity, Dada and Surrealism used cultural and artistic forms and techniques to mock and satirize the manifold alienations and moral failings of bourgeois society, with an eye to its complete transformation. What undoubtedly prompted this 'total' critique – which drew not only art but politics, lifestyle, the family, morality and urbanism into its orbit – was the unparalleled destruction and slaughter of World War One, which revealed unequivocally the gulf between the technical achievements of capitalism and its manifest failure to end human suffering and exploitation. After the European conflagration began in 1914, bourgeois values rang increasingly hollow, and such protean avant-garde movements as Symbolism and Cubism mutated into something with a much more subversive and utopian edge. Looking at these movements, Stewart Home observes, 'the essential features of twentieth-century Utopianism become apparent. The partisans of this tradition aim not just at the integration of *art* and *life,* but of all human activities. They have a critique of social separation and a concept of totality' (1988: 5). Yet however firmly Dada and Surrealism can be located in the tradition of utopian thought, they clearly represented a special manifestation of the utopian impulse. That is, rather than locate the 'good society' in a past 'golden age', or in a distant and probably unobtainable future, they sought utopia in the here and now, through the transfiguration of everyday life.

A great deal has been written about Dada and Surrealism over the years since they first appeared, both *pro* and *contra*, and what follows is not intended to be a comprehensive discussion of the aesthetic or artistic practices of this tradition. Instead, I seek to focus on the more overtly sociopolitical components of Dadaist and Surrealist thought and practice, as these pertain to the critical interrogation of daily life. It will be my contention that the critique of everyday life originally developed by Dada and Surrealism has had a significant (and oft-overlooked) impact on subsequent accounts of the 'everyday' that have proliferated subsequently in twentieth-century social and cultural theory. Indeed, we can trace a direct line of influence from Dada and Surrealism to the work of Henri Lefebvre, who was a close friend of Tristan Tzara and a participant in the 'Bureau of Surrealist Inquiries' during the 1920s, and, via the quixotic and short-lived 'Lettrist' movement, to the ideas of Guy Debord and Raoul Vaneigem, the central figures of the Situationist International.[1] Less directly, or else by way of reaction, Dadaist and Surrealist notions have coloured many other perspectives, many of which are discussed in this book, as well as the writings of Benjamin and certain postmodernist ideas.

DADA: THE 'CRUSHING JOKE'

The precise origins and influences of Dada are somewhat mysterious, and subject to much apocryphal and partisan myth-making. However, it is generally agreed that its most obvious avant-garde precursor was the Italian Futurist movement. The Futurists, led by the flamboyant Filippo Marinetti, eschewed the purely technical innovations of the Cubists – for example, the geometrical fracturing of the represented object in the paintings of Braque and Picasso – and pioneered the notion that an avant-garde movement should encompass not merely painting or writing but a complete reconstruction of the lived environment and the development of new subjectivities. To this end, the Futurists developed bold innovations in architecture, fashion and language. (Marinetti even published a 'futurist cookbook', intended to bring the jaded palates of his fellow citizens into line with the dictates and rhythms of the technological age.) Futurism also called for direct political intervention, although in practice these were mainly symbolic affairs (Davies 1988). The Futurists had a genius for self-publicity and successfully utilized the emerging mass-media to further their own agenda. They also perfected the use of staged provocations to draw public attention to their cause and wrote numerous 'manifestos', the most infamous of which advocated flooding the great museums of Venice and referred to modern warfare as a 'great purifier'.

However, Futurism was a rather ephemeral affair – although it acquired a considerable following in Russia, including the notable poet Vladimir Mayakovsky – and its sociopolitical critique of bourgeois society remained unsystematic and largely ineffectual. In any event, it was difficult to celebrate war in the twentieth century as a 'great purifier' once the carnage of World War One itself began in earnest (Eksteins 1989). To many individuals caught up in the struggle, the war's brutally imperialist and nationalistic character was a clear demonstration of the bankruptcy of technological and capitalist society. In essence, Dada arose out of the failure of the prewar avant-gardes to develop a coherent critique of modern life in its totality, combined with widespread domestic dissatisfaction in combatant nations caused by enforced conscription, rationing and military setbacks. Switzerland, being neutral, was a natural magnet for pacifists, deserters and intellectual dissenters who could congregate, write and speechify without fear of military censorship or incarceration. Consequently, it was in Switzerland in 1916 – specifically, the cosmopolitan and predominantly German-speaking city of Zürich – where the origins of the international Dada movement can be traced.

Dada's original members included the German nationals Hugo Ball, his wife Emmy Hennings, Richard Huelsenbeck, and Hans Richter, the Alsatian Hans Arp, and the Romanians Tristan Tzara and Marcel Janco. They participated in poetry readings and art exhibitions before combining their energies and talents in an artistic cabaret, the legendary Cabaret Voltaire. 'Dada' was the slogan eventually given to describe the performances, allegedly chosen at random from a dictionary, either by Tzara or Huelsenbeck. (Dada is French for 'hobby-horse', 'baby-talk' in German, 'dice' in Italian; in essence, a nonsense term.) The cabaret, which scandalized the sedate bürgers and artisans of Zürich, included musically inept performances of so-called 'Negro jazz', doggerel and nonsense verse (dubbed 'automatic poetry'), 'noise poetry' (or bruitism), and various collective performances, including one that featured poetry readings, drum-banging and singing – all done simultaneously. Such performances showed an obvious contempt for established authority and a healthy disregard for nationalistic chauvinisms. These events also prompted police harassment, although Lenin, coincidentally living only a few doors away, was free to receive visitors and to plot the overthrow of Tsarism in Russia. (The irony of this has been acknowledged by many commentators, as well as the original Dadaists themselves.) Tzara's rather imaginative description of one evening at the Cabaret Voltaire, from his *Zürich Chronicle*, captures something of the anarchic spontaneity of such events:

> February 26, 1916 Huelsenbeck arrives – bang! bang! bangbangbang. Without opposition year perfume of the beginning. Gala night – simultaneous poem 3 languages, protest noise Negro music/Hoosenlatz Hoosenlatz/piano Typperary Laterna magica demonstration last proclamation!! invention dialogue!! Dada! latest novelty!!! bourgeois syncope, Bruitist music, latest rage, song Tzara dance protests – the big drum – red light, policemen – songs cubist paintings post cards song Cabaret Voltaire – patented simultaneous poem Tzara Hoosenlatz and van Hoddis Huelsenbeck Hoosenlatz whirlwind Arp-two-stem demands liquor smoke towards the bells/a whispering of: arrogance/ silence Mme Hennings, Janco declaration, transatlantic art= the people rejoice star hurled upon the cubist tinkle dance.
>
> (cited in Richter 1965: 223)

Nothing escaped the corrosive gaze of the Zürich Dadaists: all social, political, religious, academic and moral values were considered a fair target for satire and derision. Mocking laughter and a kind of 'gallows humour' were also felt to be effective and appropriate methods of attacking the *status quo*. Little was felt to be of legitimate value in a world where mechanized death and mass destruction were justified by the emptiest and most hypocritical of abstractions, and where a kind of collective madness seems to have gripped the entire continent. 'The sustained, angry intensity generated by the Zürich group', writes Alan Young, 'was directed against the institutions and values of the Western world: nationalism, patriotism, militarism, capitalism, and culture in the form of art. They were enraged by what they considered to be the smug self-satisfaction of bourgeois institutions, especially the deep-rooted belief in natural order, authority, and progress' (1981: 15). Art was singled out for special abuse, since it had long been trumpeted by the bourgeoisie as the finest repository of lofty ideals and expressive and technical achievements. According to the Dadaists, art in modern society was thoroughly ideological, in Marx's original sense of the term. While it projected a realm of harmony and formal perfection, in reality bourgeois culture masked and thereby justified human degradation and the persistence of social divisions. In short, Dada developed a social critique of culture, one that highlighted the contradiction between the aesthetic promise of art and its repressive social and ideological functions. In this, Dada developed a position that anticipated the 'immanent critique' later developed by the Frankfurt School, especially Herbert Marcuse's notion of 'affirmative culture'.[2] As Huelsenbeck asserted, 'The Dadaist considers it necessary to come out against art because he has seen through its fraud as a moral safety valve. [Art] (including culture, spirit, athletic club), regarded from a serious point of view, is a large-scale swindle' (1971: 50).

It is significant that Huelsenbeck does not restrict his negative comments to 'art' in the traditional sense, by which is generally meant painting, sculpture or works of fiction. This is because Dada launched a wide-ranging attack on bourgeois society in all of its manifestations, including the underlying forms of rationality that underpinned modernity. Everyday life under modern capitalism was marked by repetitive and stultifying labour justified by the necessities of production, a renunciation of pleasure, and a fetishism of the 'facts', what Huelsenbeck termed a 'vulgar utilitarianism'. Gabrielle Buffet, wife of French Dadaist Francis Picabia, declared that 'Dada aspires to escape from everything that is common or ordinary or sensible. Dada does not recognize any tradition, any influence, or indeed any limits. Dada is a spontaneous product of life: a sort of cerebral mushroom which can appear and grow in every soil. Dada cannot be defined: it reveals itself' (cited in Coutts-Smith 1970: 23). This quotation nicely summarizes some of the key elements of the Dadaist vision: a nihilistic and often violent rejection of traditional values and beliefs, a libertarian or anarchistic stress on individual freedom unconstrained by proffered social roles and norms, and a celebration of spontaneity and unfettered creativity. 'Freedom' in the Dadaist lexigraphy represented emancipation from established order, logic and good sense, from the accepted and the familiar. This helps to explain the Dadaist fascination with chance, random probabilities, and unplanned configurations. Tzara, for instance, made poetry by cutting out words and phrases from magazines and newspapers, putting them in a bag, and re-assembling them at random. Similarly, in the area of visual experimentation, a frustrated Arp once tore up one of his drawings and discovered that the chance pattern the pieces formed on the floor of his apartment exactly captured the effect he had long been striving to attain through the application of formal logic. Artists like Arp and Kurt Schwitters began to incorporate fragments of daily life – bits of clothing, newspaper headlines, bottlecaps – into their multi-media collages, resulting in strange and unfamiliar juxtapositions and the production of new patterns of meaning. This 'collage aesthetic', which led directly to such now-familiar avant-garde techniques as photo- and film-montage and 'found' poetry, was part of a wider project to develop an entirely new language and a new aesthetic. It aimed to liberate humankind from the nightmare of the past weighing on the brain of the living, to paraphrase Marx, and grew out of an intense aspiration to create a relevant culture, one that took everyday life seriously as the essential locus of human dreams, hopes and desires. 'The highest art', Huelsenbeck wrote, 'will be that which in its conscious content presents the thousand-fold problems of the day' (1970: 23). Such Dadaist interventions represented a stark refusal to accept daily life as it was currently constituted. Dada suggested impudently that the routines and conventions that ordered everyday existence could be unmade and reconstructed along very different and more imaginative lines. From such a new vantage point, the individual could 'look down upon the absurdities of the "real" and earnest world' (Richter 1965: 51). If fidelity to 'common sense' meant an internalization of illegitimate authority and a wilful blindness to human suffering and destruction, then common sense itself had to be demolished along with everything else that smacked of the old world. By embracing such intuitive procedures of free association and alogic rather than accepting passively the dictates of causal 'necessity' and personal sacrifice, Dada sought to overcome the alienations of technological society and tap the well-springs of an unconstrained creativity. As Tzara wrote in his 1918 'Dada Manifesto':

Every product of disgust capable of becoming a negation of the family is Dada; a protest with the fists of its whole being engaged in destructive action: *Dada; knowledge of all the means rejected up until now by the shamefaced sex of comfortable compromise and good manners: Dada; abolition of logic, which is the dance of those impotent to create: Dada; of every social hierarchy and equation set up for the sake of values by our valets: Dada; every object, all objects, sentiments, obscurities, apparitions, and the precise clash of parallel lines are weapons for the fight: Dada; abolition of memory; Dada, abolition of archaeology: Dada; abolition of prophets: Dada; abolition of the future: Dada; absolute and unquestionable faith in every god that*

is the immediate product of spontaneity . . . Freedom: Dada
Dada Dada, a roaring of tense colors, and interlacing of
opposites and of all contradictions, grotesques, inconsis-
tencies: LIFE.

(1971: 20)

The Dadaists found theoretical support for their ideas about chance
and spontaneity in the writings of Jung (the concept of 'synchronicity') and Freud's model of the unconscious. These influences also
featured prominently in the Surrealists' 'objective chance', the
Situationists' *dérive*, Lefebvre's 'festival', and Bakhtin's carnival, as
discussed in the chapters that follow. However, it is important to
realize that there was a significant tension in the Dada movement:
between a kind of Bakuninite nihilism that celebrated the urge to
destroy as a creative urge, and a desire for reconciliation, harmony,
and the construction of a new system of positive values through
which to escape the ravages of total war and the idiocies of everyday
existence under bourgeois rule. While individuals like Tzara
routinely declared that 'the most acceptable system is on principle
to have none' (cited in Young 1981: 22), this uncompromising
iconoclasm was not met with equal favour among all participants in
the Dada movement. Arp, for example, espoused a kind of
naturalistic vitalism with almost Taoist overtones, which rejected
technological society in its entirety and yearned for a more
immediate connection with nature. He once asserted that 'Dada
aimed to destroy the reasonable deceptions of man and recover the
natural and unreasonable order. . . . Dada is for the senseless, which
does not mean nonsense. Dada is for nature and against art. Dada is
direct like nature' (1971: 28). Others, particularly the Germans Ball
and Huelsenbeck, turned to the Communist Party or various
anarchist groupings for more straightforwardly political solutions to
the perceived crisis of European civilization. Huelsenbeck proclaimed bluntly that 'Dada is German Bolshevism', and wrote a
manifesto with Raoul Hausmann advocating a strange combination
of communistic (such as the full mechanization of production and
the abolition of alienated labour) and Dadaist measures (the
introduction of a 'simultaneist' poem as the state prayer). Berlin
Dada, which gained such notable adherents as John Heartfield and
George Grosz, was particularly militant and pro-revolution, and its
adherents enthusiastically joined in the street demonstrations and
confrontations with the police that marked the abortive German
revolution of 1919. However, by the early 1920s, most of the

prominent Berlin Dadaists eventually abandoned Dadaism and joined the German Communist Party, the KDP (Sheppard 1979). These internal political and ideological differences, along with the spread of Dadaist ideas to other European and North American cities after the end of World War One, led to the disintegration of Dada as an integrated force.[3]

SURREALISM: ALCHEMY OF THE WORD

While their German counterparts turned to more orthodox forms of political agitation, Paris Dada, with the assistance of the indefatigable Tristan Tzara, seemed determined to follow the more irreverent spirit of Cabaret Voltaire. Disaffected young writers and artists flocked to the movement, including such future Surrealist luminaries as André Breton, Louis Aragon, Paul Eluard, Benjamin Péret and Philippe Soupault. (In the following discussion I will mainly draw on the writings of Breton – who earned the sobriquet the 'Pope of Surrealism' – as he is generally acknowledged as the leader and main theoretician of the Surrealist movement.) Like their Zürich and Berlin counterparts, the Paris Dadaists declaimed the follies of war, nationalism, hypocritical morality, and the tenets of bourgeois rationality (Short 1979). They also displayed a typical Dadaist penchant for scandal and provocation. Posted advertisements for one such 'Dada Evening' proclaimed that Charlie Chaplin had joined the Dada movement, and was giving a public lecture at the Salon des Indépendents. Instead of Chaplin, the curious were treated to a Dadaist shaving his head or reading aloud from a telephone book. Such provocations became something of a *succès de scandale* and garnered the movement a great deal of public notoriety. During this transitional phase, for Breton and his like-minded colleagues the figure of Jacques Vaché acquired a kind of iconic status. Vaché was a rather disturbed young soldier whom Breton met in 1916 whilst the latter was working as an orderly in a mental hospital. Rejecting war, patriotism, religion, art and just about everything else, and eventually committing suicide by an opium overdose, Vaché came to exemplify the Dadaist ethos of negativism and visceral disgust. 'In Vaché's person', suggested Breton, there was 'a principle of total insubordination undermining the world, reducing everything that then seemed all-important to petty scale, desecrating everything in its path' (1993: 18).

Residues of this extreme Vachéan outlook remained in Breton's writings for some time. For instance, in his Second Manifesto of

Surrealism, Breton argued that the 'simplest Surrealist act consists of dashing down into the street, pistol in hand, and firing blindly, as fast as you can pull the trigger, into the crowd' (1972: 128). For the most part, however, by the early 1920s he had come to reject Tzara-like provocations as stunts of limited political effectiveness. At this point, Breton suggests, he and many other Paris Dadaists fervently sought a 'radical renewal of means; to pursue the same ends [as Dada], but by markedly different paths' (1993: 51). The tools for such a positive process of sociocultural transformation, oriented toward the systematic critique of everyday life, were just beginning to emerge via a series of highly unorthodox psychological and artistic experiments. During his tenure in the mental hospital mentioned above, Breton began to read the works of Freud and attempted to utilize psychoanalytic techniques for the treatment of combat-induced psychoses and mental aberrations. From this experience, Breton gained an appreciation of the importance of dreams and free association, which for him constituted the 'raw materials' of a burgeoning Surrealist movement. Breton and others began to investigate the possibilities of 'psychic automatism', which involved releasing the creative energies of the unconscious from psychological or social constraints; various forms of collective cultural production (such as the famous 'exquisite corpse', where part of a drawing or poem was constructed by different participants but without foreknowledge of the other contributions); the use of games to exploit factors of coincidence and randomness (what they later termed 'objective chance'); and the exploration of physical space in self-induced trance-like states (Gooding 1991; Nadeau 1973). According to Breton, the goal of these explorations was 'total liberation, not only from ways of thinking but also from pre-established means of expression. Our goal was the necessary promotion of specifically new ways of feeling and saying, the search for which implied, by definition, a maximum of *adventure*' (1993: 25). Surrealism, a term first used by the prototypical avant-gardist Guillaume Appollinaire, was adopted as the new movement's appellation.

The chief enemy of Surrealism was Cartesian dualism, which posited an irreconcilable gulf between mind and matter – between, that is, an inviolate object-world of material 'facts' on the one hand, and a disembodied consciousness controlled by a rational *cogito* on the other. 'The so-called Cartesian world around [us] was indefens-ible, a humorless prankster', suggested Breton, against which 'all forms of insurrection were justified' (1993: 80). For the Surrealists, this was tantamount to accepting the empirical world as eternal and unchangeable, which in turn meant a betrayal of the human capacity for endless innovation, surprise and wonderment. In the words of Fredric Jameson, to acquiesce to such a position would represent the 'basest kind of surrender to the reality principle, since in it that purely perceptual level of things to which our most superficial waking consciousness corresponds is taken for Being itself' (1971: 97). By way of promoting a new set of values as an alternative to bourgeois rationalism, and to traverse the gap between dreams and waking life, Breton and his compatriots embraced 'poetry, dreams, and the marvelous'. More precisely, in order to grasp what the poet Rimbaud called 'real life' (authentic or de-alienated experience), Surrealism advocated the pursuit of sublime beauty, ecstatic love and eroticism. Only then could the shackles of commonsensical logic and mundane experience be thrown off, and access to what they called the 'poetic' or the 'marvellous' thereby attained. However, it is important to realize that the 'marvellous' was not a transcendental reality. Rather, it was an immanent one, located firmly in the here and now. So whereas both Christianity and Romanticism identified authentic existence with an other-worldly or supernatural domain, for Breton and the Surrealists the goal was a *transfiguration* of everyday life, and not its negation or supersession. In other words, they sought to locate the sacred *within* the profane. As Ferdinand Alquié puts it, Surrealism can therefore be described as an

> attention to everything that lifts man above himself or seems at least to draw him out of himself. It wishes to escape 'from the constraints weighing on supervised thought', from the tyranny of the laws of the sensible world, from the critical spirit, from the taboos of the current morality, from everything that corrects and dams up, and to recover, once again, the total liberty of man. The marvelous love, the hope of existence, the excitement of streets, which give surrealism its color, are not without relation to the epoch of the hypnotic sleeps. . . . In every case there is manifested a right-of-way to the world of the dream, the place where those promises may be kept that seem pledged to us in everyday reality by love and beauty.
>
> (1965: 21)

Surrealism aimed at collapsing the distinction between adventure and everyday existence, dreams and consciousness, art and life, essence and appearance. Breton spoke in favour of the 'future resolution of these two states, dream and reality, which are seemingly so contradictory, into a kind of absolute reality, a *sur-reality*, if one may so speak' (1972: 14). The key assumption here is that signs of love and the marvellous can be found in mundane objects and the experiences of daily life, provided we can free ourselves from the tyranny of a narrow rationalism. The true poet, asserted Breton, was capable of transforming 'the mediocrities of daily life into a zone of illumination and poetic infusion' (1993: 67). In such semi-fictional 'anti-novels' as Breton's *Nadja* and Aragon's *Paris Peasant*, for instance, moments of revelation, surprise and astonishment are described in the chance occurrences and meetings that take place in real-life Parisian locations within a fractured, hallucinatory narrative (Collier 1985). Rather than maintain an absolute distinction between the poetic and the everyday and to denigrate the latter, the Surrealists wanted to suffuse them, to see them as 'communicating vessels', to evoke the title of one of Breton's books. Aragon wrote in *Paris Peasant* that 'Reality is the apparent absence of contradiction. The wondrous is contradiction appearing in the real' (1971: 166; Cohen 1993). As such, the Surrealists pioneered what could be termed a 'hermeneutics of wonder', or what Walter Benjamin (1979) was later to call 'profane illumination', through which they sought to decipher everyday life and extend the boundaries of human experience and knowledge. In other words, the mundane world became the privileged site of revelation, mystery and the poetic. 'The street', Breton once put it, 'was my true element: there as nowhere else I caught the breath of the possible' (cited in Alquié 1965: 14).

Through such experiments and writings, the Surrealists tried to demonstrate that via dreams and other ecstatic or unconscious mental states, it was possible to circumvent the layer of formalized intellectual systems that usually insinuated themselves between human beings and the surrounding world, and to gain access to this 'supranatural' world in a more immediate fashion. These texts were not simply exercises in avant-garde techniques of writing and composition. Rather, they were designed to promote a reflexive awareness of the possibilities of psychic and social liberation. Breton had little patience for those 'right-wing deviationists' (particularly Dali) who utilized Surrealist techniques for purely artistic purposes, and who celebrated irrationalism for its own sake (1972: 129; Jameson 1971: 101). Following Freud, he insisted that dreams and irreason conformed to their own kind of logic; they were not in essence mysterious or ineffable but could be understood consciously and utilized practically for an emancipatory purpose. The Surrealist notion of 'objective chance', as opposed to the Dadaist cultivation of pure spontaneity, is based on the notion that under the flux and chaos of the world there is an underlying, if hidden order. Moreover, after his early, largely apolitical Dada phase, Breton consistently argued that the poetic revolution was coterminous with social revolution, in the sense that the possibility of the former was contingent upon the success of the latter. 'Surrealism's demands', he once asserted, 'have never completely overshadowed the urgent need for an economic and social upheaval that would put an end to certain glaring inequalities' (1993: 93).

I shall shortly turn to the question of the vexed relation between sociopolitical change and Surrealist doctrine. For the moment, however, I want to explore in more detail the issue of how the Surrealists proposed to circumvent the hegemony of common-sensical reason, and to reveal the marvellous within everyday life. In this context, Breton was fond of evoking Rimbaud's notion of a 'systematic derangement of the senses'. In order to demonstrate how desire and the imagination could contradict and transcend empirical reality as conceptualized by the rational *logos*, the Surrealists advocated the 'childlike and primal project of derealization' (Alquié 1965: 73). Such a 'derealization' of habitualized daily life involved techniques of shock, montage, and defamiliarization initially developed by the Futurists and Dadaists, but utilized in a much more self-conscious and systematic fashion. Only then could the potential gap be exposed between 'what is' and 'what could be'. 'Imagination alone', Breton suggested, 'offers me some intimation of what *can be*' (1972: 5). Following the influential French philosopher Henri Bergson, Breton argued that the images constructed by the mind were not insubstantial but had a material force; and, moreover, human beings were the only creatures in the natural world capable of making reality conform to their dreams. He also enlisted Freudian theory in suggesting that a society which prevented the transformation of desires into reality paid a price in the form of endemic pathologies, neuroses and violent obsessions (1972: 160n). The 'spirit is marvelously prompt in seizing the most feeble relation that may exist between two objects taken at random', wrote Breton (cited in Alquié 1965: 134). As such, the unfettered imagination is capable of refusing the logical connections proffered by common sense and mundane perception. The archetypal example of this subversive procedure of derealization is aptly expressed by

Lautréamont's famous and oft-quoted phrase: 'As beautiful as the fortuitous meeting of a sewing machine and an umbrella on an operating table'. In such an example, the juxtaposition of totally unrelated images, either verbal or visual, confounds our usual expectations and generates shock and surprise. Through the creation of such 'surrealist objects', Breton and company sought the complete transmutation of the meaning of each of the juxtaposed elements, in the process creating an entirely new configuration of meaning that reflected the vicissitudes of desire.

> What is a surrealist object? One might say roughly that it is *any alienated* object, one out of its habitual context, used for purposes different from those for which it was intended, or whose purpose is unknown. Consequently, any object which seems gratuitously made, without any other purpose than the satisfaction of its maker; further, any created object that realizes the desires of the unconscious, of the dream. Marcel Duchamp's 'ready-mades' fulfilled these conditions before the fact. What makes the *Bottle-rack* or the *Chocolate grinder* so mysterious is that they are the 'found' materialization of their creator's unconscious desires, corresponding all the more to what we are accustomed to ask of the work of art since these same desires can be shared by the spectator. Consider a bottle-rack, a banal object if there ever was one, confer upon it artistic value by isolating it from its habitual context, oblige others to consider it in itself and to forget its purpose, and you have created a strange object, catalyst of a host of unconscious desires.
>
> (Nadeau 1973: 201–2)

In discussing such defamiliarizing techniques, Breton was fond of using Hegelian language so as to describe how Surrealism could supersede the alienations and dualisms of modern society. For example, he asserted that the primary Surrealist goal was to pursue the point at which 'life and death, the real and imagined, past and future, the communicable and incommunicable, high and low, cease to be perceived as contradictions' (1993: 118), which ultimately relied on Hegel's 'idea of surpassing all antimonies'. Nonetheless, it is evident that Breton eschewed the totalizing rationalism of Hegel's grand historical dialectic, in which the reconciliation of contradictions is absolute and teleological and occurs 'behind the backs' of individual historical agents. Hegelian philosophy sub-

37

scribed to an extremely narrow conception of Reason which explicitly excluded intuition, affective sentiment, or speculative imagination – precisely those qualities that the Surrealists wanted to return to centre-stage. Ultimately, Breton affirmed the integrity of individual subjectivity as against the abstract conceptual system, and the validity of personal revolt against so-called 'historical necessity' (Breton 1972: 208). 'We are in revolt against history', as one anonymous Surrealist document put it. Put differently, Breton acknowledged the richness of the concrete and the particular, and suggested that the world and human existence could never be fully explained or encapsulated within an overarching conceptual system, whether Marxist, Freudian or Hegelian in inspiration. As against the shabby conceits of this 'positivistic realism', Surrealism pursued a very different project: it sought to extend the boundaries of human experience and understanding, rather than arbitrarily limit them by a slavish adherence to a 'scientific methodology' or a spurious notion of 'objectivity'. As Alquié characterizes Breton's position, the 'unity of man is discovered in the immediate', and not in reified theories (1965: 111).

Breton speculated that one of the greatest dangers of a Cartesian rationalism was the alienation of humanity from nature, or what Max Weber called the 'disenchantment of the world'. In this, Surrealism has proven to be remarkably prophetic, for this is a prominent and recurring theme in contemporary ecological thought. Scientific rationalism has historically conceived of the natural world as 'matter in motion', as a domain that lacks intrinsic value or non-quantifiable properties. Consequently, nature is treated in a purely instrumental fashion, as a mere 'raw material' for the satisfaction of unlimited human wants. In reacting against this perspective, the Surrealists sought to 're-enchant' the natural world, and to heal the destructive separation between humanity and nature encouraged by modernity. Surrealism abhorred the ingrained bourgeois tendency to measure everything by its functional worth, its capacity to generate tangible forms of profit. To this end, Breton and his compatriots argued that humankind had to re-discover non-cognitive and non-instrumental ways of relating to nature, as do children and non-Western peoples, rather than consider 'nature only in its relationship with the inner world of consciousness' (Breton 1972: 260). Interestingly, Surrealist narratives tended to describe the external environment and the object-world as alive, and, as such, could be related to in a playful, affective and non-purposive manner. In Aragon's *Paris Peasant*, for instance, the urban landscape is 'remythologized', transformed into exotic flora and fauna: the Eiffel Tower becomes a giraffe, or a bank is transformed into a lumbering monster. Elsewhere, Breton castigated orthodox Marxism for supposing that productive labour, or the utilitarian transformation of the external world, was humanity's sole or even primary connection with nature. 'The basis of the surrealist procedure', as Alquié put is, 'is not Hegelian reason or Marxist labor; it is liberty' (1965: 83). In so doing, the Surrealists staked out an ecologically progressive position that evokes Marx's youthful comments about the possibility of the 'humanization of nature and the naturalization of humanity'. Parenthetically, it also helps to explain the pervasive Surrealist preoccupation with lived experience, sensuality and the body. To quote Breton, the Surrealists

> in no way accept that nature is hostile to man, but suppose that man, who originally possessed certain keys that kept him in strict communion with nature, has lost these keys, and that since then he persists more and more feverishly in trying out others *that don't fit*. Scientific knowledge of nature can be worthwhile only on condition that *contact* with nature via poetic and, dare I say, mythic routes be reestablished. It remains understood that any scientific progress achieved within a defective social structure only works against man, and further worsens his condition.
>
> (1993: 206)

In their attempt to reconcile reason and unreason, natural necessity and human imagination, the Surrealists argued that access to the marvellous and the realization of desire was a universal human capacity. In this context, Lautréamont's dictum 'Poetry should be made by all, not by one' was a key Surrealist maxim. Previous avant-garde movements, particularly those of a Romanticist bent, usually subscribed to the notion of the individual creative genius, and often expressed contempt for the backwardness and intellectual limitations of the masses. Surrealism, by contrast, stressed the *collective* nature of cultural production and sought to radically democratize the process of poetic revelation, insofar as the wellspring of creativity resides within an unconscious that is shared by all. Rather than espouse the familiar communist slogan 'To each according to his needs', Breton declared 'To each according to his desires'. Moreover, Breton often condemned the petty-bourgeois egocentrism displayed by certain of the Surrealists, which led them to exaggerate the uniqueness of their artistic talents and to adopt an 'Olympian attitude' with respect to the labouring classes. Surrealist images are not the product of individual genius, Breton argued; rather, they come to a person 'spontaneously, despotically. He cannot chase them away; for the will is powerless now and no longer controls the faculties' (1972: 36). This 'collective unconscious', of which all humankind partakes, was for the Surrealists a unifying factor that overcame superficial considerations of race, class, or nationality.[4]

> I believe that Surrealism aims, *and is the only one to aim systematically,* at abolishing differences. You know that with Surrealism the accent was moved off the *ego,* which is always somewhat despotic, and onto the *id* common to all men. [Surrealist] thought [seeks] to overthrow the hegemony of consciousness and daily life, in order to conquer the realm of *revelatory emotion.*
>
> (Breton 1993: 193)

Spiritual liberation, Breton and the other Surrealists eventually came to realize, was entirely dependent upon social liberation, insofar as the existing organization of society blocks or sublimates the realization of authentic desire. In his 'Second Manifesto of Surrealism', Breton declared: '"Transform the world," Marx said; "change life," Rimbaud said. These two watchwords are one for us' (1972: 241). Again, however, Breton's utopianism must be understood as the expression of a desire for the *immediate* transformation of everyday life and the realization of human passions, rather than as an advocacy for some grand (and unrealizable) future utopia.[5] This, parenthetically, explains why he found much of value in the writings of nineteenth-century utopian socialist Charles Fourier.[6] 'I always forbade myself to think of the future', wrote Breton in 1924 (cited in Alquié 1965: 13), which accurately sums up his idiosyncratic utopianism of the everyday.

The Surrealists' attempt to translate the unbound imagination into practical action was initially prompted by general outrage at French imperialist designs on North Africa in the Moroccan 'Riff' War of 1925. However, this new-found interest in rendering Surrealist ideas in concrete political practice proved to be exceeding difficult. Some, like Benjamin Perét, enlisted in the International Brigades during the Spanish Civil War in order to defend the beleaguered Republic. Others preferred less direct contributions to the cause, such as street demonstrations or pamphlet writing. By 1927, many of the Surrealists (including Breton) had joined the French Communist Party (PCF), although most subsequently left after finding its authoritarianism and aesthetic and intellectual conservatism intolerable. This is not the place to chronicle the complex and tension-fraught history of the relation between the Surrealists and the official communist movement (Lewis 1990; Short 1966). Suffice to say that the essentially anarchistic orient-ation of Surrealism and its proclivity for 'total revolt' rather than the more limited aims of economic or social reconstruction espoused by established communist and socialist organizations made the Surrealist vision difficult to translate into tangible forms of political action.

CONCLUSION

From the perspective of the early twenty-first century, Dada and Surrealism represent a complex and by no means unambiguous legacy. Their concerted attempts to engage in effective sociopolitical change were less than successful, and their call for total critique and the transformation of everyday life was largely ignored by the orthodox socialist and communist movements. They were also much less resistant to recuperation and commodification by powerful social interests than most of the founders could have possibly imagined. Fifty years after the Cabaret Voltaire set out to shock and scandalize the bourgeoisie, for instance, the city fathers of Zürich dutifully placed a bronze plaque on the building where the cabaret was originally held in 1916. Similarly, many of the Surrealists aban-doned revolutionary principles as the lure of cultural capital and financial success proved to be too attractive to forgo. In an effort to retain the revolutionary purity of the Surrealist movement, Breton took to routinely excommunicating dissident Surrealists who showed signs of favouring a mainstream artistic career. This internal crisis in the Surrealist movement, combined with its political shortcomings, eventually led to the degeneration of Surrealism into mysticism, a mere parody of its former self. But even in its more robust phase, certain elements of the Surrealist vision have not endeared it to its many critics. A number of feminist writers, for example, have justifiably singled out the Surrealists' penchant for patronizing sexism and paeans to an idealized femininity as cause for concern (Pierre 1992; Caws et al. 1991). Moreover, although not directly addressing Surrealist arguments, Michel Foucault (1978) exposed a darker side to human sexuality by demonstrating its close relation to systems of power and domination. Finally, the historical experience of Nazism has led many to question the liberatory potential of irrationalist cultural politics.

Nonetheless, Dada and Surrealism remain of considerable interest. They were among the first to develop a systematic critique of idealist aesthetics, not out of purely academic considerations, but with the intent of overcoming the false dichotomy between art and life in order to transform everyday life. In this, they developed a wide-ranging and unflinchingly critical perspective on modern social relations, including morality, lived space, the commodity form, and many others. They took daily life seriously as the essential terrain of sociopolitical change, although the central role of aesthetics in Dada and Surrealism has tended to become less important in subsequent critiques of everyday life, as evinced by the work of the thinkers discussed in the following chapters. Finally, in their stress on the ubiquity of desire and the limits of rationality, their suspicion of totalizing intellectual systems, and their exploration of the connection between politics, sexuality and the imagination, Dada and Surrealism anticipated many poststructuralist and postmodernist notions, as found within such works as Deleuze and Guattari's *Anti-Oedipus* or Jean-François Lyotard's *The Postmodern Condition*.

3

BAKHTIN'S PROSAIC
IMAGINATION

I possess nothing but the everyday out of which I am never taken. The mystery is no longer disclosed, it has escaped or it has made its dwelling here where everything happens as it happens.

Martin Buber

INTRODUCTION

The ideas of the Russian social philosopher and cultural theorist Mikhail M. Bakhtin (1895–1975) have, over the last two decades, become virtually ubiquitous in many humanities disciplines. Although his influence has been slower to take root in the social sciences, there are signs that this situation is changing (Bell and Gardiner 1998; Mandelker 1995). In particular, there is a growing realization that certain aspects of Bakhtin's approach – especially involving the concept of 'prosaics', a neologism coined originally by two pre-eminent Bakhtin scholars, Gary Saul Morson and Caryl Emerson[1] – have much to offer to a critical theory of everyday life. This chapter will sketch out Bakhtin's ideas regarding the centrality of this 'prosaic' dimension in human social existence. I will begin with a brief outline of Bakhtin's life and intellectual milieu, followed by a discussion of his early phenomenological writings, where the notion of prosaics and his life-long concern with ethics and inter-subjectivity were initially formulated. The key theme in such texts is that the values and meanings that most directly shape our lives emerge from the existential demands of daily living and our immediate interpersonal relationships. The everyday therefore constitutes the central ground upon which our judgements and actions, particular those of a moral or normative character, are exercised. I

43

will then consider Bakhtin's 'linguistic turn' of the mid-1920s. In this phase of his career, Bakhtin locates prosaics primarily within the dialogical properties of language-use, as found both in life and literature, and he asserts that the incorporation of everyday speech genres and idioms into various cultural forms (especially the novel) helps to transform human consciousness in a more open, reflexive and dialogical direction. The concluding section will examine the relationship between Bakhtin's writings on carnival and everyday life, in which the prosaic outlook of his earliest writings is somewhat problematized and accorded a more overtly critical and sociopolitical character.

BAKHTIN'S LIFE AND WORK:
A BRIEF SKETCH

Mikhail Mikhailovich Bakhtin was born in Orel, Russia, in November 1895, the son of a bank clerk and *déclassé* aristocrat.[2] He grew up in Odessa, in the Crimea, and studied philology and classics at the University of Odessa. He was eventually transferred to the University of Petrograd where he graduated in 1918. After graduation, Bakhtin taught elementary school in several provincial towns in Russia, and ended up in the Russian provincial town of Nevel'. Here a group of like-minded musicians, scientists and writers gravitated towards him – the so-called 'Bakhtin Circle'. The Circle was a tightly knit group of scholars, artists and scientists who met regularly during the early 1920s, first in Nevel' and later Vitebsk, to indulge in 'strong tea and talk until dawn', as one member put it (Brandist 1996). Bakhtin was undoubtedly the leading intellectual force; other important members included V. N. Voloshinov (poet, musicologist, linguist) and P. N. Medvedev (literary critic and essayist). The Circle gave a number of informal talks, and, together with such other participants as L. V. Pumpian'ski (literary theorist) and M. I. Kagan (philosopher), published an extraordinarily wide-ranging body of work. The members were strongly influenced by neo-Kantian philosophy; several had studied in Germany under such prominent neo-Kantians as Hermann Cohen. Others, such as Voloshinov and Medvedev, were more overtly Marxist. Medvedev even occupied several important government positions in education and culture in the nascent Soviet regime. During this Nevel'/Vitebsk period (1918–24), Bakhtin wrote a series of essays which were marked by the influence of classical

German philosophy, in which he sought to develop a general aesthetics of artistic creation and a theory of 'alterity', or intersubjectivity. Unfortunately, in this period Bakhtin contracted osteomyelitis, a serious bone disease, which led to the amputation of most of his right leg in 1938. He was plagued by chronic ill-health throughout much of his life, and Bakhtin owed much to the caregiving skills of Elena Aleksandrovna Okolovich, whom he married in 1921.

In 1929, Bakhtin published his first book under his own name with the original title *The Problems of Dostoevsky's Art*, although several essays and books by Medvedev and Voloshinov had already appeared by this time.[3] The Dostoevsky book received a generally hostile response from the cultural organizations of the Communist Party, which were beginning to adopt the official aesthetic of socialist realism. Bakhtin was arrested that year by the GPU (forerunner of the KGB), ostensibly for his affiliation with the Russian Orthodox Church. He was sentenced to five years in a labour camp, which would have certainly resulted in his demise, given the fragile state of his health. Fortunately, this was reduced to exile in Kazakhstan, but only due to the personal intervention of Anatoly Lunacharsky, who was then Soviet culture minister. (Lunacharsky had been favourably impressed with Bakhtin's book on Dostoevsky, and even wrote a positive review of it in a Soviet literary journal.)

Bakhtin worked in various clerical jobs in different institutions in Siberia and Kazakhstan. When his exile was completed, he was allowed to teach at a teacher's college in Saransk. During this period, he wrote his most important works, including a series of essays on the nature of language in literature and society in the context of European cultural history and a lengthy treatise on what he called the 'chronotope', concerning how temporal and spatial relationships connect and interact in the social world and literary texts. Perhaps the most important (and certainly the most controversial) work Bakhtin produced at this time was a study of the French Renaissance writer François Rabelais, which focused on the nature of 'carnival' culture during the late medieval and early modern periods. He completed this text in 1940 and submitted it as a Ph.D dissertation, but it was rejected. (It seems that it was too overly concerned with 'lower' bodily functions for the delicate sensibilities of the Soviet literary establishment.) The Rabelais book was eventually published in the USSR in 1965 and was soon translated into French and English. After the dissertation fiasco, and despite the chaos that followed in the wake of the German invasion of

Russia in 1941, Bakhtin managed to write a lengthy work on Goethe's aesthetics. Due to wartime paper shortages, and being an inveterate chain smoker, Bakhtin systematically tore it up and used it for cigarette paper. A number of other manuscripts were left to rot in a shed at his wartime residence; some were eventually recovered by his students in the 1960s. After the end of the war, Bakhtin moved back and forth between a small town near Moscow and Saransk until the early 1960s, when he retired and was allowed to move to Moscow, where he died in 1975. Some of his final projects included an extensive reworking of his Dostoevsky book, published as a second edition in Russia in 1963, and a series of brief notes and fragments, including some programmatic essays on the human sciences, which returned to the more philosophical themes of his early period.

THE PHILOSOPHY OF THE ACT

As mentioned, during the so-called Nevel'–Vitebsk phase Bakhtin wrote a series of complex and allusive texts that borrowed extensively from a bewildering welter of philosophical influences, including neo-Kantianism, Husserlian phenomenology and Bergsonian vitalism. The result was a rich and distinctive synthesis that contained in embryonic form many of the key ideas that were to sustain him throughout his long and productive career. Although never originally intended for publication, many of these works were eventually made available in Russia in the 1970s, and have, in recent years, been translated into English as *Toward a Philosophy of the Act* (1993) and *Art and Answerability: Early Philosophical Essays by M. M. Bakhtin* (1990). Beginning with the former, earlier study, Bakhtin meditates at length on the implications of the disjuncture between immediate experience and our *a posteriori* symbolic representations of this experience. As Michael Holquist adroitly puts it, Bakhtin's primary interest at this formative stage in his intellectual development was to

> get back to the naked immediacy of experience as it is felt from within the utmost particularity of a specific life, the molten lava of events as they happen. He seeks the sheer quality of happening in life before the magma of such experience cools, hardening into igneous theories, or accounts of what has happened. [Bakhtin] wants to understand how the

constantly aeteiolating difference between what is *now* and what is *after-now* might be bridged in the relation I forge between them in all the singularity of my unique place in existence.

(1993: x)

What Holquist here terms the 'molten lava of events' is crucial for Bakhtin, because this is where the unique character of our everyday actions and deeds, and indeed our very selfhood, is constituted. It is the paramount reality where 'we create, cognize, contemplate, live our lives and die – the world in which the acts of our activity are objectified and the world in which these acts actually proceed and are actually accomplished once and only once' (Bakhtin 1993: 2). Life must be understood as a continuous series of singular acts, and each act, or 'event', must be grasped on its own terms, as an 'experiential and sensuous given' (1993: 4). This is not to say that human existence is coterminous with a continuous, inchoate flow of fragmentary sensations and events, akin to Henri Bergson's notion of *durée*. Rather, we seek to organize such events symbolically and cognitively (or 'architectonically', in Bakhtin's terminology), in order to give them an overarching meaning and significance (Bender 1998: 181). Yet this process of transforming life into a coherent whole, or what Merleau-Ponty would call a *gestalt*, cannot rely exclusively on abstract, theoretical cognition. Our judgements, values and behavioural orientations must emerge 'organically', as it were, out of the terrain of the everyday, and we must be acutely aware of and responsive to the moral and existential demands of this realm of ordinary existence. Of course, it is undeniable that abstract cognition is an important facet of human life, and in such realms as science and technology it is seen as essential to our physical survival. At the same time, the limits of such formal rationalities must be acknowledged, and kept within clear boundaries. Otherwise, as Jürgen Habermas would have it, theoretical reason would threaten to colonize and displace the centrality of everyday life.

Bakhtin notes that the history of Western thought has been marked periodically by perspectives that have rejected the validity of bodily, lived experience in favour of abstruse theoretical constructions – Platonism being the archetypal example. However, it is modern forms of thought that have most systematically detached what he terms 'Being-as-event' – that is, Being as constituted by ongoing, lived experience – from abstract cognition, in order to privilege the latter. The desire to supersede everyday life with theoretical abstractions is, according to Bakhtin, a 'specific peculiarity of modern times, and one could say a peculiarity of the nineteenth and twentieth centuries exclusively' (1993: 8). Scientific rationalism has encouraged the transcription of Being-as-event into a series of universalistic abstractions that cleave Being from becoming, by stifling the potential for continual growth and development. As such, what Bakhtin terms 'discursive theoretical thinking' denigrates the sensuous and tangible character of the lived event, perpetrating a 'fundamental split between the content or sense of a given act/activity and the historical actuality of its being' (1993: 2). Once alienated from the lifeworld, grand theoretical systems acquire a proxy life and operate according to their own internal laws, bypassing the experiential world of practical consciousness and action. But there is a terrible price to be paid for the epistemic certitude sought by scientific rationalism, in which the irrepressible complexity and ambiguity that marks the everyday world is eliminated in the relentless search for what Descartes liked to call 'clear and distinct ideas'. The sociocultural conditions of modernity have therefore encouraged us to privilege a purely cognitive relation to the other and our lived environment, which in turn reinforces an instrumental, disengaged attitude towards the world. Such a necessitarian logic – or 'theoreticism', as Bakhtin calls it – is reflected in the unabashedly utilitarian character of modern science and technology, in which any activity is justified by reference to the overriding goal of technical efficacy and control. As Morson and Emerson usefully summarize, theoreticism can be understood as the rationalist project of subordinating everyday life to a formalized, metaphysical system projected by a hypostatized consciousness, which devalues or expunges any experience or viewpoint that it cannot fully assimilate. Such a 'transcendent-logical transcription' inevitably suppresses the 'eventness', or sensuous particularity, of embodied social existence, and encourages a 'blind faith in "technical" systems and laws, unfolding according to their own immanent logic' (Morson and Emerson 1989: 9).

This orientation helps to explain Bakhtin's pronounced hostility to positivistic social science and idealist philosophy, mainly because these have had profound, largely negative effects on society. For instance, echoing the Frankfurt School's concept of 'instrumental reason', Bakhtin asserts that technology, 'when divorced from the once-occurrent unity of life and surrendered to the will of the law immanent to its development, is frightening; it may from time to time irrupt into this once-occurrent unity as an irresponsibly destructive and terrifying force' (1993: 7). For Bakhtin, one of the central imperatives of modernity therefore lies in the attempt to transcend our situatedness in concrete time/space by recourse to what Heidegger (1977) has called the 'technological world-picture'. This has palpable sociopolitical consequences: we cease to be present in the world as 'individually and answerably active human beings' (Bakhtin 1993: 7). Abstract, dispassionate contemplation from afar supplants our active and incarnated participation in the world of everyday values and meanings. This yearning for transcendence from the ambivalence and 'messiness' of daily life allows us to abrogate the difficult existential and moral demands that profane existence places upon each of us as incarnate subjects. 'As disembodied spirit', writes Bakhtin, 'I lose my compellent, ought-to-be relationship to the world, I lose the actuality of the world' (1993: 47). The quest to live such a 'non-incarnated fortuitous life' can only result in a ghostly, illusory existence separated from the world, an 'indifferent Being not rooted in anything' (1993: 43). Such a privileging of the cognitive, incorporeal subject results in a pronounced tendency to equate the self with egocentric mental processes, what Bakhtin calls 'psychic being'. This, in effect, is a form of extreme, egocentric subjectivism or solipsism, which Donna Haraway has described as the 'standpoint of the master, the Man, the One God, whose Eye produces, appropriates and orders all difference' (1995: 184).

In order to counter the abstractions of idealist philosophy and scientific positivism, Bakhtin argues that we must grasp the nature of the concrete deed or 'act' as it constitutes the essential 'value-centre' for human existence. His position is, in an important sense, a gloss on Goethe's famous dictum that 'In the beginning is the deed'. For Bakhtin, the self must be understood as a dynamic, embodied and restlessly creative entity that strives to attribute meaning and value to its life and surroundings. We are forced to make certain choices and value-judgements with respect to our Being-in-the-world, to transform the proffered 'givenness', the objective facticity of our environment, into a coherent 'world-for-me'. In making the world a meaningful place, one that is steeped in personal values, the subject actively engages with and alters its lived situation; and, in so doing, continuously transforms itself. This is an ongoing process: the self is continually 'reauthored' as its life and circumstances change, and is hence 'unfinalizable', always open to further development and transformation. What Bakhtin is striving to outline here is a phenomenology of what he terms 'practical doing', one that focuses on our incarnated activities within a lifeworld, which, much like Merleau-Ponty's 'primordial being', exists 'prior' to the more rarefied operations of abstract cognition. Only if we think and act in a 'participative' fashion, in tune with the rhythms and textures of everyday life, can we be wholly 'answerable' for our actions, in the sense that we are reflexively conscious of the existential and ethical implications of our acts. Being-as-event must therefore be lived through, and not passively comprehended from afar. The impoverishing and necessitarian mode of thought perpetuated by modernity, which tends to overlook the inherently value-laden, interactive and embodied character of human life, can only be combatted by a repudiation of theoretical abstraction pursued as an end to itself, so as to grasp the concrete deed as the axiological centre around which our existence revolves. Answerability demands the presence of an incarnated and participative subject. In challenging the logic of formalist reason, Bakhtin argues, first, that there is no possibility of surmounting our 'unique place in once-occurrent Being'; and secondly, that theoretical cognition is only one aspect of a wider 'practical reason'. Abstract philosophical or aesthetic contemplation in and of itself can never gain entry into this universe of lived Being; it requires 'actual communion' with the concrete actions that I perform, through my living corporeality.

In taking this position, Bakhtin is rejecting the common supposition that everyday life is the realm of the trivial and the habitual, and hence devoid of intrinsic value, which implies that meaning must be brought to our lives from such external value-spheres as philosophy, religion or politics. At the same time, it should be clear that Bakhtin is not espousing a form of proto-postmodernist relativism. Although we have to understand Being-as-event 'from the inside', as it were, this is not a descent into subjectivism or psychologism. What Bakhtin terms the 'answerably performed act' is a synthetic or architectonic activity that brings together the 'sense and the fact, the universal and the individual, the real and the ideal' (1993: 29). Answerability often seems to mean, in an almost Habermasian sense, the ability to express the particularistic truths of a given situation in a manner that can be comprehended rationally by others, within the context of a shared lifeworld. So the meaning of acts are shared, jointly constructed within particular situations, and not purely subjectivistic. Just as there are no 'private languages' for Wittgenstein, answerability for Bakhtin implies continual communication with, and responsibility to, concrete others. Indeed, at one point Bakhtin suggests that we must be 'answerably rational' creatures. Through practical action we can bridge the gap between our 'small scrap of space and time' and that of the 'large spatial and temporal whole' (1993: 51) – or, in more sociological terminology, between the 'micro' sphere of personal life and intimate interaction and the more public realm of politics and culture. This is a *practical* rationality, rooted in the concrete deed, and not detachable from specific situations and projected as some sort of speciously universalistic and decontextualized 'Truth'. We must, Bakhtin argues, always put our personal 'signature', or 'emotional-volitional tone', upon the act in question, and any expressions or objectivations that emanate from such a deed must bear the mark of this signature.

What the foregoing discussion demonstrates is that Bakhtin strongly rejects what Emmanuel Levinas characterizes as the 'primacy of intellectual objectivism, which is affirmed in science, taken as the model of all intelligibility, but also in Western philosophy, from which that science emerges' (1994: 22). The penchant for abstract theory and the objectification of the world on the part of the modernist paradigm represents a retreat from lived experience, a symptom of profound alienation from the everyday world. For Bakhtin, moral reasoning can only emerge out of specific situations, and not simply deduced from *a priori* concepts. If our norms and values do not remain in constant contact with the immediacy of everyday life, then the 'detached content of the cognitional act comes to be governed by its own immanent laws, according to which it then develops as if it has a will of its own'. When we have performed such an 'act of abstraction, we are now controlled by its autonomous laws or, to be exact, we are simply no longer present in it as individually and answerably active human beings' (Bakhtin 1993: 7). Again, this explains Bakhtin's hostility to absolutist ethical systems along Kantian lines (a position he shares with Agnes Heller, as discussed in Chapter 6), mainly because such systems rely on overgeneralizing and spuriously universalistic principles. Because my participation in the world is unique and non-recurrent, shared by no other person, no one else can accept responsibility on my behalf: 'That which can be done by me can never be done by anyone else' (1993: 40). This explains Bakhtin's recurring, and haunting phrase: there is no 'alibi' in Being. We cannot justify our deeds by recourse to abstractions like the Categorical Imperative, the Unconscious, the Historical Mission of the Proletariat; nor can we act out of mere habit or convention. These provide us with just such an alibi for evading our responsibility, in which case we do not have 'an answerable deed but a technical or instrumental action', one that is devoid of existential meaning and a capacity for answerability.

> The world in which an act or deed actually proceeds, in which it is actually accomplished, is a unitary and unique world that is experienced concretely: it is a world that is seen, heard, touched, and thought, a world permeated in its entirety with the emotional-volitional tones of the affirmed validity of values. The unitary uniqueness of this world [is] guaranteed for actuality by the acknowledgment of my unique participation in that world, by my *non-alibi* in it. [I] *come upon* this world, inasmuch as I *come forth* or issue from within myself in my performed act or deed of seeing, of thinking, of practical doing.
>
> (Bakhtin 1993: 56–7)

What is of particular interest here is that Bakhtin seems to be sketching out, at least in a tentative fashion, the lineaments of a post-Cartesian social theory, in which the traditional subject/object dualism of Western philosophy is discarded in favour of what Wald Godzich (1991) has termed a 'subject/subject' paradigm. In the latter approach, our relation to others and the world is necessarily embodied, situated in concrete time/space, and saturated with normative evaluations. A non-indifferent, sensuous relation to the object is not an external relation of necessity or 'givenness', suggests Bakhtin, but is part and parcel of a 'changing moment in the ongoing event of my experiencing [in which] what-is and what-ought-to-be, of being and value, are inseparable' (1993: 32). These central values and meanings are immanent within the relationships and activities of everyday existence. Hence, our incarnate participation in the world is what effectively breaches the subject/object dichotomy – which, for Bakhtin at any rate, is a false dualism born out of the aporias of modernity and the valorization of abstract rationality as against the kind of broader, practical reason that he envisages. Only the 'prosaic imagination' can grasp the sheer contingency, complexity and 'messiness' of everyday life, and recognize the very phenomenon of difference or 'otherness' itself; only participatory thinking can appreciate

> all this multiformity and diversity, without losing and dissipating it, without leaving behind a mere skeleton of basic

lines and sense-moments. [An] indifferent or hostile reaction is always a reaction that impoverishes and decomposes its object: it seeks to pass over the object in all its manifoldness, to ignore it or to overcome.

(Bakhtin 1993: 64)

INTERSUBJECTIVITY: THE 'I/OTHER' RELATION

In *Toward a Philosophy of the Act*, Bakhtin stresses the situated and embodied character of lived existence and its consequences for ethics and aesthetics. The result is the construction of a distinctive social philosophy, characterized by 'a form of thinking that presumes the importance of the everyday, the ordinary, the "prosaic"' (Morson and Emerson 1990: 15). Curiously, Bakhtin has relatively little to say here about the phenomena of intersubjectivity – or, more precisely, what Nick Crossley (1996) calls 'intercorporeality'. In the concluding segment, however, Bakhtin does gesture to the importance of what Edmund Husserl once called the 'problem of other people'. Here, Bakhtin suggests that a genuine moral philosophy cannot be formulated outside the 'contraposition' of self and other. Any attempt to answer the solicitation of the world must be sensitized to the fact that I and other commingle in the ongoing event of Being, that we are equal participants in a shared lifeworld, yet remain uniquely incarnated. Although this insight is not sufficiently elucidated here, in his next major essay, 'Author and Hero in Aesthetic Activity' (included in *Art and Answerability*), the I–other relation becomes Bakhtin's central leitmotiv. In this essay, he reminds us that life is always directed toward the 'yet-to-be'. As such, Being is properly understood as an 'open process of axiological accomplishment' (1990: 129), a continuous activity of creating existential meaning. Yet when engaging with the world as embodied beings, our ability to attribute meaning and significance solely through our own thoughts, deeds and perceptions is subject to certain limitations, particularly with respect to the 'authoring' of our own selfhood. Bakhtin places singular emphasis on the phenomenon of 'transgredience' – that which transcends or lies outside our immediate subjective existence and cognitive activity, and which necessarily partakes of 'otherness'. His central argument is that just as we are impelled to attribute meaning to the object-world around us, we need to envisage *ourselves* as coherent and meaningful entities. But from our own vantage-point (the 'I-for-myself'), we are manifestly incapable of envisioning our outward appearance, and of comprehending our location within the 'plastic-pictorial world' (i.e. the lived environment of objects, events and other selves). To be able to conceptualize ourselves as cohesive meaningful wholes is fundamental to the developmental process of individuation, self-understanding and moral awareness. 'Each of us *is* a singular narrative', Oliver Sacks points out, 'which is con-structed, continually, unconsciously, by, through, and in us – in our perceptions, our feelings, our thoughts, our actions, and, not least, our discourse, our spoken narrations' (1987: 110–11). However, to Sacks's assertion, Bakhtin would add the following qualifier: that this process of constructing our singular life narrative requires an additional, external perspective to our own. The other exists in a relation of externality or 'exotopy' *vis-à-vis* ourselves, in a manner that transcends, or is transgredient with respect to, our own perceptual and existential horizon.

Invoking a visual metaphor, Bakhtin contends that we can only exist through the 'borrowed axiological light of *otherness*' (1990: 134). Since each of us occupies a unique time/space, we can see and experience things others cannot, within our sphere of self-activity. The reverse is equally true, in that the other can visualize and apprehend things that we are unable to. Hence, the other has a 'surplus of seeing' with regard to ourselves, and vice versa. Bakhtin insists that this co-participation in the everyday world, through which our visual fields overlap and complement one another without completely coinciding, cannot occur solely through the medium of 'cognitive discursive thought'. This would be to suc-cumb to the error of what he calls 'epistemologism'. Genuinely participative thinking and acting requires an engaged and embodied – in a word, *dialogical* – relation to the other, and to the world at large. Otherwise, the intrinsically affective and moral character of the self–other encounter is fatally undermined. Our capacity for abstract cognition and representational thinking is incapable of grasping the incarnate linkage between self and another within the fabric of everyday life, cannot comprehend our 'organic wovenness' in a shared social and natural world: 'only the other human being is experienced by me as connatural with the outside world and thus can be woven into that world and rendered concordant with it' (Bakhtin 1990: 40).

This stance again reveals starkly the deleterious consequences of a subjectivistic idealism. Solipsism, Bakhtin remarks, might be a compelling argument if one were the only sentient creature in the world. But inasmuch as we always engage with other persons within the lifeworld, it would be 'incomprehensible to place the entire world (including myself) in the consciousness of *another* human being who is so manifestly himself a mere particle of the macrocosm' (1990: 39). Moreover, insofar as values are present or embodied in all human actions and experiences, moral or ethical considerations must be rooted in the common lifeworld, in tangible, everyday circumstances (Gardiner 1996a, 1996b). The ability to recognize the other's words and gestures as analogous to one's own, as part of the same lifeworld and structure of perceptual experience, is ultimately what makes a viable interhuman ethics possible. Yet Bakhtin is adamant that this commingling of self and other within the lifeworld does not erase their 'radical difference', inasmuch as outsideness or exotopy must be successfully maintained in any genuinely intersubjective encounter. Another's existence can be enriched by me, and vice versa, 'only insofar as I step outside it, actively clothe it in externally valid bodiliness, and surround it with values that are transgredient' (Bakhtin 1990: 70). The encounter with the other forces us to abandon our natural inclination toward an inward-looking subjectivism, and thereby connects us to the outside world and other selves. The upshot is that the other is I-myself – my body and self can only have a *value* in the presence of another: 'I-myself cannot be the author of my own value, just as I cannot lift myself up by my own hair' (Bakhtin 1990: 55).

For Bakhtin, therefore, the architectonic value of the incarnated self can only be affirmed in and through its relation to a concrete other: 'the body is not something self-sufficient: it needs the *other*, needs his recognition and form-giving activity' (1990: 51). Because we are ultimately responsible for any 'answer' given to others and to the world in the course of (co-) authoring our life, alterity necessarily involves a normative dimension as well. Sharing is not simply an economic or abstractly ethical imperative, as Michael Holquist puts it, but rather a 'condition inherent in the very act of being human' (1990: 34). Insofar as each of us occupies a unique position in time/space, the self–other relation is mutually enriching, so long as exotopy or 'outsideness' is successfully maintained. However, Bakhtin asserts that if the 'event is transposed in all its constituents to the unitary plane of a single consciousness, and it is within this single consciousness that the event is to be understood and deduced in all its constituents' (1990: 87), impoverishment rather than enrichment is the result. This reifies the live event, and transforms the particularity of lived experience into an empty abstraction. What is lost in this transcription is the actual, living creative forces at work in the encounter between self and other on the terrain of daily life – the integrity of the 'living and in principle non-merging participants of the event' (Bakhtin 1990: 87). Following on from a position he initially sketched out in *Toward a Philosophy of the Act*, Bakhtin suggests that this reification occurs because, under modernity, a purely cognitive relation to the other is encouraged and deemed to be of the highest value. In so doing, we relate to the other, not as another subject, but as an object. Abstract, dispassionate contemplation from afar supplants active co-participation within a shared horizon of value and meaning. A properly *ethical* relation to the other requires a 'loving and value-positing consciousness', within the context of everyday existence, and not a neutral, objectifying gaze projected from the Archimedean vantage-point of an isolated, solipsistic ego. For Bakhtin, 'cognitive-discursive thought' is, at least on its own terms, inherently non-ethical, because it cannot tolerate 'another consciousness outside itself, cannot enter into relations with another consciousness, one that is autonomous and distinct from it' (1990: 88).

DIALOGISM AND THE 'LINGUISTIC TURN'

To recapitulate briefly the central argument thus far: in Bakhtin's view, as for the phenomenologist Alfred Schütz, the 'paramount reality' of human beings is our embodied existence within the everyday lifeworld. Unlike Schütz, however, the realm of the everyday is not a simple repository of habitualized, unreflective actions and inchoate and unsystematic thoughts. Rather, it constitutes the primary terrain on which our values are actively constructed, in which a world of contingency is transformed into one of meaningfulness. As Graham Pechey astutely puts it, Bakhtin's thoughts on this subject 'turn not on the meaning of life but the life of meaning' (1993: 61). Moreover, by the time he wrote 'Author and Hero' in the early 1920s, he came to realize that this process of value-creation could not take place outside of the 'contraposition' of self and other, in which incarnate subjects live their lives in distinct times and places, but co-participate in a shared lifeworld and act to 'consummate' each other's life narrative by providing an exotopic viewpoint, a 'surplus of vision'. It is noteworthy that although Bakhtin does concern himself with the nature of language in these early phenomenological writings – in 'Author and hero', for instance, he observes that 'Language or, rather, the world of language [is] actualized in an utterance of lived life within myself and within the other' (1990: 230) – it remains of largely secondary interest. This observation is perhaps surprising, mainly because Bakhtin is usually construed as a philosopher of language and dialogue *par excellence*. What is distinctive about his writings from the mid-1920s onwards is that language – or, more specifically, the dialogical properties of language-use, as inscribed within both everyday speech-acts and cultural texts of all sorts – tends to occupy centre-stage. Dialogue, in Bakhtin's view, is not simply a form of linguistic exchange that occurs between two existing entities or consciousnesses. Indeed, this is precisely what he finds objectionable about Ferdinand de Saussure's famous structuralist model of language-use. For Bakhtin, dialogism constitutes a generalized perspective, a 'model of the world' that stresses continual interaction and interconnectedness, relationality, and the permeability of both symbolic and physical boundaries. A central element of this worldview is the notion that entities are not pre-constituted monads, but are formed in and through their dialogical relations with other things, a process that is ongoing and without ultimate closure or finality.

In terms of the sociocultural world *per se*, Bakhtin is emphatic that the phenomenon of 'self-ness' is constituted through the operation of a dense and conflicting network of discourses and signifying practices that are themselves bound up with the intricate phenomenology of the self–other relation, within the everyday lifeworld. His essential point is that a self-sufficient, Cartesian *cogito* cannot possibly exist, except as a mythical construct projected by egological, idealist philosophies. This is because the very process of acquiring self-consciousness and a sense of distinctiveness *vis-à-vis* others is something that is utterly dependent upon our verbal interaction with another 'I'. 'I realize myself initially through others: from them I receive words, forms, and tonalities for the formation of the initial idea of myself', asserts Bakhtin. 'Just as the body is formed initially in the mother's womb (body), a person's consciousness awakens wrapped in another's consciousness' (1986: 138). A total separation from the other and the aspiration to pure autonomy does not lead to mastery or ennoblement *à la* Robinson Crusoe, but can only result in the loss of self, a figurative death: '*To be means to communicate.* Absolute death (non-being) is the state of being unheard, unrecognized' (Bakhtin 1984b: 287). The presence of the other in oneself must be recognized and respected. Only then can we gain an awareness of a self that is not egocentric but profoundly social and intersubjective. Everything relevant to the self enters through the words of others, insists Bakhtin. Even the most rigidly solipsistic or monologic voice is premised upon a 'firm social support, presupposes a *we*' (1984b: 280–1). We must realize that every aspect of consciousness and every practice a person engages in is constituted dialogically, through the ebb and flow of a multitude of continuous and inherently responsive communicative acts. Unlike the monologic word, which always 'gravitates towards itself and its referential object', the dialogic word is locked into an intense relationship with the word of another. It is always addressed to someone, real or imagined – a witness, a judge or simply a listener – and it is accompanied by the keen anticipation of another's response. Nor is the dialogic word a passive vehicle of neutral description or information: because it is designed to provoke a response, to initiate dialogue, it is an 'arena of battle between two voices'. 'The word, the living word, inseparably linked with dialogic communion, by its very nature wants to be heard and answered' (Bakhtin 1984b: 300). Hence, dialogism renounces the imposition of abstract theoretical schemas onto the concrete sociohistorical world. It begins the task of inquiry by assuming the absolute integrity of real, flesh-and-blood human beings and the symbolic exchanges that occur within the realm of the everyday. Real dialogue is ultimately open-ended and 'unfinalizable'. It does not conform to an inherent logic of development; it does not unfold temporally in a given, predetermined manner in any necessitarian sense. Rick Bowers usefully characterizes this stance as 'a refusal of closure, a celebration of difference, an insistence on socially-in-scribed discourse' (1994: 569). Insofar as social life involves at its core intersubjective communication, and dialogue itself is constitu-tively open-ended, it follows that human beings, and the socio-cultural practices they engage in, are bound up in a continual process of non-teleological 'becoming'.

By the time Bakhtin wrote *Problems of Dostoevsky's Poetics*, he recognized that the primary medium through which intersubjective relations occur, and our values and meanings are articulated, is language itself. The ceaseless flow of living dialogue expresses most fully the nuances and ambiguous shades of meaning within every-day life, the rich and irrepressible potentialities inherent in prosaic human experience, and the complex intertwining of the self–other relationship. Speech, as Oliver Sacks puts it, 'does *not* consist of words alone, [but] consists of *utterance* – an uttering-forth of one's whole meaning with one's whole being' (1987: 81). However, it is important to understand that Bakhtin's 'linguistic turn' is also, *inter alia*, a 'social turn', in that he starts to realize the inherent limitations of a purely phenomenological approach to the study of aesthetics and intersubjectivity. This 'social turn' is one of the central themes of Michael Bernard-Donals's study *Mikhail Bakhtin: Between Phenomenology and Marxism* (1994). Bernard-Donals suggests that phenomenology, particularly in the work of Edmund Husserl and Roman Ingarden, has generally been concerned with the process by which individuals relate cognitively to objects and develop an awareness and understanding of their world, particularly in terms of aesthetic judgement. By contrast, more sociological approaches, particularly Marxism, tend to focus on the level of social relations. *Toward a Philosophy of the Act* is the most straightforwardly phenomenological of Bakhtin's texts, but 'Author and Hero' can be viewed as a transitional work, because here Bakhtin places especial emphasis on the phenomenon of intersubjectivity. He does so, however, mainly by extrapolating from the self–object model of phenomenology articulated by Husserl and others. At this point, the actual *sociological* content of Bakhtin's notion of everyday life, and the virtues of a prosaic outlook, remain sketchy and under-developed. Yet by the time language comes to occupy Bakhtin's attention, he begins to adumbrate a more recognizably materialist and historicizing approach to the study of human relations and communicative praxis. Bernard-Donals characterizes this second paradigm as an idiosyncratic and anti-reductionist form of Marxism. In such a materialist theory, the focus shifts away from pheno-menology as such to the process by which subjects are constituted through their instantiation within wider social factors, particularly the ideological and linguistic superstructure. Accordingly, in his later writings, Bakhtin places the lingual dimension of human life centre-stage with respect to the formation of selfhood and social relations in general, which gives us considerable insight into how subjects are 'positioned' ideologically within particular cultural and discursive formations that are marked by asymmetrical relations of power. This conceptual shift, in turn, sensitized Bakhtin to the importance of sociocultural critique. He contends, for instance, that subordinate social groups can 'dialogize' authoritative or mono-logical discourses and reinscribe them with new meanings, values and significances. But he also realizes that our ability to subvert or dialogize such monologic ideologies is contingent upon an aware-ness of – and capacity to transform – the material or sociohistorical conditions within which particular discursive formations are located and such ideological conflicts played out. Bakhtin therefore developed, at least tacitly, a 'theory that maintains a distinction between rhetorical (that is, linguistically-embedded) knowledge and material (that is, extra-linguistic) knowledge, but that nevertheless functions with relation to – and reveals valid knowledge about – both' (Bernard-Donals 1994: 171).[4]

Despite this drift towards a more recognizably materialist social theory, Bakhtin continued to oscillate between phenomenological and sociological concepts throughout his career, without fully re-conciling or synthesizing them. In terms of his preoccupation with the everyday, we can see its influence in his 1930s writings on European cultural history and the novel, including such essays as 'Discourse in the Novel', 'From a Prehistory of Novelistic Discourse' and 'Forms of Time and of the Chronotope in the Novel'. In the remainder of this section, I will focus on two central themes that run through these writings: first, how the phenomenon of 'hetero-glossia', or the multiform speech genres and modes of discourse found in the everyday lifeworld, is incorporated into the novel form; and secondly, how Bakhtin elaborates on the 'prosaic epistemology' he advanced initially in his phenomenological writings.

With respect to the concept of heteroglossia, it is important to note that what animates Bakhtin's approach here is the intention to critique various theoretical and aesthetic positions which, in his eyes, serve to buttress and legitimate the centralization and hier-archization of what he terms the 'verbal-ideological' sphere, in the context of the everyday lifeworld. Bakhtin argues that a cursory examination of the modern European novel reveals the presence of a diversity of 'social speech types'. Hence, the 'concrete social context' of discourse, and the time–space referents or chronotopes they contain, must be revealed before the dialogical nature of the novel can itself be comprehended. Whilst this multi-voiced quality of the novel has long been recognized, traditional approaches have explained this by reference to the stylistic idiosyncracies of a given author. In Bakhtin's view, this approach can be faulted because it assumes that the individual author is responsible for all aesthetic creativity and constitutes the epicentre of meaning. He dismisses the latter as a vestige of egological idealism, and argues that the authorial voice is secondary to the incorporation of social hetero-glossia into the novel form. Indeed, the fetishization of the authorial voice has other, more ominous ramifications: for Bakhtin, it is nothing less than an ideological expression of forces that strive to unify hegemonically the social world and smother the concrete particularity of everyday life. According to him, a myriad of philosophical, literary and linguistic movements, from Aristotle's poetics to Saussure's structuralism, can be implicated in this reifying and centralizing process. Far from being innocent examples of 'pure scholarship', these traditions have actively contributed to the consolidation of a unified language throughout European history. This official language takes its cue from the rarefied conversational and literary generic forms characteristic of the educated elites, and it defines itself in contradistinction to the 'low' or everyday speech types found in the street, in the marketplace, and the public square. Officialdom attempts to stamp a fixed order on these heteroglot languages, to introduce a canonical style to which the latter must submit, so as to 'preserve the socially sealed-off quality of a privileged community' and solidify the boundary between 'legitimate' and 'illegitimate' language-use. Nevertheless, argues Bakhtin, this drive to unify the verbal-ideological world is never completely successful. Accompanying this centripetal tendency towards integration are (more or less powerful) centrifugal processes that continue unabated. The latter – which Bakhtin identifies increasingly with 'folk-festive' genres of ordinary people – operate to ensure the subversion and dis-unification of the officially sanctioned language system from within. As such, he views the social world as the terrain of a ceaseless battle between the official forces of stasis and fixity, and the 'unofficial' impetus towards movement, change and diversification. The proliferation of socio-ideological points of view in modern society effectively ends the hegemony of a single and unitary official language and worldview, and it frees a plurality of 'cultural-semantic and emotional intentions' that are inscribed within everyday social relations from the one-dimensional constraints of earlier forms of mythical thought. 'The internal speech diversity of a literary dialect and of its surrounding extraliterary environment [undermines] the authority of custom and of whatever traditions still fetter linguistic consciousness', writes Bakhtin. 'It erodes that system of national myth . . . destroying once and for all a mythic and magical attitude to language and the word' (1981: 368–9). For Bakhtin, then, language is unitary only in the abstract; in reality, there exists a irreducible plurality of 'verbal-ideological and social belief systems'. Within any given official 'national language', there are always present numerous 'social languages' and everyday speech genres, including oratory or journalistic forms, the language of the marketplace, or rural dialects. The latter incorporate different modes of intentionality, intonation and social evaluation; they emerge out of the everyday world and enter into struggle, invest and animate human consciousness with specific patterns of motivation and action, coexist and interrelate dialogically. It is this capacity of the novel to assimilate such a variety of everyday speech genres and utterances that makes it an important site through which wider discursive and ideological struggles are condensed and refracted. By carving artistic images of social languages out of the raw material of everyday heteroglossia, the novel constitutes a privileged vantage-point from whence to grasp the 'great dialogue' of the age. The novel, in short, 'denies the absolutism of a single and unitary language [by incorporating] the languages of social groups, professions and other cross-sections of everyday life' (Bakhtin 1981: 366–7).

This brings me to a second leitmotiv of Bakhtin's 1930s writings on the novel: that the puncturing of 'epic distance' through the introjection of heteroglossia into the novel form makes possible a heightened understanding of our intercorporeal embeddedness in everyday life. Prior to the emergence of the novel, literary genres such as the epic were located exclusively in mythological time and space, an abstract chronotope that bore no relationship to temporality and spatiality as it was actually experienced by real people in historical societies. What is most remarkable about the novel, according to Bakhtin, is that it is structured, not by reference to the absolute distance of a mythologized past, a long-dead and unreachable 'golden age' that is 'outside any possible contact with the present in all its openness', but rather by a 'zone of maximally close contact between the represented object and contemporary society' that is infused with 'personal experience and free creative imagination' (1981: 19, 31). Again, this shift to a form of 'direct and even crude contact' with actual history and sensuous, embodied experience helps to precipitate a shift in human consciousness itself away from the reifications of mythopoetic societies towards a more nuanced and critical appreciation of the material circumstances of our daily social lives. The modern period, he writes, 'is characterized by an extraordinary complexity and a deepening in our perception of the world; there is an unusual growth in demands on human discernment, on mature objectivity and the critical' (1981: 40). In taking this position, it should be noted that Bakhtin demonstrates his adherence to a sophisticated and essentially dialectical view of modernity, one that is cognizant of its dangers and excesses as well as its potentially emancipatory qualities.[5]

PROSAICS AND CARNIVAL

What we can detect in Bakhtin's writings on cultural and literary history is a revisioning and extension of his earlier phenomenological notion of the prosaic into the realm of social discourse and various literary genres. 'Bakhtin adheres to the idea that social and aesthetic forms are produced under particular circumstances', as Stanley Aronowitz observes, 'and the task of language study is another kind of historiography: the analysis of everyday life' (1994: 140). We also see the rudiments of a more overtly sociopolitical consciousness emerging, as evinced by Bakhtin's comments about the ceaseless 'battle' between official (monologizing, centralizing) and 'unofficial' (dialogizing, multiform) sociocultural forces, and the latter he identifies with the popular or 'folk-festive' culture of the people, the 'eternally living element of unofficial speech and unofficial thought'. What Stallybrass and White (1986) call Bakhtin's 'cosmic populism' reaches its apotheosis in what is arguably his most important, and certainly his most politically-charged text: namely, *Rabelais and His World*. Here, Bakhtin turns his attention towards the boisterous, disruptive and libidinous qualities of popular cultural forms and the collective body, within a historical period marked by the collapse of medievalism and the emergence of a more open and humanistic Renaissance culture.

Before entering into a fuller discussion of this text, however, is it important to clarify what Bakhtin had in mind by the critique of theoreticism, as well as the precise nature of the relationship between prosaics and carnival. With respect to the former, Bakhtin's post-Cartesian stance is clearly suspicious of the more extravagant and aggrandizing claims of rationalist and positivist-inspired traditions. Since he feels that dialogue, in the widest possible sense, is the most important medium through which selfhood and social relations are expressed and realized, Bakhtin continually emphasizes the presence of what Roland Barthes once called the 'grain of the voice', the trace of the flesh-and-blood personality that lies behind every utterance. His acute sense of the dense particularity of lived experience, of the thing-in-itself, leads him to decry the reification of language and concrete human actions effected by formalist and rationalist approaches. Bakhtin's ongoing concern with value and existential meaning explains why some of his sharpest critical barbs were reserved for the arid abstractions of philosophical idealism. Dialogism must come to grips with the ambivalent, sensuous materiality of human existence, and also with the pragmatic moral demands that 'lived life' continually makes upon us. Yet at the same time it is important not to give the impression that Bakhtin is arguing against the utility of theory *per se*. This point is made forcefully by Ken Hirschkop, who suggests that the frequent interpretation of Bakhtin as an 'anti-theoretical theorist' overlooks the fact he did not hesitate to utilize abstract concepts and modes of analysis throughout his writings. There are clear dangers in fetishizing the everyday as the *locus classicus* of all that is valuable about human existence, which can have the effect of encouraging a naive empiricism that affirms uncritically the *status quo*. 'The greatest possible abstractions, and a refusal to engage in conceptual argument', as Hirschkop puts it, 'lead to the grossest and most dogmatic empiricism, whereby individualized opinions and pre-judices (our common, unargued sense of what dialogism and responsibility consist of) are put forward as philosophical truths' (1990b: 23). This interpretation is reinforced by Bakhtin's own comment that Enlightenment and modernist modes of thought have tended to encourage a static and narrowly empiricist concep-tion of reality, thereby sanctioning the immediately 'given' at the expense of an awareness of a deeper, processual reality. Such an empiricism manifestly fails to recognize the 'embryo, the shoots, the seeds, the prophecies and revelations' of possible future becomings (1984a: 124).

Hence, an appeal to the prosaic as a kind of guarantor of the non-ideological simply ignores the extensive colonization of the everyday by the dominant discourses and practices of power, what Michel Foucault has described as the disciplining of the lifeworld through the various technologies of social control, which, for many, is an important feature of modernity. As Gayatri Spivak (1988) has cogently argued, the tendency for phenomenology to privilege immediate or direct experience sometimes entails the conclusion that 'theory' as such can only function to suppress difference and heterogeneity. Such a position results in a vague populism that is 'utopian' in the pejorative sense, because it assumes that the oppressed can effect their own liberation without the translation of rebellious energies into effective forms of political organization, and because it precludes the Gramscian project of 'the difficult task of counterhegemonic production'. To stress the importance of the everyday should not lead us to overlook the need to 'defetishize the concrete', as Spivak puts it. Her stance is echoed by Michael Bernard-Donals, when he suggests that we have to be cognizant of the broader sociohistorical conditions within which everyday activities occur. Bakhtin, he argues, was acutely aware of the 'connection between ethics and an anti-theoretism of lived life on the one hand and the need for an understanding of the material that comprises the lived life on the other. [He] knew full well the elements of a social criticism or theory that were required in order to fully [understand] cognitive-ethical action' (1995: 51). In other words, some element of abstraction or theoretical cognition will always be present in our reflexive understanding of self and experiential situation, particularly if we accept the possibility that our everyday consciousness might be influenced by ideological factors. Insofar as our 'common sense' can be shaped profoundly by the wider sociopolitical forces and the imperatives of dominant social groups, ideological criticism, what Paul Ricoeur calls a 'hermeneutics of suspicion', must be on the agenda of any genuinely critical, emancipatory social theory.

Secondly, it is important to stress that the carnival (especially its 'defamiliarizing' and utopian qualities) and prosaics are not anti-thetical notions, as is sometimes implied in the literature on Bakhtin. 'Carnival is steeped in the everyday, and the everyday cannot be divorced from its other – the carnival', as Wall and Thomson cogently assert. 'Bakhtin's theorization of the everyday as inextricably intertwined with the carnivalesque emphasizes the traces of otherness in the most insignificant of utterances' (1993: 66). Or, as Bakhtin himself suggests, we should not remain deaf to the 'carnivalesque overtone [that] remains everyday in life' (1986: 154). What Bakhtin's usage of the concept of 'carnival' does is to problematize uncritical and naively empiricist interpretations of everyday life, by drawing our attention to the underlying socio-cultural forces that transgress and disrupt our received common-sensical notions and habitualized viewpoints (Polan 1989: 7; Eagleton 1986: 118). The carnivalesque image 'brings together, unifies, weds, and combines the sacred with the profane, the lofty with the low, the great with the insignificant, the wise with the stupid', writes Bakhtin (1984b: 123), and in so doing underscores the inevitability of change and transformation. In transgressing the usual norms and rules that govern the more routinized and habitual aspects of daily life, carnival represents 'life turned inside out': 'incompleteness, becoming, ambiguity, indefinability, non-canon-icalism – indeed, all that jolts us out of our normal expectations and epistemological complacency' (Clark and Holquist 1984: 312). Hence, Bakhtin's evocation of the 'carnivalesque' is best understood as a continuation and extension of the theme of prosaics in a new and innovative direction. It is indicative of his desire to de-reify the sociocultural world, to overcome the alienation fostered by contemporary society and to encourage a renewed awareness of what he calls 'the dregs of an everyday gross reality', the hidden and all-too-often suppressed potentialities that lie within the sensuous, the bodily and the profane.

In *Rabelais and His World*, Bakhtin celebrates the sixteenth-century writer François Rabelais and his novel *Gargantua and Pantagruel* for many reasons, but primarily because this work of fiction managed to incorporate the lived, everyday culture of the 'common folk [that] was to a great extent a culture of the loud word spoken in the open, in the street and marketplace' (1984a: 182). According to Bakhtin, the earthy, sensuous, even scatological qualities of popular daily life had a tremendous symbolic power to combat the 'monolithic seriousness' of officialdom. The characteristic images and tropes of a 'thousand-year-old popular culture' (symbolic inversions, ritualized parodies, and so forth) were, in his opinion, capable of deflating the pompous idealism of the 'agelasts', the self-appointed scholastic guardians of order, propriety and respectability, thereby undermining the ideological foundations of a gloomy and moribund medieval system. In repudiating the asceticism and other-worldly spirituality of medievalism, this folk-festive culture laid primary emphasis on the embodied aspects of human life within the context of an everyday, informal sociality. 'These utopian tones were immersed in the depths of concrete, practical life, a life that could be touched, that was filled with aroma and sound', writes Bakhtin. 'This was completely in accord with the specific character of all Rabelaisian images, which *combine* a broad universalism and utopianism with extraordinarily concrete, obvious and vivid traits, strictly localized and technically precise' (1984a: 185; my emphasis). *Rabelais and His World* constitutes Bakhtin's most thorough-going and radical attempt to demolish the notion of the sovereign, monological subject and its ontological basis in a rigid dualism between subject and object, mind and body, nature and culture, and to replace this orientation with an alternative conceptual and sensory regime that privileges the somatic and the everyday. In particular, he 'fleshes out' the nascent themes of embodiment and intercorporeality that he sketchily developed in his early phenomenological writings, by giving these phenomena a markedly higher degree of socio-historical specificity and concreteness. 'Alterity' in the context of the carnivalesque becomes less a matter of the intersection of different visual fields or verbal exchanges than the bodily intertwining of self and other, including the 'other' of nature, within what Merleau-Ponty liked to call the overarching 'flesh of the world' (Gardiner 1998).

This orientation is best evinced in Bakhtin's discussion of the 'grotesque body' and his analysis of a succession of different 'body canons' that he claims has occurred in European history since the Middle Ages. Repudiating the asceticism and other-worldly spirituality of medievalism, the grotesque stresses the sensual and intercorporeal aspects of human existence. All that is abstract and idealized is degraded and 'lowered' by the transferral of these images and symbols to the material, profane level, which represents the 'indissoluble unity' of earth and body. Grotesque realism acts to 'degrade, bring down to earth, turn their subject into flesh' (1984a: 20). Bakhtin's quirky, 'scatological' materialism is designed to challenge resolutely the arid abstractions of idealist philosophy, which is demonstrated clearly when he writes that the grotesque image 'materializes truth and does not permit it to be torn away from the earth, at the same time preserving the earth's universal and cosmic nature' (1984a: 285). Accordingly, acts of defecation and bodily expulsion, sex, birth, eating, drinking and conception perform a major symbolic role in folkloric texts and practices. As Renate Lachmann puts it, 'The material and corporeal are namely the manifest as such, they are what is really "real." What matters to Bakhtin is matter' (1989: 126). For instance, the act of tasting and consuming food and drink, an image so often evoked in *Rabelais and His World*, reveals the body as open, unfinished; its connection with the universe is most fully revealed because this body transgresses its own limits by assimilating the material world and by merging with the other beings, objects and animals that populate it. 'The encounter of man with the world, which takes place inside the open, biting, rending, chewing mouth, is one of the most ancient, and most important objects of human thought and imagery. Here man tastes the world, introduces it into his body, makes it a part of himself', asserts Bakhtin, whereby the 'limits between man and the world are erased' (1984a: 281). In promoting the idea of a sensuous, direct and familiar contact with everything, rather than through the rarefied abstractions of scientific thought or obscure theological systems, Bakhtin demonstrates effectively that the body as depicted in grotesque realism is not an autonomous, self-sufficient object. It is irrevocably opposed to the 'completed atomized being' of bourgeois culture. In blurring the distinction between mind and body, self and other, and between humanity and nature, carnival presents a profound challenge to the traditional bourgeois ideals of predictability, stability and closure (Gardiner 1993b, 1999).

The crux of the grotesque aesthetic therefore lies in its portrayal of transformation and temporal change, of the contradictory yet interconnected processes of death and birth, ending and becoming. Grotesque symbolism explicitly denies the possibility of completion, of ending, of finality. For instance, carnival images often involve the playful combination of animal, vegetable and human forms, or the metamorphosis of one into another, so that 'the borderlines that divide the kingdoms of nature in the usual picture of the world were boldly infringed' (Bakhtin 1984a: 32). The system of images associated with the grotesque body takes innumerable forms in the rituals, language and artefacts of folk culture: in the colloquial oaths and curses of 'marketplace speech' and the symbolic oppositions of praise/abuse and crowning/ uncrowning, in folklore and myth (such as tales of giants and griffins, harpies and demons), in diableries and mystery plays, the bodily relics of saints, and the circuses and comic performers of the marketplace. The carnivalesque functions to reverse the estrangement of humanity from nature fostered by the hierarchical medieval order, to re-familiarize human beings with the natural world (including human nature) and thereby bring it 'closer to man'. Folk-festive culture, in short, promised a better and happier future, one characterized by material abundance, equality and freedom – a distinctly utopian vision epitomized by the mythical 'Land of Cokaygne'. 'The popular conquest of the world', Bakhtin says, 'destroyed and suspended all alienation; it drew the world closer to man, to his body, permitted him to touch and test every object, examine it from all sides, enter into it, turn it inside out, compare it to every phenomenon, however exalted or holy, analyze, weigh, measure, try it on. And all this could be done on the one plane of material sensual experience' (1984a: 380). Perhaps a concrete sociohistorical example would help to clarify Bakhtin's concept of carnival and the grotesque body. In his book *Popular Culture in Early Modern Europe*, the noted cultural historian Peter Burke discusses at length the famous 'feast of fools'. This celebration typically occurred in late December, and the central event was the election of a mock bishop or abbot – the 'lord of misrule'. This was followed by dancing, street processions, a mock mass enacted by clergy in women's clothes or dressed back to front, the recital of bawdy songs and verses, card-playing at the altar, and the usual feasting and drinking – especially the consumption of large blood sausages, an obvious phallic/fertility symbol. The feast of fools was, as Burke puts it, a perfect example of the 'literal enactment of the world turned upside down' (1978: 192).

Bakhtin's decision to focus on Rabelais and the folk-festive culture of this period is clearly not an arbitrary one. He consciously sets out to identify a historical conjuncture of great significance, a relatively brief interregnum marked by the breakdown of feudalism (with its denial and mortification of the flesh), but before the consolidation of Cartesian dualism and the valorization of an abstract visuality, and the construal of the social self as a unified and autonomous ego. As Stephen Toulmin asserts in *Cosmopolis: The Hidden Agenda of Modernity*, the brief flourishing and great promise of Renaissance humanism, exemplified in the writings of Rabelais, Montaigne and Erasmus, was effectively squandered when thinkers like Descartes and Leibniz came to dominate European intellectual life after the seventeenth century. Whereas the former emphasized the sensual, local, oral and particularistic aspects of human life and language – in essence, the prosaic viewpoint that Bakhtin valorized – the latter transferred cosmology and philosophy to a 'higher, stratospheric plane, on which nature and ethics had to conform to abstract, timeless, general and universal theories' (1990: 35). The Enlightenment, Toulmin suggests, consolidated this intellectually imperious and reifying trend, with deleterious results that are still being felt today. Bakhtin would have undoubtedly concurred with Toulmin's assessment. In successfully combatting premodern mythological and metaphysical forms of thought, Bakhtin argues in *Rabelais and His World* that modernity's preference for formalized reason encouraged a condensation and purification of reality. By adhering dogmatically to 'abstractly moral or abstractly rational criteria', the idealist, metaphysical systems developed under modernity have prevented humankind from understanding and participating in the immanent dynamism and open-endedness of the world. The Enlighteners' mechanistic view of matter and penchant for abstract typification has served to impoverish the world, and has precluded a proper appreciation of the 'culture of ambivalence' that he so clearly favours. 'In the age of the Enlightenment', Bakhtin writes, 'cognitive reason became the yardstick of all that existed. This abstract rationalism and anti-historicism . . . prevented the Encyclopaedists from grasping theoretically the nature of ambivalent festive laughter' (1984a: 118).

CONCLUSION

What I have tried to demonstrate is that the work of Mikhail Bakhtin is marked by an ongoing concern with the nature and dynamics of everyday life. Despite the myriad shifts and transformations in his thinking, what we witness in all of his writings is a profound distrust of abstract, metaphysical idealism and reductive and deterministic social theories. He seeks to return us to the terrain of sensuous, embodied human existence and concrete inter-human relations. In this, Bakhtin's thinking evinces a recognizably Marxian rejection of the effects of reification and alienation on human consciousness and social relations, although his idiosyncratic, 'somatic' materialism is perhaps closer to Nietzsche's ecstatic Dionysianism than Marx's more sober vision of *homo faber*. At the same time, particularly in *Rabelais and His World*, Bakhtin pursues this agenda without wholly abandoning emancipatory and utopian aspirations. A Bakhtinian prosaics promises a novel way (pun intended) of conceptualizing in a critical fashion the nature of sociocultural relations, one that places especial stress on the subtleties of human dialogue and the phenomenological 'depth' of the self–other relation, the inherent creativities and irrepressible potentialities that inhere in everyday activities, and the limits and dangers of an abstract rationality. At the heart of this preoccupation with the everyday, finally, is an ethical concern, highlighted by his insistence that 'A philosophy of life can only be a moral philosophy' (1993: 56). Only a prosaic orientation can foster an intense awareness of the nuances of situation, of the timbre of voice, of what Bakhtin calls 'radical difference'. By promoting a heightened cognizance of the indeterminate, 'impure' and ambivalent character-istics of everyday life, Bakhtin alerts us to the very phenomenon of difference or 'otherness', and the moral imperative behind its nurturing and preservation. As William H. Thornton has cogently observed, 'the very possibility of cultural difference hinges upon a politics of impurity – one without final solutions or "finalizable" (positivistic or "poetic") representation' (1994: 92).

4

HENRI LEFEBVRE: PHILOSOPHER OF THE ORDINARY

The physicalist image presented by positivism impoverishes the human world, and its absolute exclusiveness
deforms reality, because it reduces the real world to but *one*
dimension and aspect, to the dimension of extensity and of
quantitative relations. In addition, it cleaves the human
world, when it declares the world of physicalism, the world
of idealised real values, of extensity, quantity, mensuration
and geometric shapes to be the only reality, while calling
man's everyday world a fiction.

Karel Kosík

INTRODUCTION

The French Marxist Henri Lefebvre (1901–91) is the quintessential
critical theorist of everyday life. His prolific and remarkably wide-
ranging writings, which span some sixty years, touch on virtually
every topic discussed in this book: language, the body, space, and
the imagination, to name but a few. During his long and productive
career, once free of the intellectual straightjacket of the French
Communist Party (PCF), Lefebvre productively engaged with many
theories and perspectives ancillary to Marxism, including existentialism, phenomenology and structuralism. This engagement was
registered in his open-ended and constantly evolving perspective,
one that never threatened to harden into dogma. Yet despite a brief
period of interest in his work in the early 1970s – which, perhaps
not surprisingly, coincided with the ascendency of the New Left –
Lefebvre's ideas have been greatly neglected in the English-speaking
world, outside of intellectual histories of postwar French political
and social thought,[1] although this situation has been rectified in

part by the recent publication of Rob Shields's masterful intellectual biography *Lefebvre, Love and Struggle: Spatial Dialectics* (1999). Given the current popularity of other French thinkers, such as Foucault, Baudrillard and Derrida, in Anglo-American social and cultural theory, this disregard is hard to fathom. One could speculate that it may be because Lefebvre – although he developed many insights that anticipated certain aspects of postmodernist and poststructuralist thought – remained unrepentant about his fidelity to a critical Marxism and the utopian project of human liberation. Indeed, shortly before his death, he proclaimed himself the last of the French Marxists (Davidson 1992: 152). This profession would no doubt strike most contemporary French intellectuals as hopelessly *gauche* and retrograde. Despite, or perhaps because of his commitment to currently unfashionable ideas and causes, I hope to demonstrate here that Henri Lefebvre articulated an exceedingly valuable and multifaceted critique of everyday life, one that has continuing importance and relevance.

LEFEBVRE'S LIFE AND WORK: AN OVERVIEW

Before discussing Lefebvre's concept of 'everyday life' in detail, I will begin with a brief overview of his life and work and situate it within the context of twentieth-century French political and theoretical debate. Born in 1901, Lefebvre grew up in the town of Navarreaux. Deeply religious in his youth, he studied Catholic thinkers like St Augustine and Pascal at the University of Aix-en-Provence, with an eye to eventually becoming a college instructor. However, whilst studying philosophy at the Sorbonne in Paris, Lefebvre came to reject religion as an abstract and reified system of belief that denied and dissipated human potential, and thereafter declared himself a militant atheist. Finding little of interest in the prevailing currents of academic French philosophy (such as Cartesianism or Bergsonism), in the mid-1920s he helped to co-found the so-called 'Philosophies' group. This gathering included such individuals as Paul Nizan, Georges Politzer and Norbert Guterman, some of whom later had a significant impact on French intellectual life. At this time, Lefebvre was also attracted to the Surrealist movement, and, along with other members of the Philosophies circle, attended meetings of the so-called 'Bureau of Surrealist Inquiries'. Although Lefebvre's enthusiasm for Surrealism ebbed and flowed over the course of his career, an enduring result of this encounter was his exposure to the writings of Hegel. For in their search for philosophical alternatives to the prevailing hegemony of Cartesianism, the Surrealists (especially Breton) had been instrumental in introducing Hegel to French audiences, albeit in a bowdlerized version. Lefebvre was also attracted to the existentialism of Martin Heidegger and the early Sartre, even though in some ways he anticipated or prefigured many existentialist ideas (Shields 1999: 83). He was compelled to officially renounce existentialism during his Communist Party days, yet Lefebvre's work continued to display an interest in existentialist themes.

His interest in Hegel led directly to a study of Marx, in particular his youthful, humanistic texts. Lefebvre joined the French Communist Party in 1928 and helped found *La Revue Marxiste*, generally regarded as the first significant Marxist theoretical journal in France. Along with Norman Guterman, Lefebvre translated and facilitated the publication of Marx's early writings, including the *Economic and Philosophical Manuscripts of 1844*, as well as Lenin's notebooks on Hegel. In 1939, Lefebvre published his own interpretation of Marx's *oeuvre*, entitled *Dialectical Materialism*, which emphasized the Hegelian roots of Marxist thought and stressed the themes of alienation, praxis and human self-realization (Schmidt 1972; Trebitsch 1991b). Lefebvre's orientation did not endear him to the PCF, which by that time had become thoroughly Stalinized and adhered to a vulgarized dialectical materialism in matters of theory.

After the war, during which he fought in the Resistance, Lefebvre wrote an enduring classic of modern social thought, *Critique of Everyday Life*. This study extended some of the themes he explored in *Dialectical Materialism*, but in a more sociological and less speculative and philosophical fashion. The appearance of this volume prompted the Party to chasten Lefebvre as an avant-gardist in theory, and forced him to publish a humiliating 'auto-critique'. During the rest of his tenure in the Party, Lefebvre mainly wrote three kinds of works: first, rather orthodox Marxist tracts; secondly, fairly straightforward sociological inquiries, including a highly regarded study of French rural life; and thirdly, a series of books that focused on aesthetic and literary themes, including a study of Rabelais (1955). Despite his chastisement, Lefebvre persisted in his attempt to democratize and de-Stalinize the Party from within. To this end, he participated in various internal opposition groupings, an effort rewarded by his expulsion from the PCF in 1958. Freed from the constraints of Party organization and dogma, Lefebvre joined the innovative, independent Marxist circle that published the influential journal *Arguments*. This circle, which included the philosopher Edgar Morin, sociologist Alain Touraine, and semiotician Roland Barthes, strove to develop a critical and reflexive Marxism that was open to other intellectual trends. It also sought to understand the sociocultural transformations occurring within France and other Western industrial societies in the postwar era, including the impact of technology, the mass media, and consumerism (Poster 1975: 209–63). Following the cue of the *Arguments* group, during the 1960s Lefebvre was particularly concerned to bring his theory of everyday life up to date, by taking into account the changed conditions of 'neo-capitalism' that Marx's original theory could not explain adequately. This project culminated in the publication in 1968 of *Everyday Life in the Modern World*, which, like Guy Debord's 1967 book *Society of the Spectacle*, in many ways anticipated the tumultuous May–June 1968 events in France. Lefebvre was delighted by this popular upsurge against what he saw as a repressive, bureaucratic capitalism. At the same time, he was dismayed by the student movement's lack of direction and anti-intellectualism. This prompted Lefebvre to write an analysis of the uprising in 1969, translated as *The Explosion*. In the 1970s and 1980s, he broadened his interests to include urbanism, the phenomenon of space, and the reproduction of capitalism (Lefebvre 1995, 1996). This effort was crowned by his magisterial 1974 treatise *The Production of Space*. Lefebvre died in Paris in 1991 at the age of ninety.

THE CRITIQUE OF EVERYDAY LIFE

The key to understanding Lefebvre's conception of the everyday must be located in his 1947 treatise *Critique of Everyday Life*, which was supplemented by a lengthy introduction in the 1958 edition. This book contains *in nuce* many of the themes he habitually returned to throughout his lengthy career, including the dynamics of modernity and the role of leisure and cultural consumption in modern life. It is also suffused with the heady optimism of the post-liberation period in France, which was marked by a fervent desire for social transformation and a strong sense of national purpose. Later works found Lefebvre in a more reflective and cautious mood, stressing the recalcitrance of everyday life to revolutionary change and its susceptibility to bureaucratic restructuring.

Much of *Critique of Everyday Life* is taken up with a critical attack on philosophical idealism and Western philosophy in general. According to Lefebvre, the everyday has traditionally been regarded as trivial and inconsequential in Western thought at least since the Enlightenment, which has valorized the supposedly 'higher' functions of human reason as displayed in such specialized activities as art, philosophy and science. In particular, philosophers have often thought of themselves as occupying a realm of 'pure thought' unconnected to the messy vagaries of daily existence and the petty concerns of the common person. In Descartes's philosophy, for example, the paradigm of certain knowledge lay not in the evidence of the senses or the experiences of the body, but in the abstract propositions of mathematics. These axioms were located within a purely mental space surveilled by the imperious, rational Mind, the famous *cogito*. To Lefebvre's way of thinking, this Cartesian mind–body dualism, as with similar idealist philosophies, represented a systemic denigration of everyday life and of the lived experience of time, space and the body. Such an outlook had a distinct social origin: it was an expression of *alienation*, a loss of control over essential human capacities and powers that should be firmly rooted in daily existence. As such, the occlusion of the everyday in idealist thought can be linked to the historical emergence of capitalism as a socioeconomic system, and with the experience of modernity more generally. The position Lefebvre sketches out here closely follows Marx's original critique of philosophical idealism, which construed idealism as a set of beliefs severed from concrete social practices, especially labour, the latter involving the transformation of the natural world for the satisfaction of intrinsic human needs. Hence, idealist thought was best understood as a mystified inversion of real life. Likewise, Lefebvre accepts Marx's call for a fusion of theory and practice through a 'realization' of philosophy, in which the contradiction between the ideal and the real is overcome. As Michel Trebitsch puts it, 'the famous remark of Marx – that until now the philosophers have only interpreted the world; what is needed is to change it – appeared to Lefebvre as a visionary inspiration. Lefebvre defined the task he assigned to Marxism: to complete philosophy, i.e. to develop it and to go beyond it' (1991b: 11).

In order to validate his notion that the everyday should not be taken for granted or ignored, Lefebvre stresses that the everyday represents the site where we enter into a dialectical relationship with the external natural and social worlds in the most immediate and profound sense, and it is here where essential human desires, powers and potentialities are initially formulated, developed and realized concretely. It is through our mundane interactions with the material world that both subject and object are fully constituted and humanized through the medium of conscious human praxis. Moreover, it is in the everyday world where we confront the concrete 'other' in the most immediate and direct sense, and where the individual acquires a coherent identity or selfhood. In pre-modern societies, Lefebvre asserts, everyday life was not conceived of as separate from other, more specialized activities, but was fully integrated into a relatively undifferentiated totality of human practices. Such societies evinced a distinct *style of life*, a common culture, which coloured each individual's speech patterns, gestures, habits and rituals. As Lefebvre writes, each object and activity in premodern societies was 'linked to some "style" and therefore, as a work, contained while masking the larger functions and structures which were integral parts of its form' (1987: 8). Productive labour was organically connected to daily life, to the rhythms and cycles of the natural world, and the use-value of objects predominated. In short, there was no separate place or time for 'work' as distinct from everyday sociality, popular celebrations and collective rituals: 'The imperatives of the peasant community (the village) regulated not only the way work and domestic life were organized, but festivals as well' (1991a: 30–1).

With the consolidation of capitalism and bourgeois society, however, this state of affairs changed dramatically. Social activities became highly differentiated, and ceased to be consolidated into a unified whole. Labour is increasingly fragmented, regimented and specialized; family life and leisure are detached from work. Separated from organic community and from authentic intersubjectivity, the individual becomes 'isolated and inward-looking'. Consciousness is split into a public and private self, and labour divided into its mental and manual components (Sohn-Rethel 1978). Social inter-action tends to be purely utilitarian, dictated by the imperatives of production and the marketplace. People spend most of their lives constrained and defined by rigid, immobile social roles and occupational niches. Everyday life takes the form of largely un-conscious actions and performances: 'Many men, and even people in general, *do not know their own lives very well, or know them inadequately*' (1991a: 94). According to Lefebvre, under modernity imaginative and creative human activity is transformed into routinized and commodified forms, and the exchange-value of things holds sway over their utility, their use-value, leading to what Marx called the 'fetishism' of the commodity. In particular, Lefebvre feels that the centralized state represents the apotheosis of human alienation, in that human powers and capacities are increasingly transferred to an anonymous, bureaucratic apparatus. Given this essentially libertarian orientation, which locates genuine intersubjectivity or community in the sphere of everyday sociality rather than in the state (a sentiment he shares with such anarchist thinkers as Peter Kropotkin and Martin Buber), it is not surprising that Lefebvre made the 'withering away of the state' an essential component of the emancipatory project. In essence, for Lefebvre the concept of everyday life constitutes the crucial vantage-point from whence to criticize the formalized and alienated social practices characteristic of capitalism:

> The day dawns when everyday life also emerges as a
> critique, a critique of the superior activities in question
> (and of what they produce: *ideologies*). The devaluation of
> everyday life by ideologies appears as one-sided and partial,
> in both senses of the word. A direct critique takes the place
> of indirect criticism; and this direct critique involves a
> rehabilitation of everyday life, shedding new light on its
> positive content.
>
> (1991a: 87)

The tenor of Lefebvre's critique of modernity will undoubtedly strike a familiar chord with many. Despite some ostensive similarities, however, Lefebvre parts company with Romantic or conservative attacks on modern life. His view of modernity is eminently dialectical, and not prone to either nostalgic ruminations about a lost 'golden age' or abstract utopian predictions about a perfect future society. Lefebvre rejects the narrative of infinite progress, what Walter Benjamin called 'empty, homogeneous time', an essential component of the bourgeois, modernist worldview. Yet he equally repudiates theories of monolithic regress, an attitude summed up in Theodor Adorno's following statement: 'No universal history leads from Savagery to Humanity, but certainly there is one leading from the stone catapult to the megaton bomb' (cited in Connerton 1980: 114). By contrast, Lefebvre argues that modern society contains within it both repressive and emancipatory qualities. It is under capitalism where the contradiction between the material and technological potential for freedom and the subjective and objective effects of alienation is most acute, but also where the possibility of a transformed social existence is glimpsed clearly for the first time in human history. The estrangement and negation of human capacities is not, therefore, a permanent feature of the human condition, as many existentialists believed, but only a temporary phase. Lefebvre holds out the possibility of a radical dis-alienation of social life, of the complete empowerment and fulfilment of humanity's species-being, and the realization of what he calls the 'total man' (1968a: 148–65). This promise might be furtively glimpsed in premodern social formations – in the festival, for instance – but can never be fulfilled prior to modernity, due to backward social and technological conditions.

Such an emancipatory project requires a de-mystification of bourgeois ideology, which obscures the true nature of everyday life and suppresses its potentialities. As Lefebvre argues, 'to reach reality we must indeed tear away the veil, that veil which is forever being born and reborn of everyday life, and which masks everyday life along with its deepest or loftiest implication' (1991a: 57). What is required is a critical knowledge of the everyday, one that aims at the 'dialectical transcendence' of the present (*aufhebung*, to use the Hegelian term). The committed Marxist is admonished to look for the signs and foreshadowings of a transfigured social existence within the seemingly trivial deeds and gestures of the everyday, 'to search documents and works (literary, cinematic, etc.) for evidence that a consciousness of alienation is being born, however indirectly, and that an effort towards "disalienation," no matter how oblique and obscure, has begun' (1991a: 66). Only then can the critique of everyday life make a 'contribution to *the art of living*' and foster a genuine humanism, a 'humanism which believes in the human because it knows it' (1991a: 199, 232).

On a more philosophical level, Lefebvre argues for the replacement of 'abstract' by 'dialectical' reason, with the goal of healing the perennial rupture between theory and practice encouraged by capitalist social relations. Traditional philosophy, given its preference for reified abstractions that only capture isolated fragments of social reality, must be superseded. As he suggests: 'We are still learning to think via metaphysical, abstract – alienated – forms of thought. The danger of dogmatic, speculative, systematic and abstract attitudes lies ever in wait for us' (1991a: 184). Dialectical logic, which incorporates the findings of many different disciplines and sciences, is geared towards understanding society and nature as a totality, as a complex whole with multiple and mutually conditioning interconnections. What is required, argues Lefebvre, is a 'concrete, dynamic philosophy, linked to practical action as well as to knowledge – and thus implying the effort to "supersede" all the limitations of life and thought, to organize a "whole," to bring to the fore the idea of the *total man*' (1991a: 178). In this way, thought comes to coincide with the movement of reality itself, mapping its internal contradictions and grasping its tendencies toward change. Echoing Georg Lukács's *History and Class Consciousness* (1971), Lefebvre argues that bourgeois thought is mystified and fragmented, and therefore incapable of conceptualizing the whole. An understanding of totality is essential because it gives us a grasp of reality that is not abstract or ideological but concrete and many-sided. Because the crisis of modern life is global and all-pervasive, it can only be countered by a complete revolution which is cognizant of the true nature of this totality. As such, the perspective of totality gives us a kind of utopian vantage-point from whence to comprehend a transfigured social existence: 'the total conception of the world, the possibility of the *total man* – will only make sense once it stops being a "vision" and a "conception": once it penetrates life and transforms it' (Lefebvre 1991a: 251). However, it is important to realize that Lefebvre's conception of totality is open to the future, provisional and flexible. It does not correspond to a self-contained, reified system of thought, not least because a knowledge of everyday life is an essential component of this totality. Daily life is the 'connective tissue' that gives the totality its structure and coherence. Accordingly, Lefebvre makes no claims to an absolute or 'totalizing' form of knowledge of the sort normally associated with certain versions of Hegelianism, and therefore escapes the postmodernist critique that equates a holistic viewpoint or the concept of totality *per se* with totalitarian thought.

> Everyday life, in a sense residual, defined by 'what is left over' after all distinct, superior, specialized, structured activities have been singled out by analysis, must be defined as a totality. . . . Everyday life is profoundly related to *all* activities, and encompasses them with all their differences and their conflicts; it is their meeting place, their bond, their common ground. And it is in everyday life that the sum total of relations which make the human – and every human being – a whole takes its shape and its form. In it are expressed and fulfilled those relations which bring into play the totality of the real, albeit in a certain manner which is always partial and incomplete: friendship, comradeship, love, the need to communicate, play, etc.
>
> (Lefebvre 1991a: 97; also Jay 1984: 276–99)

However, this does not mean that Lefebvre found in orthodox Marxism a universal panacea for the shortcomings of philosophical idealism. Although Marxism ostensibly strives to grasp human existence as a totality, it has manifestly failed to understand the everyday in all its complexity and richness. As such, alongside the critique of idealism is a second current in *Critique of Everyday Life*: a critical interrogation of economistic, dogmatic Marxism. In essence, Lefebvre suggests that Marxism is burdened with a 'metaphysics of labour', which renders it blind to the importance of culture, ideology and other superstructural factors, as well as the vast range of human experiences external to the productive process *per se*. Put differently, praxis is not restricted to the utilitarian transformation of external nature through repetitive, instrumental action. It also involves love, sensuality, the body – a plethora of creative, emotive and imaginative practices Lefebvre calls *poesis* in his as yet untranslated 1965 work *Métaphilosophie*. These passions and needs are bound up with the individual's status as a 'being of nature'; that is, with the human self-formative process through the appropriation of nature. This is a process of 'becoming' which, as both Hegel and Marx believed, must be brought to fulfilment. In taking this position, Lefebvre shows his debt to the anti-determinist stance of existentialism, which had long criticized Marxism for its neglect of the active, transformative role played by human subjectivity. It also belies the influence of the Surrealists, who sought to expand the parameters of experience to include an appreciation of the poetic, the sensual and the non-rational. For Lefebvre, a viable social theory must be cognizant of both the subjective and objective determinants of human thought and behaviour, as these are constituted within the terrain of everyday life:

> Even when a consciousness reflects a thing, in truth it is reflecting a power together with the imperatives of action and its *possibilities*. And this involves the leap forward, the unending escape from what has already been accomplished towards images and the imaginary, towards a realm beyond the everyday and thence indeed back into the everyday so as to take cognizance of it.
>
> (1991a: 95)

In addition to the critique of work, which is the central focus of orthodox Marxism, Lefebvre called for a *critique of needs*, and maintained that human alienation evinced a wide range of psychological and moral aspects not sufficiently elucidated by Marx himself. He argued that human beings have complex and multifaceted needs and desires, the pursuit of which makes them richer and more fulfilled individuals. In the 'good society', Lefebvre asserts, the individual would be able to live his or her life in terms analogous to a 'work of art'. Capitalism, needless to say, encourages the attainment of human desire only through the medium of capital, which leads to the fetishization of money and commodities. Under modernity, needs have become atrophied and debased. Communism, as Lefebvre understood it, meant a sensuous, active appropriation of the external world, and the full development of all facets of human nature. Yet the historical experience of 'really existing socialism' did not endear Lefebvre to the Soviet experiment, because it equated socialism with purely quantitative economic expansion and the aggrandizement of state and party to the detriment of 'felt' human needs. After all, it was Lenin himself who, in all seriousness, suggested that 'communism equalled rural electrification plus Soviet power'. Lefebvre, by contrast, was always more concerned with the 'realm of freedom' as opposed to the 'realm of necessity'. For him, a genuine 'positive' freedom (freedom *to* rather than freedom *from*) meant the unconstrained opportunity to nurture and develop all human powers as ends in themselves. As with Breton, and again showing the pervasive influence of Charles Fourier on leftist French social thought, Lefebvre strongly believed that the endless deferment of human happiness to some abstract future society was something that had to be strenuously resisted, because it made a mockery of the genuine utopian impulse. Moreover, in common with the 'post-scarcity' thinkers of the 1960s, including Murray Bookchin and Herbert Marcuse, Lefebvre believed that the productive forces of capitalism had matured to such an extent that the material fulfilment of human needs was now relatively unproblematic, and thwarted only by the irrational nature of social organization under industrial civilization. As such, he felt that a genuinely communistic society was premised upon a complete mastery of the natural world – a 'Promethean' viewpoint that Lefebvre shared with the 'mature' Marx, but which, as we shall see, he later modified. In a rather optimistic spirit, Lefebvre wrote:

> Liberated from sordid necessity, needs per se are becoming suffused with reason, social life, joy and happiness. [E]specially in our era, the condition which restricted creative leisure and spiritual activities to the oppressors has

disappeared. It is a complex dialectic: needs are becoming more extensive, more numerous, but because the productive forces are broadening, this extension of needs may imply their humanization, a reduction in the number of hours worked to satisfy immediate needs, a reduction of the time spent at work generally, a universalization both of wealth and of leisure.

(1991a: 175)

Given his affinities with Breton on these issues, one might expect that Lefebvre would find much of value in the ideas and techniques developed by the Surrealist movement. Yet although there is clear evidence of such an influence, especially concerning the dual critique of philosophical idealism and mechanical materialism, Lefebvre finds fault with the Surrealist tendency to interpret the 'marvellous' as an escape or transcendence of everyday life. That is, while the Surrealists understood that daily life was repetitive and habitualized, they failed to realize that this degradation was a socio-historical condition. For Lefebvre, the notion of the 'marvellous', which pre-dates the Surrealists and can be found in such nineteenth-century artistic and literary movements as Symbolism and the Decadents, expresses a 'transcendental contempt for the real' (1991a: 29). Hence, Surrealism reinforced rather than overcame the perennial bourgeois separation between spirit and matter, mind and body, ideal and reality. For instance, Lefebvre suggests the Surrealists were right to believe that, under modernity, myth and ritual are written off as manifestations of 'irrationality', and sublimated into lesser domains like 'play', 'art' or 'dreams'. However, Lefebvre argues, rather than develop a theory of *poesis*, of the rich and manifold character of human experience, they preferred to cultivate irrationality and the 'bizarre' as an escape from the everyday. To construe the surreal as an end to itself meant that Surrealism never went beyond a purely symbolic politics; they never developed an effective praxis that was capable of transforming the institutions and practices of capitalist society. As such, their critique of bourgeois life remained abstract and mystified: 'it is clear that in the end, despite the intention to reject it, the real world is accepted, since it is transposed, instead of being transformed by knowledge' (Lefebvre 1991a: 123). By mainly restricting its critique to the aesthetic plane, Surrealism did not represent a genuine threat to the established order, and was co-opted by the culture industry with relative ease. The Surrealist penchant for shocking the bourgeoisie quickly lost its transgressive power if not connected to a wider utopian project of social transformation and to the exigencies of everyday life. As Lefebvre observes, the chief failure of Surrealism was that it 'allows the "modern" intellectual to push far from his lips the bitter chalice of an everyday life which *really is* unbearable – and will always be so until it has been transformed, and until new foundations for consciousness are established' (1991a: 120).

Lefebvre pursues a similar line of argument against phenomeno-logical existentialism, especially Heidegger, who also makes a ritualistic appeal to the everyday but profoundly misappropriates and misunderstands it. For our purposes, however, we will focus here on Lefebvre's analysis of individuality and leisure in the modern world. As suggested above, Lefebvre believed that modernity represents the dissolution of genuine intersubjectivity, and the end of popular celebrations like the premodern festival. Modernity encourages an inward-looking, solipsistic consciousness, one that is centred on an individual's particular occupational specialization, family life, and class-determined forms of commodity consumption. One result of this is that we tend to relate to others and the object-world not in a sensuous, multifaceted and affective manner, but through an 'abstract, formal, metaphysical reason'. Modernity fosters the dangerous illusion that we 'possess' objects and other individuals through our abstract cognition of them. This leads to a hyper-inflation of the self-contained, imperious ego, and encourages us to adopt a purely instrumental attitude toward the world, seeing it as a means to an end:

> Separated from the conditions in which it could flourish or even exist, [the individual] believes itself to be self-sufficient and aspires to be so. . . . When an individual life is shaped by individualistic tendencies, it is literally a life of 'privation', a life 'deprived': deprived of reality, of links with the world – a life for which everything human is alien. It is a life spilt into contradictory or separate poles: work and rest, public life and person life, public occasions and intimate situations, chance and inner secrets, luck and fate, ideal and reality, the marvellous and the everyday. . . . Crass and complacent, the individual settles down amid familiar surroundings. Consciousness, thought, ideas, feelings, all are seen as 'property' on a par with 'his' furniture, 'his' wife and his children, 'his' assets and 'his' money. In this way the narrowest, most barren, most solitary aspects of life are

taken (and with such crude sincerity) for what is most
human.

(Lefebvre 1991a: 149)

Given the degradation of work under capitalism, and the emergence
of this privatized consciousness, Lefebvre argues that many individuals seek escape from the monotony and dreariness of daily life in
such leisure pursuits as hobbies, film, sport or art. Such activities are
generally conceived of as distractions, as a compensation for work, a
'liberation from worry and necessity' (1991a: 33). Unfortunately,
leisure cannot be separated arbitrarily from other spheres of social
life, especially work. As both Hegel and Marx pointed out, necessity
does not disappear in the realm of freedom, and hence leisure under
capitalism is still an alienated practice. In modern society, leisure is
regimented and commodified, and therefore represents a passive and
manipulated way of relating to the world. 'So we work to earn our
leisure, and leisure only has one meaning: to get away from work. A
vicious circle', asserts Lefebvre (1991a: 40). The commodification of
leisure activities is an essential component of the shift from
production to consumption in postwar capitalism. Leisure is transformed into an 'undifferentiated global activity which is difficult to
distinguish from other aspects of the everyday' (1991a: 32). Indeed,
modernity creates a generalized *need* for leisure as a separate activity
and generates specific (though debased) needs via the advertising
industry, which can only be satisfied through the accumulation of
commodified objects, images and experiences. That is, the visions
and fantasies projected through advertising serve to separate leisure
from everyday life, and offer a *simulation* of non-alienated pleasure
and fulfilment, what Lefebvre terms a 'technocracy of relaxation'.
Echoing Jean Baudrillard's (1988) postmodern analysis of our
'hyperreal' and image-saturated society, although retaining a critical
and utopian perspective, Lefebvre writes:

> We are now entering the vast domain of the *illusory reverse
> image*. What we find is a false world: firstly because it is not
> a world, and because it presents itself as true, and because it
> mimics real life closely in order to replace the real by its
> opposite; by replacing real unhappiness by fictions of
> happiness, for example – by offering a fiction in response to
> the real need for happiness – and so on. This is the 'world'
> of most films, most of the press, the theatre, the music hall:
> of a large sector of leisure activities.

How strange the split between the real world and its reverse image is. For in the end it is not strange at all, but a false strangeness, a cheap-and-nasty, all-pervasive mystery.

(1991a: 35)

Lefebvre's position here bears more than a passing resemblance to the Frankfurt School's concept of the 'culture industry', including Marcuse's argument that the repressively tolerant system of late capitalism is capable of replacing genuine human needs with false ones (Marcuse 1964, 1968: 159–200). Lefebvre does at times veer dangerously close to a dystopian view of modernity, in which advertising and the culture industries obscure the degraded nature of daily life and short-circuit the possibility of negation, revolt and non-instrumentalized existence. But there are important differences. It is essential, Lefebvre argues, that leisure, work and other practices in contemporary society be analysed dialectically – that is, as a complex of activities and passivities that are partially illusory, but which simultaneously 'contain within themselves their own spontaneous critique of the everyday' (1991a: 40). The desire to transcend the routinization of everyday life is an expression of a real need, a genuine utopian impulse, however alienated and mystified it may be. Rather than subscribing to the commonplace notion that modern life foments an englobing 'false consciousness' that effectively ensnares the masses, and from which only isolated intellectuals are immune, Lefebvre clings to the belief that a project of radical dis-alienation is still a concrete possibility. Moreover, he argues that the committed intellectual can play a crucial role in this process through the practice of ideological criticism, and by distinguishing the positive versus the regressive aspects of modern life. In maintaining such an optimistic and essentially populist stance, which bears many similarities to Mikhail Bakhtin, Walter Benjamin and Ernst Bloch, Lefebvre escapes the charges of elitism and intellectualism that are often (with some justification) levelled at the Frankfurt School. At the same time, however, Lefebvre rejects the widespread proclivity within contemporary cultural studies to interpret the process of meaning-creation that accompanies cultural consumption as essentially liberatory in nature. This latter position is exemplified by John Fiske's suggestion in his book *Understanding Popular Culture* (1989) that the common practice of tearing holes in the knees of blue jeans represents an incipient revolutionary act on the part of dissaffected youth, one that exposes consumer society as fraudulent and reflects a non-mystified knowledge of capitalist social relations. This tendency to see in consumerism only the positive or pleasurable aspects, even in their most trivial and inconsequential manifest-ations, is no less deficient and one-sided than the elitist *kulturkritik* of Adorno and Horkheimer, which denigrates popular culture as a 'universal swindle'. The major point that emerges from this discussion is that consumption cannot be analysed separately from other specialized spheres of social activity (including work), but only as part of a wider totality that includes everyday life and the wider dynamics of modernity. Thus, everyday life represents a complex, multifaceted reality, a mixture of repressive and emancip-atory qualities which have to be disentangled and analysed via the application of dialectical reason, to 'extract what is living, new, positive – the worthwhile needs and fulfilments – from the negative elements: the alienations' (Lefebvre 1991a: 42).

NEO-CAPITALISM, THE FESTIVAL AND URBANISM

In the twenty years that separate *Critique of Everyday Life* from *Everyday Life in the Modern World*, Lefebvre developed a more nuanced and penetrating theory of daily life, one that altered subtly his earlier formulations and that tries to account for the trans-formation of the everyday in the wake of post-1950 socioeconomic changes. His outlook became darker and less suffused with opti-mism of the sort that marked the French left after the liberation from German occupation in 1944. He began to appreciate the enormity of the task of social transformation, especially given the precipitous decline in working-class militancy and the seeming imperviousness of consumer capitalism to radical change. Shortly after the appearance of *Everyday Life in the Modern World*, the student revolts and renewed labour unrest of the late 1960s were simul-taneously to confirm and deny Lefebvre's assessment of the possibilities of change. These events demonstrated that dissent was still possible, but also underscored the system's flexibility and capacity for recuperative self-preservation, what Marcuse (1965) termed 'repressive tolerance'.

Lefebvre begins *Everyday Life in the Modern World* by delineating more precisely what he means by 'everyday life'. Drawing on Nietzsche's concept of 'eternal recurrence', he suggests that everyday life is highly diffuse, inchoate, and marked by 'repetition' – endless, undulating cycles of birth and death, remembrance and recapitulation, ebb and flow. As he observes, 'cyclical time underlies all quotidian and cosmic duration' (1984: 6). Given the habitualized and recurrent nature of daily life, it is difficult to conceptualize or describe in theoretical terms, mainly because it is profoundly *lived*, and experienced as ceaseless recurrence. In premodern societies, this repetition is linked to the cycles and rhythms of the natural world. Under modernity, this repetition continues, but is derived from the dictates of technology, work and production rather than the natural world. The differentiation of systems and subsystems out of a formerly unified, organic totality is governed by a 'general law of functionalism', a technocratic logic. But if daily life is really marked by this Nietzschean eternal recurrence, how is it possible to reconcile this with the Hegelian and Marxian vision of the teleological character of human development, in which history 'works through' a number of internal contradictions to arrive at progressively 'higher' stages, each marking a closer proximity between the real and the rational? Lefebvre suggests that this contradiction is only apparent. The enduring character of the everyday – its 'desires, labours, pleasures' – represents a set of unsurpassable values that demand realization within concrete time/space. This gives us a critical perspective through which to view the process by which the human species engages in self-realization. Hence, Lefebvre advocates an approach which aims to synthesize the ideas of Hegel, Marx and Nietzsche.

This project requires a thorough analysis of the location where 'the quotidian and modernity take root' (1984: 28). According to Lefebvre, modernity is not a stable social formation. It is necessary to account for the tumultuous changes within modernity, and chart their effects upon daily life. Specifically, he argues that between the mid-nineteenth century and 1950, modernity was primarily characterized by the following elements: the dissociation of the everyday and more specialized activities, the destruction of organic communities, and the replacement of use-value by exchange-value. One result of these transformations is that the stable symbolic system through which premodern societies used to denote objects in the world eventually disintegrated, leading to the proliferation of 'non-referential' signs, and the emergence of a general sense of anomie and meaninglessness. These changes are traceable to the peculiar features of bourgeois society and its ideological underpinnings, such as possessive individualism, the ubiquity of private property, and the fetishization of the economic. After 1950, how-

ever, modernity was subject to a further transmutation. Consequently, the very foundation of everyday life and of individual
existence was radically altered. The stress on production, dignified
work and ascetic accumulation found in the earlier phase of
capitalism, described in detail by Max Weber's *The Protestant Ethic
and the Spirit of Capitalism* (1976), became increasingly anachronistic. According to Lefebvre (1984: 42), three major factors
distinguish this new phase of modernity: (i) the arrival of 'neo-
capitalism', which is monopolistic rather than competitive, and
state-directed instead of *laissez-faire*; (ii) a highly successful co-
option and commodification of potentially subversive creative and
revolutionary energies; and (iii) the evacuation of a sense of
historicity and change, and a feeling that contemporary society is
stuck in an 'eternal present', as reflected in the 'end-of-ideology'
arguments of the late 1950s and early 1960s (and which reappeared,
albeit fleetingly, after the fall of Eastern European communism in
1989).[2] Many social theorists would today characterize such transformative tendencies as indicative of the emergence of postmodernity. For Lefebvre, however, writing long before the postmodernist
debate began in earnest, these changes mean that the dominant
ethos of abstract rationalism has ceased to be concerned with the
disposition of individual attitudes and actions. Instead, the reigning
technocracy has become exclusively preoccupied with the
administration of ever-larger institutions and systems, which results
in a devaluation of particular human skills and expressions of
creativity. The idea that self-realization can be effected through
meaningful work, for example, is regarded increasingly as obsolete.
It is as if Saint-Simon's prophecy of the adminstration of things
replacing the administration of people in the utopian society of the
future has come to pass, but with the effect of dehumanization
rather than emancipation. Given these developments, Lefebvre asks
rhetorically:

> Does the *quotidian* still have any significance in this society
> and, if this society's basic preoccupations are rationality,
> organization and planning, is it still possible to distinguish
> a level or dimension that can be called *everyday life?* . . .
> Surely this concept must disappear at the same time as the
> singularities, survivals and extensions from an age of
> peasants and craftsmen or from that of the bourgeoisie of
> competitive capitalism.

> (1984: 45)

Lefebvre's response is that everyday life does indeed survive under neo-capitalism, but in a thoroughly reconstructed form. Neo-capitalism represents a society in which the principle of technical control has become ubiquitous and all-pervasive. Instrumentality has now become 'an autonomous economically and socially determining factor' (1984: 50). Due to this general technicization of society, the technocratic and bureaucratic strata become increasingly powerful. To utilize Pierre Bourdieu's (1977) terminology, this class fraction begins to acquire considerable symbolic, cultural and material capital. The paradox of this development – and here Lefebvre's arguments parallel those of Adorno and Horkheimer's *Dialectic of Enlightenment* (1979) – is that this process of cyber-netization lacks a clear purpose or direction, other than that of domination. It is geared towards *means* rather than *ends*, concerned exclusively with the effective regulation of isolated systems and sub-systems through the application of cybernetic techniques and forms of information monitoring and control. It has no vision of what a 'good society' might look like. As such, while neo-capitalism gives the impression of moving towards greater rationality and efficiency, the fetishization of technique masks the presence of a profoundly irrationalist ideology, the primary function of which is to shore up a technocratic hegemony. As rationality becomes increasingly special-ized and focused on discrete areas of technical control, the result is a fragmentation of society, culture and consciousness. As Lefebvre says, 'The world is fragmented and so are individual nations; we have fragments of culture, of specialized sciences and of systems and sub-systems' (1984: 70). This irrationality spills over into everyday life itself, as evinced by a pervasive interest in occultism, pop psychology, Eastern mysticism, New Age or diet fads. Thus, Lefebvre writes, 'the rationality of economism and technicity produces its opposite as their "structural" complement and reveals its limitations as restricted rationalism and irrationalism pervade everyday life, confront and reflect one another' (1984: 83).

The legitimacy of neo-capitalism is based on its oft-vaunted claim to be able to 'deliver the goods', or what Habermas has labelled a 'technocratic consciousness'. Lefebvre concedes that there has been an increased availability of commodities and services in the post-1950 era, although he does point out that pockets of indigence continue to persist in even the wealthiest, most industrialized nations. However, the main point is that the economy must con-tinually stimulate new forms of relative want and privation if it is to maintain a period of continuous expansion. One outcome is the emergence of a 'new poverty', by which Lefebvre means an enforced impoverishment of the qualitative aspects of human existence, a reality that is masked by the ubiquity of conspicuous wealth and consumption. There is no shortage of consumer durables, or the availability of manufactured leisure, but there is a dearth of genuine 'free time' (as opposed to 'compulsive time'), unrestructured urban space, or non-instrumentalized play. With regards to spatiality, for example, Lefebvre argues that under neo-capitalism, the bureaucratic state has come to thoroughly dominate space, particularly (though not exclusively) in urban centres, to incorporate it into its project of domination. It aims at the total control or homogenization of space through the application of technocratic rationality, thereby eliminating local particularities and differences and emptying daily life of its lived, affective meanings and qualities. In *The Production of Space*, Lefebvre refers to this process as the creation of 'abstract space', which strives to transform lived space and the natural world into a profitable force of production: 'The dominant form of space, that of the centres of wealth and power, endeavours to mould the spaces it dominates (i.e. peripheral spaces), and it seeks, often by violent means, to reduce the obstacles and resistance it encounters there' (1991b: 49). Space, as a commodity, is chopped up, parcelled out, and fragmented. Indeed, untrammelled nature has in a global sense been replaced by an increasingly dense 'social space', which is itself an index of the human mastery over and domination of material nature. At this stage in his thinking, Lefebvre jettisons much of the Marxian Prometheanism of his earlier work, and bemoans the ravagement of nature under late modernity. For instance, he writes that 'Nature is being murdered by "anti-nature" – by abstraction, by signs and images, by discourse, as also by labour and its products. Along with God, nature is dying. "Humanity" is killing both of them – and perhaps committing suicide into the bargain' (1991b: 71).

The main point that emerges from this discussion is that with the consolidation of consumer society, there is no active participation in commodified forms of leisure, space and entertainment. Rather, sounds and images as well as material objects are passively consumed, in a manner Lefebvre compares to the witnessing of a 'spectacle', a term also invoked frequently by the Situationists. Under neo-capitalism, leisure 'is no longer a festival, the reward of labour, and it is not yet a freely chosen activity pursued for itself, it is a generalized display: television, cinema, tourism' (Lefebvre 1984: 53–4). For neo-capitalism to continue its expansion, everyday life has to be increasingly rationalized and integrated into the cycles of production and consumption. In former phases of modernity, daily life was largely ignored, and left to its own devices. As such, it constituted a bulwark against the functionalist logic that dominated the more specialized spheres of activity, and remained the central locus for unconstrained play, interhuman dialogue, and affective relationships, what William Morris once called the 'education of desire'. By contrast, under neo-capitalism 'political and social activities converge to consolidate, structure, and *functionalize*' everyday life; they 'pursue their prey in its evasions and departures, dreams and fantasies to crush it in their relentless grip' (1984: 64–5). Hence, everyday life has become the essential site for the reproduction of capitalist social relations, rather than work *per se*. Modernity represents a 'flattening out' of the qualitative distinctions found in everyday life and their replacement by purely quantitative ones, as embodied in the abstract commodity form. This has resulted in a loss of depth, complexity and difference. The repetitive character of daily life makes it particularly vulnerable to the incursion of functionalist logic and the homogenization of human experience. Neo-capitalism – or what Lefebvre sometimes calls the *bureaucratic society of controlled consumption* – therefore represents the consolidation of a purely bureaucratic form of rationality as a generalized form of human cognition and knowledge, the predominance of consumption over production, and the total domination and commodification of everyday life:

> In the modern world everyday life had ceased to be a 'subject' rich in potential subjectivity; it had become an 'object' of social organization. . . . Everyday life has become an object of consideration and is the province of organization; the space–time of voluntary programmed self-regulation, because when properly organized it provides a closed circuit (production–consumption–production), where demands are foreseen because they are induced and desires are run to earth; this method replaces the spontaneous self-regulation of the competitive era. Thus everyday life must shortly become the one perfect system obscured by the other systems that aim at systematizing thought and structuralizing action.
>
> (Lefebvre 1984: 59, 72)

Part of this extensive colonization of everyday life by technocratic rationality involves a restructuring of the semantic field. Language is subject increasingly to bureaucratic domination and cybernetiz-ation. In premodern societies, asserts Lefebvre, language was part of an integrated culture, and consisted of an coherent symbolic system that conveyed relatively stable yet rich and multidimensional meanings. With the fragmentation of culture and the dominance of exchange-value over use-value, however, words and symbols become separated from their referents. There occurs a fundamental split between 'signifiers' (the denoting symbol) and 'signifieds' (the denoted object), precipitating a generalized crisis of meaning. What is left is a 'floating stock of *meaningless signifiers* (stray images either conscious or unconscious)', which are unconnected to real objects, to human labour, or to communal activities (Lefebvre 1984: 116). Communication within modernity is increasingly mediated by electronic forms of storage, reproduction and transmission, and hence abstracted from everyday sociality. Hearing, which is the dominant sense in premodern cultures, is largely replaced by purely visual stimuli (the written word, television, photographs). As such, the rich tonalities and personalized resonances of living speech are supplanted by the technology of writing, which, unlike spoken language, is fixed, anonymous and decontextualized. Lefebvre does not dispute the cultural and scientific achievements facilitated by the technology of writing; however, he equally asserts that writing is the handmaiden of rational administration, surveillance, and the exercise of technocratic power. Under such conditions, the multifaceted symbol is increasingly replaced by the *signal*, which reduces the semantic field to a single dimension and conveys a fixed concept or idea. Using Bakhtin's terminology, the inherent dialogic-ality of the word is supplanted by monologue, or the unilateral transferral of an single, authoritative meaning from sender to receiver. Accordingly, the richness of lived, expressive language degenerates into propaganda. Overwhelmed by this 'swarm of signs' emanating from the mass media and advertising industries, the individual is given over to passive, distracted fascination, and to an internalization of the ideological codes embedded in the signal. A profusion of signs replaces agency, and provides a *substitute* for participation, for a realization of desires within everyday life. The referentiality of words and symbols has largely disappeared because language itself has become almost entirely self-referential. Abstracted from its living social context, free-floating signs seem to acquire an autonomous power to transfigure reality. Language is increasingly about language itself (metalanguage, in Lefebvre's phraseology); it has ceased to refer to material reality.

Not surprisingly, for Lefebvre this situation parallels the arrival and consolidation of consumer society, in which the consumption of images and signs, which can be reproduced in endless identical copies at minimal cost, becomes at least as important as the consumption of tangible material goods. Again, this shift is part of the more general transition from production to consumption in the neo-capitalist economy. Commodities – and increasingly simulacra of commodities – now become the essential medium of exchange and communication. In order to survive, consumerism requires large dollops of make-believe and fantasy, and these are injected into everyday life at every opportunity. This tends to blur the distinction between the consumption of fantasies and 'real' things. Of course, the endless consumption of images results in disappointment and boredom, because they only fulfil artificial rather than genuine human needs. This potentially explosive situation must be defused by the continual manipulation of motives and incentives so that newly-induced artificial needs constantly replace 'shopworn' ones, a process that Lefebvre describes as the 'obsolescence of needs':

> Consuming of displays, displays of consuming. Consuming of displays of consuming, consuming of signs and signs of consuming; each sub-system, as it tries to close the circuit, gives another self-destructive twist, at the level of everyday life. . . . Thus every object and product acquires a dual existence, perceptible and make-believe; all that can be consumed becomes a symbol of consumption and the consumer is fed on symbols, symbols of dexterity and wealth, of happiness and of love; sign and significance replace reality, there is a vast substitution, a massive transfer, that is nothing but an illusion created by the swivel's giddy twists.
>
> (1984: 108)

For Lefebvre, these developments signal the entrenchment of a debased and inauthentic form of communication, a form of semiotic closure that is symptomatic of the advanced state of alienation and dehumanization within modern society. Under neo-capitalism, alienation has become so widespread that it is difficult to recognize, and it no longer generates widespread resentment and resistance. This helps to explain Lefebvre's antipathy towards structuralism and other sociological formalisms. He argues forcefully that the structuralist project of a 'science of signs', which makes little reference to

history or concrete social practice, is symptomatic of the technocratic rationality that has come to dominate modern society.
Furthermore, such pseudo-sciences have actively *contributed* to this
bureaucratic restructuring of the social world. By adopting the cool
and detached demeanour of the urban planner, the manager and the
administrator, academics have effectively legitimated the technocratic approach to the analysis and manipulation of society and
nature. Accordingly, such theories are, in Lefebvre's opinion,
thoroughly ideological, despite the fact they project themselves as
objective, scientific and non-partisan. Even such ostensibly radical
theories as Surrealism, existentialism and Marxism have been
successfully commodified and integrated into the *status quo*. Like the
Frankfurt School and the Situationists, Lefebvre is fully aware of the
awesome capacity of consumer society to absorb and even profit
from intellectual and cultural dissent. As he asserts, 'the "system"
makes use of everything including adaptation that becomes
fictitious and make-believe; anything can be said or nearly anything'
(1984: 119). Repressive tolerance of this sort is necessary because
neo-capitalism, despite undergoing a protracted process of internal
fragmentation and the demise of a common culture, still requires a
minimal level of system integration. However, insofar as modern
society lacks effective agencies of moral control and shies away from
mechanisms of direct repression (except in times of severe crisis),
the reproduction of capitalist social relations in the post-1950 era
can only occur at the level of consumption. Zygmunt Bauman has
cogently argued that seduction in the form of consumerism now
takes 'the place of repression as the paramount vehicle of systemic
control and social integration' (1992: 51). Consumption gives us
the illusion of freedom and choice, of spontaneity, and the successful
realization of pleasure. As such, it constitutes the perfect support
for the ideology of possessive individualism and the continued
accumulation of capital. It also marks the demise of authentic
community and intersubjective dialogue: 'Consuming creates nothing, not even a relation between consumers, it only consumes; the
act of consuming, although significant enough in this so-called
society of consumption, is a solitary act, transmitted by a mirror
effect, a play with mirrors on/by the other consumer' (Lefebvre
1984: 115). Hence, external repression has been largely replaced by
self-repression. Lefebvre suggests that this internalization of compul-
sion means that power has become habitualized, entering into the
speech, consciousness and body of the individual. The result is the
emergence of what he calls a 'terrorist society', where

terror is diffuse, violence is always latent, pressure is exerted from all sides on its members, who can only avoid it and shift its weight by a super-human effort; each member is a terrorist because he wants to be in power (if only briefly); thus there is no need for a dictator; each member betrays and chastises himself; terror cannot be located, for it comes from everywhere and from every specific thing; the 'system' (in so far as it can be called a 'system') has a hold on every member separately and submits every member to the whole, that is, to a strategy, a hidden end, objectives unknown to all but those in power, and that no one questions.

(1984: 147)

Lefebvre's theory of a 'terrorist' society is certainly more pessimistic than anything found in his earlier writings. Indeed, it bears numerous affinities with Foucault's (1977) account of power/knowledge and disciplinary apparatuses. Nonetheless, he still rejects the view that contemporary society has become totally 'one-dimensional' and incapable of sustaining negation and revolt. Referring specifically to Marcuse, Lefebvre argues against the notion that the power structures of neo-capitalism are monolithic and all-pervasive. This is to confuse the appearance of the terror society, its idealized self-image, with reality. Modernity represents a 'system' insofar as all sectors of society conform to a common organizational logic – namely, the logic of bureaucratic domination. However, technocratic ideologies, as Habermas (1976) has also suggested, are highly prone to legitimation crises, and their ultimate effectiveness in regulating thought and behaviour has definite limits. Lefebvre argues that while in the earlier phases of modernity, universalistic claims about the supremacy of abstract reason and ideologies of nationalism or ethos of infinite progress had strong integrative powers, in the contemporary context the 'channelling of such universalizing ideologies into the restricted rationalities of technology and the state has reduced their former strategical power to nothing, with the result that impotence prevails in cultural and especially in integrative spheres' (1984: 95). Perhaps most importantly, while consumerism is heavily dependent upon the manipulation of needs and motives (both conscious and unconscious), the system inadvertently stimulates authentic desires that it cannot possibly satisfy through the proffering of commodities and images. That is, 'satisfaction' is the aim and objective of consumer society, and remains its official justification. Although neo-capitalism strives to attain a totally controlled consumption – not only in terms of the production of objects for consumption but also the forms of satisfaction obtained from them – it cannot sell happiness, however much it claims to. The result is a generalized sense of unrest and dissatisfaction, and a profound crisis of values that shows no sign of ending within the existing horizon of consumer capitalism. This, according to Lefebvre, is the Achilles' heel of neo-capitalism:

> the anomie of desire, its social-extrasocial nature, resists social and intellectual systematizations attempting to reduce it to a distinct, classified need satisfied as such. Desire stifles in everyday life, but it dies in a specialized context; to organize desire its signifiers must be captured and signified, it must be stimulated by signs, by the sight or rather the action of undressing, forms of torment that recall those of desire. But desire refuses to be signified, because it creates its own signs as it arises – or simply does not arise; signs or symbols of desire can only provoke a parody of desire that is never more than a pretence of the real thing.
>
> (1984: 172)

Hence, modernity contains within itself its own self-criticism. Neo-capitalism seeks to emulate the Platonic ideal of a closed, cybernetically controlled, self-referential system which has no value or meaning outside itself. But contradictions remain; cracks and fissures appear in the smooth wall of controlled consumption and the visage of ubiquitous panoptic power. Despite this process of systematization and bureaucratic domination, 'moments' of difference survive in the desiring body, everyday sociality, and the dense, non-instrumentalized spaces of urban life. As to the former, Lefebvre suggests that late modernity is marked by the appearance of an 'elaborated body' that resists the homogenizing abstractions of bureaucratic neo-capitalism. In detecting such a body-based culture, Lefebvre claims to have located a desire to return to the sensible and sensuous qualities of premodern societies, to 'break with the monotony of the everyday, to find spaces of freedom and *jouissance*' (1988: 82).[3] In essence, Lefebvre argues that the body retains a expressive or sensuous quality by which it constitutes a rallying point against the reifying and quantifying forces of modernity:

The body will not allow itself to be dismembered without a protest, nor to be divided into fragments, deprived of its rhythms, reduced to its catalogued needs, to images and specialisations. The body, at the very heart of space and of the discourse of Power, is irreducible and subversive. It rejects the reproduction of relations which deprive it and crush it. What is more vulnerable, more easy to torture than the reality of a body? And yet what is more resistant? [The] human body resists the reproduction of oppressive relations – if not frontally, then obliquely. It is of course vulnerable. But it cannot be destroyed without destroying the social body itself: the carnal, earthly Body is there, every day. It is the body which is the point of return, the redress – not the Logos, nor 'the human'.

(1976: 89)

Similarly, Lefebvre suggests that although modernity attempts to homogenize and commodify space, this state-sponsored project of 'normalization' ultimately provokes opposition and negativity. A plurality of what he calls 'differentiated' spaces continues to persist under neo-capitalism, where difference is registered and 'linked to the clandestine or underground side of life' (1991b: 4). Accordingly, Lefebvre advocates a transformation of urban existence which will extend these differentiated spaces to the furthest possible limits. In *The Production of Space*, he asserts that a revolution that does not involve a transformation of lived space is not worth the effort: 'A social transformation, to be truly revolutionary in character, must manifest a creative capacity in its effects on daily life, on language and on space – though its impact need not occur at the same rate, or with equal force, in each of these areas' (1991a: 54). Such a transformed urban space will be based on the idea of the 'city as play', where 'everyday life would become a creation of which each citizen and each community would be capable' (1984: 135). Lefebvre conceives of a liberated urban locale as the time and place where desire is fulfilled and where authentic human needs are catered to, a place where speech will triumph over metalanguage, and where a coherent cultural style will again emerge to supersede the fragmented, utilitarian culture that currently exists. The 'city as play' will have a transfigured everyday life that will banish 'quotidianness', or habitualized drudgery, and 'terror' will be successfully challenged. In the liberated city,

play and games will be given their former significance, a
chance to realize their possibilities; urban society involves
this tendency towards the revival of the Festival, and,
paradoxically enough, such a revival leads to a revival of
experience values, the experience of place and time, giving
them priority over trade value. Urban society is not opposed
to mass media, social intercourse, communication, intimations, but only to creative activity being turned into
passivity, into the detached, vacant stare, into the consumption of shows and signs; it postulates an intensific-
ation of material and non-material exchange where quality
is substituted for quantity, and endows the medium of
communication with content and substance.

(Lefebvre 1984: 190–1)

Above all, the task of social transformation requires a 'decolonization' and transformation of everyday life and a resurrection of the
vast human potentialities lying dormant within it. The exemplar of
such a transfigured everyday life lies in the festival, which is
curtained by modernity but never completely overshadowed. In
premodern times, the Dionysian ecstasies represented by the festival
were fully integrated into everyday life, and resonated with the
rhythms and cycles of communal existence and the natural world. It
involved the participation of all of the individual's sensuous, bodily
and intellectual qualities in a spontaneous and non-repressed
fashion, with the full and non-hierarchical participation of all
members of the community. As social stratification emerged and
became institutionalized, reaching its pinnacle in modern neo-
capitalism, festivals became ritualized and separated from daily
existence, subject to sublimation and commodification. Metaphysical
anxiety (expressed most clearly in existentialism) and a profound
fear of nature have replaced the joyful communion with humanity
and the natural world exemplified by the premodern festival.
According to Lefebvre, the rebirth of the festival represents an
overcoming of the conflict between play and everyday life, a
transcendence of human alienation and a reawakening of the spirit
of popular celebration:

The revolution of the future will put an end to the
quotidian. . . . This revolution will not be restricted to the
spheres of economy, politics and ideology; its specific
objective will be to annihilate everyday life; and the period

of transition will also take on a new meaning, oppose everyday life and reorganize it until it is as good as new, its spurious rationality and authority unmasked and the antithesis between the quotidian and basis of society.

(1984: 36–7)

In the events of May 1968 in Paris, Lefebvre claimed to detect just such a re-emergence of the genuine festival. He felt the uprising was premised on a total rejection of hierarchy and specialization, of the faded and tawdry trappings of a rampant consumerism. It represented a reinvigoration of the metaphorical richness of human speech and language and a desire to recapture urban space from the clutches of the bureaucrats and planners and invest this space with qualitative meanings and significances. For Lefebvre, May 1968 was a project suffused with an undercurrent of popular celebration, playfulness and laughter. During this revolutionary 'dress rehearsal', the radical workers and students voiced their preference for *autogestion*, or self-management, as opposed to elitist, centralized and hierarchical forms of sociopolitical organization. Lefebvre interpreted this as an aspiration for collective responsibility and the direct control of daily existence. Like the 1871 Paris Commune, May 1968 represented what Lefebvre called the 'moment', an evanescent glimpse of a transformed social world, which, if only temporarily, broke decisively with the monotonous and relentless advance of 'official' history.

CONCLUSION

Despite the pessimistic tenor of his later writings, in many ways Lefebvre remains the archetypal revolutionary optimist. His almost boundless faith in the regenerative capacity of everyday life, the resistant qualities of the body, and the unquenchable spirit of contestation and radical subjectivity, mark him as a thinker with very few analogues in contemporary intellectual life. In these postmodern times, few of us are quite so sanguine about the liberatory potentialities of Eros, popular celebrations, urban space, or dialectical reason. However, many of the young French intellectuals who avidly read Lefebvre in the 1960s or attended his lectures, and consequently participated in the events of May–June 1968 in Paris, were inspired by his utopian vision of a transformed social world based on the abolition of work, *autogestion*, and the realization of desire. Later, these same intellectuals appropriated Lefebvre's theses and fashioned them into something quite different, indeed something he would not have recognized, in a manner which conformed more closely to the post-1968 *Zeitgeist*. By the 1970s, it was Nietzsche, and not Marx or Fourier (and certainly not Hegel), who was the main source of inspiration for disillusioned Left Bank intellectuals. At this point, human history only made sense by reference to a ubiquitous 'will to power', and not the process of human self-realization that Marx described in his *1844 Manuscripts*. Rationality, even 'dialectical reason', was only an embodiment of this will to power, and hence it was implicated in a power structure from which there was no escape. Moreover, the severance between signifier and signified that Lefebvre analysed in *Everyday Life in the Modern World* ceased to be understood as a historically specific condition, linked to the domination of exchange-value and the commodity form and the bureaucratic usurpation of language. For postmodernists like Jean Baudrillard, the 'floating signifier' had no anchor in the real; consequently, 'the "real" table does not exist' (1981: 155). There is no escape from the endless proliferation of signs and images, no possibility of accessing the 'real' or distinguishing between appearance and essence, and certainly no chance of fulfilling Marx's dream of dis-alienation. What we are left with, as Baudrillard puts it, is a 'hyperreal henceforth sheltered from the imaginary, and from any distinction between the real and the imaginary, leaving room only for the orbital recurrence of models and the simulated generation of difference' (1988: 167).

Christopher Norris has detected in the post-1968 writings of Baudrillard and like-minded postmodernists a version of politics that ends up 'effectively endorsing and promoting the work of ideological mystification' (1990: 191), because it embraces an extreme epistemological scepticism, based on their view of the radically unstable nature of meaning, and rejects any attempt to project a utopian alternative to existing social arrangements. What is interesting about Lefebvre is that his diagnosis of neo-capitalism identifies many of the same changes with regard to language, subjectivity and social relations. But at the same time he refuses to believe that the ideological *appearance* of the system, its self-image, tells the whole story. For him, no matter how advanced the 'crisis of representation', or how difficult it is to gain a reflexive awareness of alienation or understand society as a multifaceted totality, neo-capitalism continues to generate internal contradictions and crises that erupt in periodic manifestations of social revolt which evinces a desire for a better world, a better way of life. At the heart of this belief is an image of the human subject as an active, creative force that always seeks to transform the conditions of its very existence, to turn one's life into a 'work of art'. In such a project, the transform-ation of everyday life from a habitualized and degraded 'dead time' into a space/time ripe with human potential and oriented towards self-realization, occupies a central place in Lefebvre's theoretical universe. We can still find much of value in his project, not least his critical utopianism, which towards the end of his career he defined as that which 'concerns what is and what is not possible. All thinking that has to do with action has a utopian element. Ideas that stimulate action, such as liberty and happiness, must contain a utopian element. This is not a refutation of such ideals; it is, rather, a necessary condition of the project of changing life' (1988: 87).

5

THE SITUATIONIST INTERNATIONAL: REVOLUTION AT THE SERVICE OF POETRY

Behind the most radical elements in the student movement lie the fantastications, the lyric anarchy, the Dada gestures and search for hallucination which mark symbolist literature and the art and drama of the 1920s and 30s. The world is a collage subject to spontaneous rearrangement, a Kurt Schwitters assemblage to be taken apart and brushed into the corner.

George Steiner

INTRODUCTION

When Steiner wrote these words in 1967, just a few months before Paris and all France was caught up in the convulsive events of May–June 1968, he recognized presciently that the main force behind the more provocative and creative aspects of the French New Left movement was the politico-cultural organization known as the Situationist International (SI). The SI, which officially existed between 1957 and 1972, developed what is easily the most intransigent and uncompromising critique of modern society and everyday life of any of the thinkers and traditions discussed in this book. In their total rejection of both consumer capitalism and what used to be called 'really existing socialism', and their demand for a 'generalized permanent revolution', they exceeded the demands of even most ultra-leftist organizations. As one of the SI's main theorists, Raoul Vaneigem, put it: 'People who talk about revolution and class struggle without referring explicitly to everyday life, without understanding what is subversive about love and what is positive in the refusal of constraints, such people have a corpse in their mouth' (1983: 15). At the same time, the innovative ideas and forms of political intervention developed by the SI had clear antecedents. They drew heavily upon the humanism of the early Marx, the neo-Hegelian Marxism of Georg Lukács, Surrealist provocations and techniques of defamiliarization, and existentialist notions of authenticity. In particular, they heeded Lefebvre's call for a 'critique of everyday life'. As with Lefebvre, the Situationists felt it was necessary to identify sociopolitical analogues for Surrealist notions of aesthetic transgression and sublimity (the festival, urban space, and *autogestion*); they excoriated abstract utopianism, while simultaneously defending what they took to be a genuine utopian impulse; and they sought a positive transfiguration of daily life and intersubjectivity, especially language. The overarching goal of both Lefebvre and the SI was to achieve an 'authentic existence' through the establishment of non-commodified social relations, thereby overcoming the alienations and passivities induced by modern consumer capitalism. SI theses about modern life were, until very recently, virtually ignored in the English-speaking world, partly because of the professed Situationist antipathy for 'impartial' scholarship and the academy, which they viewed as bulwarks of the 'spectacular economy'. However, there has lately been a resurgence of interest in the activities of the SI. A strong Situationist influence can now be detected in alternative cultural practices (such as music, film and graphics), in architectural design and urbanism, and in the tactics of numerous oppositional social movements, as well as in more orthodox scholarly studies.[1] This interest has been supplemented by a flood of English-language translations and anthologies of Situationist material.[2] In this chapter, after a brief look at the history of the SI, I will examine the central ideas of the Situationist movement, focusing on their concept of the 'spectacle' and the commodity, and the possibility of resistance and social transformation under the conditions of late capitalism.

THE SITUATIONIST INTERNATIONAL (1957–1972): A SCHEMATIC HISTORY AND OVERVIEW

The SI did not emerge *ex nihilo*, but as the result of a coalition between various postwar avant-gardes, especially the Lettriste Movement and the International Movement for an Imagist Bauhaus (IMIB). The original Lettriste Movement, led by the strange, flamboyant Romanian poet and theorist Isidore Isou, was premised

on the idea that a moribund poetry could only be revitalized if words were broken down into their constituent elements and reconstructed, so as to create entirely new words, sounds and poetic images. Although it derived its central impetus from existing Dadaist and Surrealist techniques, Lettrism did pioneer the transferral of such practices to film-making and the manipulation of visual images for the purpose of defamiliarization and the awakening of a critical consciousness. However, as the cultural theorist Stewart Home points out, although Lettrism located itself within the utopian and avant-garde traditions, it 'lacked a materialist critique of reigning society' (1988: 15). Some of this missing component of social critique was supplied by Guy Debord and Gil Wolman, who joined Isou's organization in 1950. Shortly thereafter, however, Debord, his future wife, Michele Bernstein, and Wolman left the Lettriste Movement and formed the breakaway Lettriste International (LI). The LI denounced Isou's aestheticism and instead committed itself to continuous artistic innovation and the transformation of daily life through cultural revolution. What set the LI apart from previous and contemporaneous avant-gardes was their highly inventive vision of architecture and ideas about a new style of urban life. In a highly prescient 1953 text called 'Formulary for a New Urbanism', published in the LI journal *Potlatch*, Ivan Chtcheglov wrote: 'We have already pointed out the need of constructing situations as being one of the fundamental desires on which the next civilization will be founded. This need for *absolute* creation has always been intimately associated with the need to *play* with architecture, time and space' (1981: 3). Chtcheglov's aim was to realize 'forgotten desires' via spontaneous and random wanderings through a transfigured urban space full of unexpected surprises and unusual architectural forms, including mobile buildings and fantasy castles. Although he was shortly excommunicated from the LI for failing to maintain the requisite level of revolutionary purity – a practice that was later continued in the SI as well – Chtcheglov's ideas regarding the city had a major impact on Debord's thinking about the urban environment and its relationship to human freedom and creativity. About the same time, in 1953, the International Movement for an Imagist Bauhaus (IMIB) was formed. Led by the Dane Asger Jorn, Italian Enrico Baj and Belgian Christian Dotremont, the IMIB was itself the product of a fusion between two earlier organizations, the so-called 'COBRA' group and the Nuclear Art Movement. The IMIB dabbled in musical, photographic and visual experimentation, and

pursued researches which paralleled those of the LI, such as architecture, urban nomadism and cultural anthropology.

In September 1956, the 'First World Congress of Visual Artists'
brought together disparate avant-garde groups from all over Europe.
Realizing that they shared similar ideas about the nature of modern
capitalism and cultural revolution, and were agreed on the importance of a revitalized urban space for a future style of life, elements
of the LI and IMIB decided to join together under the new title
'Situationist International'. This amalgamation was formally completed in 1957, followed by the emergence of the flagship SI journal
Internationale Situationniste in 1958. This publication remained the
chief venue for the development of Situationist ideas until it ceased
publication in 1969. According to Debord, the creation of the SI
was fuelled by a shared belief that such an umbrella organization,
which was comprised of the most advanced avant-garde tendencies
in modern society, had considerable potential to realize the initial
promise of Surrealism – namely, the transformation of life and the
realization of desire. However, it could only fulfil its potential if it
avoided Surrealism's obsession with the unconsciousness and the
aesthetic, which had made it extremely vulnerable to an inward-
looking mysticism and to co-option by the culture industry. In his
1957 text 'Report on the Construction of Situations and on the
International Situationist Tendency's Conditions of Organization of
Action', Debord suggested that

> Our central idea is that of the construction of situations,
> that is to say, the concrete construction of momentary
> ambiances of life and their transformation into a superior
> passional quality. . . . The construction of situations begins
> on the ruins of the modern spectacle. It is easy to see what
> extent the very principle of the spectacle – nonintervention
> – linked to the alienation of the old world. Conversely, the
> most pertinent revolutionary experiments in culture have
> sought to break the spectator's psychological identification
> with the hero so as to draw him into activity by provoking
> his capacities to revolutionize his own life.
>
> (1981a: 22, 25)

As Debord's comments indicate, the revolutionary project of the SI
aimed to supersede the aesthetic and largely symbolic political
stance of the Surrealists, through a systematic sociopolitical critique
of modern consumer society and the development of a viable

strategy for social transformation. This project required a thorough understanding of post-war capitalism, particularly the epochal shift from production to consumption that Lefebvre also detected. Yet at the same time, the ultimate goal of the Situationists remained more or less the same as that of André Breton: the synthesis of art and life, and the actualization of the creative potential of each and every human being. Accordingly, for the SI the task of the *engagé* artist or intellectual was not simply to create objects or texts to be bought and sold in the capitalist marketplace; rather, it was to facilitate the theory and practice of constructing *situations*. Such freely constructed situations would end the alienation of daily life under capitalism by achieving a congruence between affective desire and the urban environment, thereby ushering in an entirely new way of life. Without such a 'free creation of events', consumer capitalism would be able to refine continually its techniques of domination, and perfect what Lefebvre called the 'bureaucratic society of controlled consumption'. Hence the necessity for 'total revolt' and the complete supersession of the capitalist system.

The SI's uncompromising radicalism, however, precipitated a number of internal schisms. A less militant wing, comprised mainly of artists rather than theorists and activists, split off to form the Scandinavian-based 'Second Situationist International' in 1962. The remaining members, grouped around Debord, Vaneigem and Bernstein, rejected art except as a technique to de-mystify bourgeois ideology, and concentrated instead on a 'global' critique of Western society. The critique and transfiguration of everyday life figured prominently in this project, a legacy of Lefebvre's influence, who taught sociology to Debord and Vaneigem at the University of Nanterre in 1957–8. Other key influences included Marx's analysis of alienation (as developed in the *1844 Manuscripts*), Georg Lukács's account of reification and commodity fetishism, and Karl Korsch's ideas about left-wing or 'council' communism, the latter forcefully condemned by Lenin in his 1920 pamphlet *Left-Wing Communism: An Infantile Disorder* (Home 1996; Plant 1992; Wollen 1989). The Leninist disapproval of council communism, or self-government through workers' councils, made it all the more attractive to the SI. The Situationists largely adopted the critical analysis of orthodox communism or 'state capitalism' developed by the Socialisme ou Barbarie group, which included the formidable theorist Cornelius Castoriadis and the later pioneer of postmodernism, Jean-François Lyotard (Hirsch 1982: 108–38). Accordingly, state socialism of the sort exemplified by the Eastern Bloc nations held little attraction for the SI. Despite this, they never abandoned a faith in the proletariat as the agent of social revolution, and in this sense they remained more orthodoxly Marxist than critical theorists like Adorno or Marcuse, or indeed Socialisme ou Barbarie itself.

The *locus classicus* of the Situationist critique of consumer capitalism can be found in its concept of the 'spectacle'. In the spectacle, lived experience is increasingly replaced by the media and advertising image, and active participation is supplanted by the passive gaze. This leads to social atomization, alienation and pacification. Debord developed his most thorough analysis of the spectacle in his 1967 book *Society of the Spectacle*, but also in a series of pamphlets, films and articles dealing with everything from the Watts riots to the Algerian revolution, in tandem with the other members of the SI. For his part, Vaneigem's main theoretical contribution was *The Revolution in Everyday Life*, also published in 1967. A related and no less important concern for the SI, which again belied the influence of Lefebvre, was the investigation and critique of lived space. According to the Situationists, space was not 'empty' or 'neutral'. Rather, it was the site of power and contestation *par excellence*. Under late capitalism, space had been commodified and effectively transformed into a mechanism of social control. As Vaneigem put it, 'the space of everyday life is encircled by every form of conditioning' (1981a: 128). Hence, the SI postulated that space had a crucial and largely unnoticed sway over our psychological and behavioural dispositions. Space was a socially constructed and historically specific phenomenon, acquiring different forms in divergent social contexts. The Situationists referred to their inquiries into the relation between lived space, consciousness and behaviour as 'psychogeography'.

Along with these sociopolitical analyses, the SI expounded methods of contesting the spectacle, including *détournement*, the 'hijacking' and reorganization of cultural and textual materials for the purpose of ideological criticism, and *dérive*, a kind of play-driven 'urban nomadism'. Their goal was the creation of non-alienated 'situations' outside of the power structure of consumer capitalism. In so doing, they outlined a positive vision of a non-hierarchical and de-alienated society, one which owed a considerable debt to the ninteenth-century utopian socialist tradition of Proudhon, Kropotkin and Fourier no less than to a humanistic Marxism.

By the mid to late 1960s, the ideas of the SI had percolated through the most militant sectors of the French student and cultural left. In 1966 a group of Situationist-inspired students managed to get elected as the student government of Strasbourg University. They subsequently published a widely distributed pamphlet called 'On the Poverty of Student Life', a text that displayed an advanced understanding of SI concepts and tactics. The ensuing scandal raised the profile of the Situationist movement considerably. The Strasbourg events precipitated a series of student demonstrations and occupations, which eventually culminated in the May 1968 upheaval. Many of the famous slogans that appeared during this period – such as 'Be worthy of your dreams!', and 'Humanity won't be happy till the last bureaucrat is hung with the guts of the last capitalist' – can be directly traced to Situationist concepts, as were the political stratagems and forms of propaganda utilized by the students themselves (Viénet 1992). Despite their apparent break-through, however, after 1968 the SI gradually disintegrated amid recriminations, purges and further splits, and officially disbanded in 1972. Debord himself committed suicide in 1994, under rather murky circumstances that have never been satisfactorily explained.[3]

THE SPECTACLE AND EVERYDAY LIFE

Any discussion of SI theory must logically begin with their concept of the 'spectacle', which is the key to their analysis of consumer capitalism and everyday life. As Debord bluntly put it in *Society of the Spectacle*, in late capitalism 'all of life presents itself as an immense accumulation of spectacles' (1987: 1).[4] In essence, Debord accepted Lefebvre's suggestion that late capitalism is qualitatively different from its *laissez-faire* predecessor. In its initial phase, industrial capitalism was mainly concerned with *production* – that is, with the organization of space, machines, labour power and raw materials in the most efficient manner possible. Here, the com-modity itself is of secondary importance; it is simply a means to further the accumulation of capital. During capitalism's 'second industrial revolution', by contrast, the commodity acquires para-mount significance, insofar as the economic system becomes premised on *consumption* rather than production. The commodity becomes the motor of socioeconomic reproduction, and the locus of social control. Given its centrality to the reproduction of capitalism, consumption is judged to be too important to be left to the autonomous judgement of individual consumers. Consumption must be thoroughly managed and regulated, with nothing left to chance. This monitoring and control is effected through a vast information and communications network that operates 'from the top down', and which imposes a set of artificially constructed needs onto the populace. The spectacle makes its début on the world-historical stage at the point where the commodity totally dominates everyday life. 'In the advanced regions', Debord writes, 'social space is invaded by a continuous superimposition of geological layers of commodities' (1987: 40). Alienated consumption supersedes alien-ated production, and specialized sciences of domination (cybernetics, industrial management, sociology) emerge to monitor and regulate the entire cycle of consumption and leisure. Moreover, the trans-formation of the proletariat from producer to consumer requires a new relation of domination between bourgeoisie and worker. Whereas in the earlier phase of capitalism, the proletariat was left to its own devices after the working day ended – that is, everyday life retained a semblance of autonomy from the economy – the cycle of endless consumption requires that all leisure and everyday time be commodified and manipulated. As a result, exchange-value has completely supplanted use-value, because consumer capitalism reduces the usage of all goods and services to the 'mercy of exchange' (1987: 47). When the economy dominates all social life, the formation of authentic human needs is replaced by manufactured pseudo-needs. When this stage is reached, Debord argues, 'The real consumer becomes a consumer of illusions. The commodity is this factually real illusion, and the spectacle its general manifestation' (1987: 47).

The construction of 'pseudo-needs' is the prerogative of the mass media and advertising agencies, which generate an endless series of glittering and seductive images for consumption by the masses. Such visions – of plenitude, total satisfaction, and fulfilment – encapsulates an 'ideal-typical' fantasy life that acts as a substitute for genuine, lived existence. Stars and celebrities from every conceivable walk of life (sports, actors, even academics) are the virtual embodi-ment of this fantasy existence – they not only extol particular commodities for a fee, they *are* living, breathing commodities themselves. 'In the final analysis', Debord writes, 'stars are created by the need we have for them, and not by talent or absence of talent or even by the film industry or advertising. Miserable need, dismal, anonymous life that would like to expand itself to the dimensions of cinema life' (1981b: 33). Consequently, daily life is 'invaded' by the image or, more precisely, the spectacle. The spectacle, for all intents and purposes, has the guise of reality. It becomes increasingly difficult to distinguish between spectacular appearance and the 'real':

'In a world which *really is topsy-turvy*, the true is a moment of the false' (1987: 9). The spectacle is a negation of life and a simultaneous '*affirmation* of appearance'. As such, it demands passive acceptance, and is consumed with a kind of dumbfounded astonishment. The domination of the spectacle is a central element of the subordination of human needs to the dictates of economic expansion and the purely technical or utilitarian logic this implies. 'Being' is equated with 'having' under consumer capitalism, and 'having' increasingly means the passive absorption of ephemeral images and signs.

For Debord, the endless consumption of the spectacle supplants authentic human existence, because authenticity requires an immediate engagement with the material world and a process of self-realization. Consequently, the world under late capitalism can no longer be grasped directly, but only through a series of *mediations* and abstractions. Individuals are separated increasingly from the terrain of lived life, and are more and more isolated. Given this, Debord speculates, the spectacle is best understood as a symptom, or rather a refinement, of philosophical idealism. Idealism, to briefly reiterate, attempts to capture the real through a 'visionary' process of abstract conceptualization. To Debord's way of thinking, the technicist ethos that dominates modern life – the desire to re-make the world along the lines of abstract models of perfect symmetry and formal elegance – grew out of this original idealist impulse. As he writes: 'The spectacle does not realize philosophy; it philo-sophizes reality. The concrete life of everyone has been degraded into a *speculative* universe' (1987: 19).

In essence, the spectacle represents a secularization of religious and metaphysical illusions. Like religion, it banishes human powers to a nebulous fantasy-world, and thereby perfects the alienation of humanity's species-being. What Debord accomplishes, in effect, is the transferral of Marx's original theory of alienation, itself premised on a 'sociological' reading of Ludwig Feuerbach's philosophical anthropology, to the conditions of late capitalism. He manages this feat by synthesizing the Marxian concept of alienation with Lukács's account of commodity fetishism, as developed in the latter's essay 'Reification and the Consciousness of the Proletariat', included in *History and Class Consciousness*. For Lukács, commodity fetishism occurs when social actors are alienated from the things they pro-duce, and thereby fail to recognize the social character of commod-ities in the process of exchange. As a result, mystified beliefs about the nature of these social processes replace or mask their objective social character. Individuals therefore come to view their social relations as relations between *things*, and hence as natural, eternal and unchangeable. Hence, for Debord the spectacle is an expression of commodity fetishism, but exacerbated to a degree that Marx or even Lukács could not have foreseen. The spectacle manages to replace the concrete world with ghosts, images and abstractions. Because the commodity form represents a purely quantitative essence, its domination over the social world through the medium of the spectacle results in a fundamental 'loss of quality'. Reified thinking has come to dominate all areas of sociocultural life, and has virtually eliminated the qualitative and human aspects from capitalist society. History is arrested; the present system thus appears as natural and inevitable, completely insulated from human intervention. By its perfection of domination, the spectacle manages to project itself as a totalizing entity, the expression of a seamless and monolithic power. It represents the idealized self-image of power; as such, it accurately reflects the realities of bureaucratic hier-archy, repressive control and specialization under late capitalism:

> The spectacle is the existing order's uninterrupted discourse about itself, its laudatory monologue. It is the self-portrait of power in the epoch of its totalitarian management of the conditions of existence. [The] generalized cleavage of the spectacle is inseparable from the modern *State*, namely from the general form of cleavage within society, the product of the division of social labor and the organ of class domination.
> (Debord 1987: 24)

In other words, the spectacle projects itself as the alpha and omega of reality, and manifestly superior to non-spectacularized social relations. Like myth (its most obvious predecessor), it aims at a spurious unification of society, by masking or obscuring its internal conflicts and contradictions, especially of a class-based nature. Under the reign of the spectacle, a person finds it difficult to visualize themselves outside of the 'dominant images of need', images that eventually become absorbed into each individual's psyche, unconsciousness, gestures and speech. 'This is why the spectator feels at home nowhere', writes Debord, 'because the spectacle is everywhere' (1987: 30). Alienation, because ubiquitous, has become 'comfortable', and hence generally unrecognized as such. The result is the construction of a totally manipulated and spectacularized environment, encompassing all of time and space, and the world *in toto* appears to each individual as foreign and alien.

111

Time is dominated by the spectacle because the commodity places its stamp on the very meaning of chronological change itself. Time becomes irreversible and linear, a reflection of the temporal succession of secular power and the endless accumulation of things, of commodities. This domination of time, which was also noted by Lefebvre, is made possible by the technology of writing and mechanical reproduction. According to Debord, writing signals the appearance of 'a consciousness which is no longer carried and transmitted directly among the living: an *impersonal memory*, the memory of the administration of society' (1987: 131). Under modernity, the domination of time by things entails the elimination of 'lived' or qualitative time, and the emergence of a 'new immobility within history' (1987: 143). Blocks of time, consisting of 'abstract fragments' of a fixed value, are packaged and sold to the highest bidder (the 'complete vacation', the 'total' leisure experience). Time thus accumulated is unified, one-dimensional and irreversible. Hence, commodity time is a specialized time reflecting specific class interests and lacking a true use-value, but it manages successfully to project itself as universal and eminently desirable: 'In the spectacle, the lower the use value of modern survival-time, the more highly it is exalted. The reality of time has been replaced by the *advertisement* of time' (1987: 154). Real time, which incorporates the micronarratives of daily struggle and resistance, is expunged. This results in a historical amnesia, or what Debord calls the 'false consciousness' of modernity: 'Because history itself haunts modern society like a spectre, pseudo-histories are constructed at every level of consumption of life in order to preserve the threatened equilibrium of present frozen time' (1987: 200). Moreover, the spectacle unifies and dominates *space* as well as time. Space has become homogenized and 'banalized', and actual geographical distance has been replaced by spectacular separation. As Debord puts it, modern life is marked by 'capitalism's seizure of the natural and social environment; developing logically into absolute domination, capitalism can and must now remake the totality of space into its *own setting*' (1987: 169). Urban space is transformed into a *pseudo-community* based on the privatized family and the atomized individual, and structured according to the requisites of consumption and the reproduction of capitalism. However, the spectacle is not satisfied with the assimilation of space and time. In its frenzied attempt continually to reproduce the circuit of capital, culture (including past and non-Western cultures) is considered fair game for commodification. Culture, in the anthropological as well as the narrower sense, is increasingly severed from everyday life, and subject to a process of formalization and specialization. Lifestyles, spirituality, sexuality, knowledges, ideology – all are grist for the mill of the spectacle. Spectacular culture 'preserves congealed past culture', rather than producing genuinely new and innovative cultural and artistic forms. As such, a major function of the spectacle is '*to make history forgotten within culture*' (Debord 1987: 191, 192).

> Under the shimmering diversions of the spectacle, *banalization* dominates modern society the world over and at every point where the developed consumption of commodities has seemingly multiplied the roles and objects to choose from. The remains of religion and of the family (the principal relic of the heritage of class power) and the moral repression they assure, merge whenever the enjoyment of *this* world is affirmed – this world being nothing other than repressive pseudo-enjoyment.
>
> (Debord 1987: 59)

SI analysis concentrated especially on the deterioration of language. Under the reign of the spectacle, language is robbed of its rich, metaphorical textures rooted in everyday experience, and turned into a 'cascade of hierarchic signals' (Debord 1987: 202). In almost Bakhtinian terms, as discussed in Chapter 3, Debord regards the unilateral forms of communication engendered by the spectacle a 'metalanguage of machines', and hence the 'opposite of dialogue'. 'The acceptance and consumption of commodities', he writes, 'are at the heart of this pseudo-response to a communication without response' (Debord 1987: 219). The theme of the debasement of language is taken up more fully by Vaneigem in his text 'Basic Banalities', and also by another SI member, Mustapha Khayati. According to Khayati, the bourgeoisie has always desired to impose a universal, unitary language upon the social world. Under the guise of developing universal citizenship within the framework of the nation-state, modernity has encouraged a process of cultural-linguistic homogenization that 'attacks language and reduces its poetry to the vulgar prose of its information' (1981: 172). The reduction of living speech and language to codified information and unambiguous signals, streamlined to facilitate the bureaucratic regulation and control of social relations, results in the mutilation and destruction of language: 'Power presents only the falsified, official sense of words' (Vaneigem 1981c: 114). Because communication in the society of the spectacle is mediated by bureaucratic agencies, people are less able to engage in authentic dialogue, and are increasingly transformed into passive receivers of information and orders. To quote more fully from Khayati's 'Captive Words: Preface to a Situationist Dictionary':

> Language colonized by bureaucracy is reduced to a series of blunt, inflexible formulas in which the same nouns are always accompanied by the same adjectives and participles; the noun governs them and each time it appears they automatically fall in around it and in the correct order. This 'falling into step' of words reflects a more profound militarization of the whole society, its division into two basic categories: the caste of rulers and the great mass of executants.
>
> (1981: 173)

The spectacle also displays a remarkable capacity for what the Situationists termed *recuperation*, or the absorption of dissent and oppositional culture and their transformation into commodities. Through recuperation, the original intent of even the most radical critique is deflected and rendered harmless, translated into just another lifestyle choice. Debord terms this 'spectacular rebellion': 'dissatisfaction itself became a commodity as soon as economic abundance could extend production to the processing of such raw materials' (1987: 59). In short, the spectacle represents the perfection of ideology, or rather its *materialization*, because it has tailored the world to fit this abstract appearance. It is the absolute negation and impoverishment of everyday life, which 'obliterates the boundaries between true and false by driving all lived truth below the real presence of fraud ensured by the organization of appearance. One who passively accepts his alien daily fate is thus pushed toward a madness that reacts in an illusory way to this fate by resorting to magical techniques' (1987: 219). For Debord, the spectacle is a 'pseudo-festival', a usurpation and redirection of creative energies and utopian desires into commodified and alienated forms.

VANEIGEM AND THE CRITIQUE OF 'SURVIVALISM'

Vaneigem, particularly in his book *The Revolution of Everyday Life*, developed a slightly different line of inquiry than did Debord.

Although Vaneigem was also concerned with analysing the forms of power and domination bound up with the spectacle, especially its relationship to myth and religion, he mainly concentrated on the effects of the spectacularization of social relations upon subjectivity and consciousness in the context of daily life. Moreover, his writing style tended to be even more densely poetic and metaphorical than Debord's, inasmuch as Debord preferred to parody the style of academic and philosophical treatises. Vaneigem was particularly concerned to critique the specialization of social roles under late capitalism and the emergence of a rapacious individualism, together with the ethos of 'survivalism' that accompanies these developments.

Like Lefebvre, Vaneigem argues that everyday life in the society of the spectacle has become trivialized and 'neutralized', with the result that the creative potentialities inherent within daily existence have been subordinated to powerful interests. Everyday life has attracted the gaze of power, mainly because the belief systems of previous epochs – including myth and religion, but also Enlightenment ideologies like liberalism and official communism – no longer retain any legitimacy, and have become anachronistic. Vaneigem speculates that this power vacuum, resulting from what Lyotard (1984) has termed an 'incredulity towards metanarratives', has subsequently been filled by the more diffuse but no less effective ideology of consumerism. Consumerism, as a form of social control, is more 'rational' and less mysterious than mythopoetic forms of legitimation, such as the 'divine right of kings'. It is also far more insidious, because it becomes ingrained into the everyday consciousness and behaviour of individuals, constituting part of their 'common sense'. Echoing Foucault's (1977) notion of the 'carceral society', Vaneigem writes: 'Docility is no longer ensured by means of priestly magic, it results from a mass of minor hypnoses: news, culture, city planning, advertising, mechanisms of conditioning and suggestion ready to serve any order, established or yet to come' (1983: 12). Consumerism offers a cornucopia of delights, and the promise of both material abundance and human fulfilment. Natural scarcity, which justified earlier systems of domination and hierarchy, has by and large been eliminated, at least in the industrialized West – or so it seemed to many in the post-war years of relative affluence. However, there is a price to be paid for this leap in productive efficacy: the loss of sovereignty over self, and the transformation of the human subject into object. Objectification signals the demise of authentic intersubjectivity and dialogue, encouraging the phenomena of isolation and psychological dependency. According to Vaneigem,

'People touch without meeting; isolation accumulates but is never realized; emptiness overcomes us as the density of the crowd grows. The crowd drags me out of myself and installs thousands of little sacrifices in my empty presence' (1983: 26). As a system of domination, however, consumerism adroitly turns this loneliness and acquisitive egoism into an unassailable good, something inherently and eminently desirable. The result is that modern society has erected a 'palace of solipsist madness', which it blindly worships. In an economy based on consumption, however, individuals cannot be transformed into any object. They have to take on the attributes of a specific *type* of consumer, so that they can be more easily identified, pigeon-holed and manipulated by the spectacular economy. People are treated as conforming to discrete 'categories', each of which is supposed to have certain lifestyle and purchasing proclivities. As Vaneigem puts it, 'the present economic system can only be rescued by turning man into a consumer, by identifying him with the largest possible number of consumable values, which is to say, non-values, or empty, fictitious, abstract values' (1983: 50).

For Vaneigem, Marx's oft-criticized thesis of 'immiseration', in which the proletariat was subjected to increasingly brutal forms of exploitation and degradation until it was literally forced to rebel, was incorrect only in that Marx identified immiseration with the quantity of material goods rather than with the overall quality of life. The key contradiction of consumer capitalism is that the perfection of material abundance is paralleled by the impoverishment of lived existence and human potential. Vaneigem concurs with Debord that time under the spell of the spectacle is measured primarily by the accumulation of commodities, which is a static and purely quantitative form of temporality. It ceases to be an expression of the richness and multiplicity of human experience. Since money and commodities are the measure of all things, we seem to have no option but to consume faster, to make the treadmill turn more quickly. The result, according to Vaneigem, is the emergence of an ideology of *survivalism*, which is a powerful prophylactic against social revolution. Survival is paramount, and survival means life reduced to its basic essentials, to an abstract form. Existence is increasingly lived on the minimum level required for the reproduction of the system of consumption. As Vaneigem writes: 'Work to survive, survive by consuming, survive to consume: the hellish cycle is complete. Under the reign of "economism," survival is both necessary and sufficient. This is the fundamental truth of bourgeois society' (1983: 51). The logic of commercial exchange and quantification permeates daily existence and dominates our lives: 'Strictly quantified, first by money and then by what might be called "sociometric units of power," exchange pollutes all our relationships, feeling and thoughts. Where exchange dominates, only *things* are left, a world plugged into the organization charts of cybernetic power: the world of reification' (1983: 58).

For Vaneigem, a central aspect of this process of reification and the devaluation of everyday life is the extreme specialization and hierarchization of tasks under late capitalism. Society now consists of a number of fixed 'roles' that strictly regulate each person's horizon of activities, access to social networks, and 'appropriate' personality and behavioural dispositions. Essentially, roles are formal constructions which drain life of its spontaneity and creativity; they fragment what Lefebvre called the 'total man'. To adopt a specialized role is to identify totally with it. As such, the role represents the consumption of power, in that it locates people within a pre-existing hierarchy and system of domination. The specialist, argues Vaneigem, is a 'chimerical being, a cog, mechanical *thing*, housed in the rationality of a perfect social order of zombies. . . . Knowing everything about a small area, he enlists others to produce and consume within the confines of this area so that he himself may receive a surplus-value of power and increase the significance of his own hierarchical image' (1983: 108–9). To illustrate his point, Vaneigem contrasts the modern role with its premodern counterpart. To be a 'worker' or 'peasant' in the past did not mean the occupation of a role in its modern sense, because there was little internal differentiation of such activities and no expectation that one had to conform to stereotypical ways of thinking and acting. In contemporary society, however, roles have become firmly established and increasingly internalized. 'Taken over body and consciousness by the blandishments of a succession of images', Vaneigem writes, the modern consumer 'rejects authentic satisfaction and espouses a passionless asceticism' (1983: 101). The function of such roles is to facilitate the continuation of the spectacular economy through the adaptation of the individual to the 'well-policed universe of things'. Evoking the work of the renegade Austrian psychoanalyst Wilhelm Reich, Vaneigem (1983: 105) links this process of adaptation to the redirection of potentially subversive erotic and creative energies into more consumer-friendly forms, what Herbert Marcuse (1955) has called 'repressive desublimation'. Identification with a role might give an individual a limited degree of access to the system of power and the spectacular economy, but at the cost of abandoning one's autonomy and capacity for self-realization. 'What is gained at the level of appearances', suggests Vaneigem, 'is lost on the level of being and becoming' (1983: 105). To dwell in the realm of appearances is the compensation offered by the spectacle to people for their dehumanization and loss of authenticity:

> Dislodged from its essential place by the bombardment of prohibitions, limitations and lies, lived reality comes to seem so trivial that appearances become the centre of our attention, until roles completely obscure the importance of our own lives. In an order of *things,* compensation is the only thing that gives a person any weight. The role compensates for a lack: ultimately, for the lack of life; more immediately, for the lack of another role. A worker conceals his prostration beneath the role of foreman, and the poverty of this role itself beneath the incomparably superior image of a late-model car. But every role is paid for by self-injury (overwork, the renunciation of 'luxuries', survival, etc). At best it is an ineffective plug for the gaping wound left by the vampirization of the self and of real life.
>
> (Vaneigem 1983: 106)

RESISTING THE SPECTACLE

The spectacle is a formidable power, which cripples the imagination and induces an acceptance of alienation, fragmentation and passivity. Despite its apparent ubiquity, however, the SI believed that the reification of society had definite limits. The apparently invincible society of the spectacle had certain points of vulnerability that, if broached, could bring the entire system tumbling down like a house of cards. As Vaneigem put it, 'All the springs blocked by power will one day burst forth to form a torrent that will change the face of the world' (1981a: 124). In moving from traditional or mythopoetic forms of legitimation to an ideology of possessive individualism based on the principle of consumption, the grasp of anonymous power had been extended into every sphere of social existence, including private life and the everyday. However, this was something of a Faustian bargain. According to the SI, it has transferred the social basis of power from a secure, if restricted foundation, to a wider but less stable one. Power seeps into the most microscopic spaces of everyday social life; yet at the same time few people accord the system any real legitimacy. Social reproduction relies more on passivity and *ressentiment* than active assent, a situation accurately summed up by Peter Sloterdijk (1984) in his phrase 'enlightened false consciousness'. As such, the hierarchical power structure can be effectively contested, as long as a descent into pure nihilism is avoided. However, successful revolt requires a relentless attack on the 'general science of false consciousness' perfected by the spectacle (Debord 1987: 194). In taking this position, the Situationists operated with a fairly orthodox view of ideology – again, mainly derived from Lukács's *History and Class Consciousness*. As it appears in the spectacle, ideology is the basis of class society, and it represents a deformed consciousness of reality. The spectacle as ideology strives to obliterate the distinction between truth and falsity, reality and illusion. Yet this mystification (*contra* Baudrillard) can be challenged and reversed: 'Emancipation from the material bases of inverted truth – this is what the self-emancipation of our epoch consists of' (Debord 1987: 221; Plant 1990). In classical Marxist fashion, Debord argued that this process of supplanting true for false consciousness was not a matter of correcting individual error, the position taken by the Enlighten-ment philosophers. It could only be effected through practical action on the part of what Marx called the class with 'radical chains': the proletariat. In overcoming the ideological obfuscation and political inertia fostered by the spectacle, the proletariat would, through the realization of 'practical theory', construct its own lived situation, and make history in a conscious fashion. The masses would take control of space and time for their own uses, rather than those proscribed by the spectacle. This would itself require direct democracy, a politics without specialization or mediation. As exemplars of direct democracy, the Situationists pointed to the Paris Commune of 1871 and the soviets and workers' councils of the early twentieth century, as theorized by libertarian Marxists like Karl Korsch, Otto Bauer and Antonie Pannekoek (Jacoby 1981).

According to Situationist theory, the revolutionary organization must be a microcosm of the future society itself. For all of its elitist posturing, the SI refused to consider itself as a political vanguard *à la* Lenin, for this would mean a return to specialized politics, a separation between leaders and led. Instead, the Situationists strove to operate as a catalyst, to trigger the dissolution of false conscious-ness perfected by the spectacle and thereby enable the masses to actualize their own liberation. Another, more Freudian metaphor they utilized to characterize the role of the SI was that of 'therapist'. Situationist activities could be understood as therapeutic in the sense that they brought to consciousness the repressions and distortions fostered by the spectacle. The Situationists, Sadie Plant remarks, 'defined themselves as the last specialists: in the post-revolutionary world, there would be no need for elite groups of revolutionaries, and art, politics, and all other disciplines would no longer exist as separated areas of thought' (1992: 5). Moreover, the SI argued that their theses and ideas were not specialized concepts, comprehensible only to an educated elite. Rather, Situationist 'theory' was grounded in the practice of everyday life and grasped instinctively by the proletariat, which would correctly intuit the debased character of work and the machinations of power behind the spectacle. For instance, Vaneigem suggested that 'all Situationist ideas are nothing other than faithful developments of acts attempted constantly by thousands of people to try and prevent another day from being no more than twenty-four hours of wasted time' (1981a: 123). This explains why the Situationists found considerable succour in the seemingly 'trivial' acts of revolt and contestation found within the daily life of urban capitalism. Vandalism, petty theft and looting, industrial sabotage, provocative graffiti, squatting in abandoned properties – these were interpreted by the SI as latently revolutionary, as signs of a liberated consciousness and the collective refusal to accept passively the boredom and stultification induced by consumer capitalism. '*Boredom*', as the SI said in their journal *Internationale Situationniste*, '*is counterrevolutionary*' (1981a: 86).

Not content simply to draw attention to such spontaneous acts of refusal, however, the SI sought to articulate an effective political strategy and to 'illuminate and coordinate the gestures of refusal and the signs of creativity that are defining the new contours of the proletariat, the irreducible will to freedom' (1981b: 139). This praxis hinged on the transformation of culture from a tool of the spectacle into one of contestation and demystification. Because culture was the 'star commodity' of the spectacular commodity, the SI argued that the initial skirmishes of social revolution would be fought on the terrain of culture, information and the media – not as an end to itself, but as a prelude to a total revolution of everyday life. For Vaneigem, this revolution hinged on the negation of three aspects of consumer capitalism – the *spectacle*, or the replacement of reality by appearance; *separation*, the atomization of social life; and *sacrifice*, the renunciation of desire and personal happiness for the empty promise of the commodity – and their replacement by *participation*, *communication* and *realization* (1981b: 121).

To this end, the Situationists developed two key strategies, *détournement* and the *dérive*. *Détournement* – a 'game of subversion' – was for the SI equivalent to Marx's dialectical critique of Hegel's idealism (Fields and Best 1986: 386). Just as Marx argued that Hegel's *Geist* or 'World Spirit' obscured the real basis of society (the production and reproduction of material existence), the commodity replaces lived experience with a series of spectral abstractions. The lie of the spectacle could be exposed through the construction of a 'new semantic field for expressing a new truth' (Khayati 1981: 170), thereby prompting what the Situationists called a 'reversal of perspective'. *Détournement* involved the utilization of materials proffered by the spectacle itself – photographs, films, graphics, advertising slogans – transforming the original meaning by placing such materials in a new context or through the addition of other texts or images. By this technique, the Situationists sought to fulfil Lautréamont's injunction that 'Plagiarism is necessary. Progress demands it.' For instance, the Situationists appropriated and redirected the original meaning of comic strips by erasing the existing talk or thought bubbles and inserting their own text, usually to both humorous and consciousness-raising effect. Similarly, Debord's numerous avant-garde films consisted of fragments from a variety of sources, including television advertisements, newsreels and fiction films, to form a collage of images, accompanied by an oblique voice-over usually provided by Debord himself. Indeed, Anselm Jappe (1999: 60) goes so far as to claim that many SI writings, especially Debord's *Society of the Spectacle*, were in themselves elaborate *détournements* of texts by Hegel, Marx and Lukács. To successfully *détourn* meaning in this way helped to reveal the spectacle's monologic desire to project itself as the sole source of meaning and value as a hollow sham, and to undercut the bourgeois cult of the author-genius. As Khayati put it, *détournement* demonstrates 'the insubordination of words, of the impossibility for power to *totally recuperate* created meanings, to fix an existing meaning once and for all' (1981: 171). Lived experience, argued the SI, could be the only legitimate arbiter of meaning; true communication is impossible outside of the context of 'free creative activity' located within the sphere of everyday life.

The Situationists were adamant that the creative *détournement* of meaning was not the sole prerogative of artists working with such traditional materials as painting or sculpture. Following the Surrealists, the SI asserted that the well-spring of creative and spontaneous self-actualization was a subversive capacity that everyone shared, regardless of their position within the spectacular hierarchy. Such an inherent creativity can be found in 'seething unsatisfied desires, daydreams in search of a foothold in reality, feelings at once confused and luminously clear, ideas and gestures presaging nameless upheavals' (Vaneigem 1983: 147). The spectacle, of course, attempts to co-opt this energy and forces it into prearranged and commodified forms. Yet no matter how alienated or repressed an individual is, every person harbours a creative spark that seeks expression and consummation. Like Heller and Lefebvre, the SI insisted that the desires stimulated continually by the consumer system could not be fulfilled within the present socioeconomic organization of society. This irreversible tension signals the system's eventual downfall: 'The more oppression is justified in terms of the freedom to consume, the more the malaise arising from this contra- diction exacerbates the thirst for total freedom. [The] laboratory of individual creativity transmutes the basest metals of daily life into gold through a revolutionary alchemy' (Vaneigem 1983: 147, 149). Spontaneous creativity, which maintains an immediate connection to lived existence and the qualitative, is incapable of being totally co-opted or reified; as such, it constitutes the most efficacious vehicle through which the 'slave consciousness' propagated by the spectacle can be challenged and overturned.

The *dérive*, which the SI defined as a 'mode of experimental behavior linked to the conditions of urban society: a technique of transient passage through ambiances' (1981c: 45), evinced a similar desire to introject the 'play' element into everyday life. Under the spectacle, people live in constructed situations that are monotonous, homogeneous and predetermined. Accordingly, the Situationist goal in the *dérive* was to produce novel environments that were more closely attuned to personal desire and affect. In order to deflect the preferred meanings inscribed in the spaces and places of the capitalist city, individuals were admonished to engage in a 'playful reconstructive behaviour' of the lived environment. In the *dérive*, the 'social text' of urban space is effectively rewritten according to a very different set of priorities, meanings and desires, which serves to 'extend the terrain of play to all desirable constructions' (Debord 1981c: 57). As mentioned above, the term given by the Situationists to the concrete practice of refashioning the city landscape along these lines was 'unitary urbanism'. As a theory and practice of urban life, it was totally opposed to the ideology of 'urban planning', which had domesticated urban space according to the bureaucratic requirements of state and capital. Unitary urbanism was a 'living critique, fuelled by all the tensions of daily life, of this manipulation of cities and their inhabitants' (Kotányi and Vaneigem 1981: 66). The Situationist vision of a transfigured urban space involved the maximum degree of participation, communality, and interaction between individuals. Free dialogue, non-instrumental exchange, and play would supersede the atomized and purely contractual relations of consumer capitalism. As Debord put it, 'Revolutionary urbanists will not limit their concern to the circulation of things and of human beings trapped in a world of things. They will try to break these topological chains, paving the way with their experiments for a human journey through authentic life' (1981c: 58). The following quotation, from the SI text 'Theory of the Dérive', may help to render Situationist intentions more comprehensible:

> Thus a loose lifestyle and even certain amusements considered dubious that have always enjoyed among our entourage – slipping by night into houses undergoing demolition, hitchhiking nonstop and without destination through Paris during a transportation strike in the name of adding to the confusion, wandering in subterranean catacombs forbidden to the public, etc. – are expressions of a more general sensibility which is nothing other than that of the dérive. Written expressions can be no more than passwords to this great game.
>
> (1981d: 53)

Situationist critique in the service of demystification does not, therefore, rely on the postulation of a realm of abstract, transcendental values. Rather, it is an immanent critique because it seeks to 'expose the appalling contrast between the possible constructions of life and its present poverty'. Utopia, according to Debord and Vaneigem, is about the realm of the possible, in the sense that the here and now contains within it all the necessary materials for a transfigured social existence. However, Situationist theory is future-oriented in that it refuses a romanticist nostalgia and anticipates the arrival of a new society and a new way of life. 'The revolution of everyday life cannot draw its poetry from the past, but only from the future', as one SI text put it, paraphrasing Marx's *Eighteenth Brumaire* (1981e: 64). Such a revolution represents a triumph of the present and the future over the dead hand of the past, and a casting off of repetitive, stultified behaviour and the ethos of survivalism and sacrifice. In the non-spectacular society of the future, 'work' as it is currently understood would be abolished, and exchange-value would be replaced by use-value. The outlines of such non-commodified social relations could be glimpsed in the forms of gift-giving and 'nonproductive expenditure' found in premodern societies (Bataille 1988). For example, as an anonymous SI text argued, 'real desires begin to be expressed in festival, in playful self-assertion, in the *potlatch* of destruction' (1981f: 155). This revolution, unlike all previous rebellions, would be marked by the abolition of work and a full flowering of the creative potential of daily life, and a supersession of capitalist isolation and possessive egoism. The return of authentic community would not, however, be marked by the tyranny of the group over the individual. As the SI understood it, community could only be based on the full participation of sovereign and free individuals. Liberated from the despotism of specialization, each person would be able to cultivate all the different sides of human nature and develop their full potentialities. The realization of true community was premised on the self-realization of each of its members, and with the 'liberation of the inexhaustible energies trapped in a petrified daily life' (Kotányi and Vaneigem 1981: 67). In Plant's words, the SI envisaged the revolution as

> the first freely constructed game, a collective transformation of reality in which history is seized by all its participants. Play, pleasure, and participation were to be the hallmarks of a new form of social organisation appropriate to a world in which the imperatives of survival no longer legitimise relations of domination, alienation, or the separation between the individual and the world. The euphoric fluidity of the revolutionary moment, in which experiences gain a tangible immediacy which makes a few days seem like years, comes out of the free and experimental play unleashed by the total rejection of existing rules. [The] joy of freely assumed roles is rediscovered in the midst of the contestation of those previously prescribed, and out of the ruins of commodified lifestyles and definitions emerge new patterns of playfully chosen and flexible identities like those one fleetingly adopts when playing charades or childhood games of make-believe. And play is also the charm with which the revolution is protected from hierarchy and mediation.
>
> (1992: 71)

CONCLUSION

In their analysis of the spectacle, consumerism and specialization, the SI developed a trenchant and insightful critique of modernity and everyday life. Any revolutionary project that ignored the stultification of daily life in industrial society, the repressive and repetitive character of alienated labour, and the perennial human demand for immediate freedom and happiness, was a revolution that was not worth the effort. Yet, at the same time, they managed largely (though not entirely) to avoid the pandering elitism of so many other avant-garde cultural and political movements with a similar ideological orientation. To their credit, they also articulated concrete and highly successful strategies for sociocultural contestation. Perhaps what is most important about the Situationists, however, is their intransigence and optimism, especially given the present cultural and intellectual climate. They argued convincingly that a commodity-based economy was irredeemable, a barrier to the project of human disalienation, individual sovereignty, and the achievement of genuine community. This position presents a serious challenge to current intellectual fashion, which has largely made its peace with the consumer capitalism, by stressing the latently creative side of consumption, or by denying any possibility of its transformation. The SI therefore subscribed to what we can term 'immanent utopianism', which does not broach compromise with consumer capitalism, nor locate an 'alternative' in some abstract blueprint of the future or an irretrievable past. It is a message which has found favour with certain elements of the radical left – for instance, in the activities of the US group centred around the (unfortunately now defunct) San Francisco-based publication *Processed World*.

This is not to say that Situationist theory is unproblematic. For example, its almost complete preoccupation with class fails to take into account the 'everyday life' of other sectors of the population, most notably women and ethnic minorities. Its fairly orthodox Marxist faith in the revolutionary agency of the proletariat seems increasingly anachronistic today, when some kind of 'rainbow coalition' and the new social movements appear to many as a more viable expedient of social change. Moreover, its almost complete stress on ideological and cultural criticism, which itself relies on a dubious notion of 'false consciousness' and an equally mechanistic 'reversal of perspective'. In this, the SI seriously underestimated the stubborn resilience of existing socioeconomic structures and

125

overlooked the material bases of class power, as opposed to the system's ideological underpinnings. Finally, like many radical critiques of capitalism developed in the 1950s and 1960s (seen also in the contemporaneous work of Herbert Marcuse and Murray Bookchin, for example), the SI were simply incorrect in suggesting that post-war capitalism had definitively solved the problem of scarcity, and that 'poverty' in the West was purely qualitative rather than quantitative in nature. A viable utopian, non-market society does not only have to be fun; it has to achieve a harmonious balance with the natural world. This is a consideration that the Situationists paid no heed to whatsoever. Despite this, however, the SI are to be admired for asking many uncomfortable and provocative questions about the means and ends of social change, the nature of community and individualism, and the limits of capitalism and reification. Their approach must be given serious credence in a properly critical theory of everyday life.

6

AGNES HELLER: RATIONALITY, ETHICS AND EVERYDAY LIFE

Whatever you are doing, as a scientist or anything else, you always start out from problems of everyday life.

Georg Lukács

INTRODUCTION

The philosopher and social theorist Agnes Heller has produced an impressively variegated and challenging body of work, which to date encompasses over fifty volumes and literally hundreds of articles in several languages. It is an *oeuvre* that has undergone dramatic transformations over the past thirty-five years, from critical Marxism to 'post-Marxism' through to a qualified post-modernism, changes that have mirrored wider developments within the critical discourse of the European left intelligentsia. At the same time, her massive output has been largely overlooked in the social sciences and humanities literature, at least in the English-speaking world, although the publication of a recent *Festschrift* may alter this (Burnheim 1994). Born in Hungary in 1929, Heller was a star pupil and research assistant of the Marxist theoretician Georg Lukács, a towering (if controversial) intellectual figure who has had a major impact on twentieth-century social thought, especially aesthetics, sociology and political theory.[1] In the wake of the failed Hungarian uprising of 1956, Heller was expelled from the Hungarian Communist Party and the University of Budapest for her 'revisionist' views. Heller taught in a secondary school until her 'rehabilitation' in 1963, which coincided with the partial liberaliz-ation of the Communist regime. During this period, she conducted historical research into Renaissance culture at the Hungarian Academy of Sciences, which culminated in her 1965 book *Renaissance*

Man. From this historical inquiry, Heller developed a keen interest in the problems and social constitution of everyday life, which eventually led to the publication of *Everyday Life*. In the 1960s and early 1970s, Heller was a key member of the so-called 'Budapest School', a group of young critics and intellectuals who gravitated around Lukács, and which included Ferenc Fehér (her late husband and frequent collaborator), György Márkus, István Mészáros and Mihály Vajda (Frankel and Martin 1973; Gabel 1975). The Budapest School's vocal support for democratization and liberalization in Czechoslovakia during the 'Prague Spring' era, which ended abruptly with the Soviet and Eastern Bloc invasion of 1968, led to a permanent marginalization of the group by the Kádár regime and their relegation to 'dissident' status. Most members of the School left Hungary soon thereafter. Heller and Fehér emigrated to Australia in 1977, whereupon she took up a position in sociology and philosophy at La Trobe University. After her departure from Hungary, Heller's work became increasingly sophisticated and wide-ranging, addressing such areas as the theory of needs, historiography, political philosophy, methodological issues in the human sciences, ethics, postmodernism, and the sociology of state socialism. More recently, Heller was appointed Hannah Arendt Professor of Philosophy at the New School for Social Research in New York.[2] In this chapter, I will concentrate on Heller's analysis of everyday life, although other related aspects of her work will also be considered, especially her thoughts on ethics, rationality and utopia.

THE SOCIAL ONTOLOGY OF EVERYDAY LIFE

Heller's most sustained and systematic work on everyday life falls within her critical Marxist phase, a period spanning from the early 1960s to the late 1970s. At this time, Heller subscribed to a humanistic and Hegelian interpretation of Marx that focussed primarily on the latter's early texts concerning alienation, self-realization and 'species-being', and which embraced a project of radical political transformation. This Marxist humanism was synthesized with existentialist and phenomenological elements derived from Kierkegaard, Sartre, Heidegger and the Czech philosopher Karel Kosík, traditions that stress the 'lived' or experiential situation of the individual within the concrete lifeworld (Heller 1977). Indeed, many of her categories are a subtle blend of Hegelian and Heideggerian concepts (Wolin 1987). A third major influence upon

Heller's work is the legacy of classical Western philosophy, especially the ideas of Aristotle and Kant. It is worth noting that her writings of this period defend a 'strong programme' of human rationality and the critical orientation of Enlightenment philosophy, and bring questions of value and morality to the fore of theoretical discussion. More recently, however, Heller has come to question many aspects of the Marxian project (and more generally what she labels 'radical universalism'), especially its perceived Promethean, messianic and dogmatic tendencies. In particular, Heller singles out Marxism's obsession with the paradigm of production and its adherence to a very narrow definition of materialism as being especially problematic, for this has encouraged a devaluation of such 'bourgeois' conceptions as ethics, human rights, and the need to nurture and sustain a vibrant, autonomous civil society. *Pace* Jean-François Lyotard, she has come to reject the 'grand narratives' characteristic of modernity and of 'totalizing' philosophical perspectives, and has raised doubts about the Marxian and Enlightenment belief in an inherent *telos* or progressivist trend in history, which in her opinion has led to a simplification of social reality and a suppression of difference and plurality. Modernity, she claims, is a historically-contingent phenomenon that does not conform to any single, underlying logic or purpose; as such, it presents itself to us as a horizon of unfulfilled possibilities. In these claims, Heller has staked out a position that she describes as a 'limited scepticism'.

Yet despite her acceptance of such postmodern values as complexity, openness and difference, and her efforts to rethink the relation between theory and praxis, Heller remains highly critical of the irrationalist and politically compromising tendencies of certain versions of postmodernism. Moreover, she has remained committed to the view, formulated with particular vigour in her earlier studies, that the sphere of everyday life remains the essential 'value-horizon' for human beings, and that it is here where human ethical and intersubjective relations must be forged. Indeed, Heller continues to defend the human capacity for rationality as central to the achievement of responsibility and autonomy, although by this she means an Aristotelian/Kantian 'practical reason' that is not dissimilar to Lefebvre's notion of dialectical rationality, as opposed to the 'Absolute Reason' of Hegel and other philosophical idealists. The essential difference between her early and later work does not so much concern her substantive analysis of spheres like everyday life, but rather the task of the intelligentsia and the status of critical knowledge. To use Zygmunt Bauman's (1987) terminology, Heller now sees the role of the critical intellectual as being that of an 'interpreter' of the sociocultural world, as a facilitator of self-understanding *vis-à-vis* the options facing humankind, and not a 'legislator' who seeks to impose a particular political or theoretical programme on an increasingly pluralistic and variegated society.

In spite of her recent re-evaluation of the Marxian tradition and her retreat from radical universalism, Heller's writings continue to explore themes and issues that she has never abandoned completely. Briefly stated, her writings on the everyday attempt to utilize the methodological tools of historical materialism, as influenced by Lukács's later work on 'social ontology', in tandem with certain insights developed by the phenomenological tradition, in order to shed light on the nature of daily existence and human intersubjectivity. Heller's essential position is that everyday life cannot be considered in isolation, and abstracted from wider social relations and institutions. As with Lefebvre *et al.*, she insists that it is necessary to view everyday life in contemporary society from a broader sociohistorical perspective. Indeed, the structural differenti-ation of everyday life from other social spheres is, in her opinion, a relatively recent development. In premodern societies, daily life is fully integrated into a wider range of productive, ritualistic and sacred practices. Everyday life becomes detached from other activ-ities when 'higher' or more specialized pursuits, such as science, religion and art, become the prerogative of elites.

However, this process of differentiation, at least in its initial phases, does not necessarily imply the degradation of everyday life. Echoing Bakhtin's analysis of the Renaissance in *Rabelais and His World*, Heller argues that during this period there was a fruitful interchange between scientific and cultural pursuits and the 'lived' or experiential qualities of everyday life. With the demise of traditional social hierarchies and mythopoetic forms of legitimation, there ceased to be such a sharp distinction between 'high' and 'low' culture. For example, science in Renaissance Europe had not yet become highly technical and abstract, but had a 'sensuous' quality that was strongly linked to pragmatic forms of thinking and action (Toulmin 1990). Similarly, philosophical investigation was con-cerned with the articulation of a practical ethics, and dealt with certain epistemological problems associated with everyday percep-tion. Finally, art in the immediate post-medieval era was no longer subordinated to religious worship. In acquiring a specificity and autonomy that it did not formerly enjoy, art became 'this-worldly', a source of pleasure and entertainment within daily life, yet at the same time separate from it. As Heller writes, Renaissance society 'no longer simply generated art as an integral part of daily life itself, but created, honoured, and exalted it *as art*; while art, obedient to its own laws, reacted back upon everyday life as art, and permeated it' (1978: 151). By the end of the seventeenth century, however, this creative osmosis between everyday life and more specialized activities had by and large ended. Needs, both individual and social, were increasingly subordinated to the technical requirements of a rapidly expanding apparatus of production, rather than 'organically' connected to the rhythms and textures of daily life. Within learned discourse, particularly science and philosophy, everyday life became the target of ridicule and vilification. Francis Bacon, for instance, derided everyday thinking as confused and mystified, because it was based on unsubstantiated prejudices rather than the verifiable principles of objective science. 'Everyday life', asserts Heller, 'came to be thematized from the standpoint of a "truth" which then defined this life as void of truth' (1985a: 80). As such, daily existence in the early modern period came to be overshadowed by the 'brutality of primitive accumulation' (1978: 152).

Accordingly, Heller insists that everyday life has only rarely been considered a worthy object of contemplation during the last two and a half thousand years of Western thought. This situation has only begun to change in the twentieth century. In part, this can be explained by the emergence of social theories and philosophies like hermeneutics, phenomenology, and *Verstehen* sociology, which contain the necessary conceptual and methodological tools for a systematic analysis of the everyday lifeworld. In this context, Heller mentions the likes of Max Weber, Georg Simmel and Alfred Schütz. Because these figures successfully focused on the intersubjective constitution of the social world, their work represented a significant advance over purely idealist approaches, which had only considered the world from the perspective of the isolated, monadistic subject (Heller 1986; Outhwaite 1975). However, Heller also asserts that these intellectual developments could only have arisen if everyday life was recognized as *problematic*, and hence deserving of study in the first place. As intimated above, modernity represents a distinct threat to the integrity of everyday life, because it subjects daily existence to an extensive process of bureaucratic restructuring and rationalization. Although this situation has forced modern social thought to at least be aware of the existence of 'everyday life' as a distinct ontological category within the social world, it has led to a strangely polarized state of affairs. On the one hand, some approaches do indeed make reference to everyday life, but interpret it in a negative fashion. For instance, in his *magnum opus Being and Time* (1962), Heidegger considered the everyday world to be 'fallen', because it was not attuned to the truth of 'Being', and hence devoid of authenticity. On the other hand, theories such as Schütz's version of phenomenology, or the more recent approach of ethnomethodology, tend to valorize the ongoing accomplishments and practices of everyday life but in an uncritical and essentially descriptive fashion, and conceptualize the underlying structures of the lifeworld as unchanging and immutable.

Heller strives to avoid the shortcomings of both extremes. She insists that everyday life and forms of intersubjectivity have to be analysed on their own terms, and not reduced to something more 'fundamental', or subjected to arbitrary value judgements. Yet she wants to retain a dialectical and critical focus, by asserting that everyday life has hidden or suppressed potentialities that need to be brought to fruition. In this phase of her career, Heller subscribes to a political project that aims at the rehabilitation and transformation of everyday life. Her central goal is the 'humanization' and radical democratization of the everyday, so as to enrich both the individual and the human species. In this, Heller fully subscribes to Lukács's argument that the supreme moral value is the full development of the 'total' human being, a realization of manifold human powers and capacities. In taking this position, Heller argues that everyday life cannot be understood as a 'thing' or 'system', or even an 'attitude' *à la* Schütz. This would be to confuse the reified *appearance* of daily existence under commodity capitalism with its essential qualities, which are themselves subject to change and transformation. By contrast, she conceptualizes everyday life as an ensemble of historically constituted practices and forms of subjectivity that are complexly related to and mediated by other structures, institutions and practices. 'Everyday life', Heller writes, 'is not "something" but rather the shared modern life-experience on which our intersubjective constitution of the world rests' (1987: 297). As such, she sets out to analyse these practices and ensembles by relating them to the fundamental ontological categories of the sociocultural world. Heller's main supposition is that we can never fully comprehend any part of society without considering the context of social existence in its entirety.

Whereas Marxism has traditionally been concerned with examining the 'macro' structures of the capitalist economy as the primary site of social production and reproduction, Heller focuses on the reproduction of the individual human being within the sphere of everyday life. Indeed, she defines everyday life as 'the aggregate of those individual reproduction factors which, *pari passu*, make social reproductions possible' (1984a: 3). The reproduction of society, including the institutional sphere, is therefore contingent upon the reproduction of the individual, inasmuch as society can only survive if human beings discharge particular functions. Accordingly, Heller argues, everyday life is a human universal: it exists in all societies, although of course the actual form and content of the everyday lifeworld is historically variable. In order to grasp this dualistic process of reproduction and the relationship between them, Heller develops a social ontology that comprises three basic categories: (i) 'objectivation-in-itself'; (ii) 'objectivation-for-itself'; and (iii) 'objectivation-for-and-in-itself'. Before discussing each of these in detail, it is important to realize that the key element connecting these three spheres is the human capacity for *work*. (It must be noted that Heller distinguishes between *labour*, which she sees as alienated and essentially individual, and *work*, which is social and non-alienated.) For Heller, following Marx and Lukács, work is a primary social activity, and one that is exclusively human. It is best understood as a 'teleological project' through which we externalize basic human powers and capacities by appropriating and transforming nature, thereby creating the things we require to satisfy our material and social needs. In so doing, we 'humanize' nature and transform ourselves into reflexive and purposive beings, and we activate and utilize powers that are intrinsic to the human species. As Marx put it in the *Economic and Philosophical Manuscripts of 1844*: 'The practical creation of an *objective world*, the *working upon* inorganic nature, is vindication that man is a conscious generic being, that is, a being which is related to his genus as to its own essence or is related to himself as a generic being' (cited in Márkus 1978: 5). This process, which Heller labels 'objectivation', can be either material or ideational in nature.

According to Heller, what she terms 'objectivation-in-itself' is the first major ontological category of society. It is the backbone of everyday life, mainly because it 'embodies and explains the inter-subjectivity of our knowledge, action and communication' (1985a: 81). It is here where we find the fundamental *a prioris* (in the Kantian sense) that enable any form of human experience or social interaction to take place: namely, language, objects (or tools) and customs (or norms). That is, it is within this sphere that a human being acquires certain skills and competencies, through acculturation and socialization, that allow one to become a functioning member of society. An individual must learn to 'use the concrete things and custom patterns of the world into which he is born, however great their variety and their complexity' (1984a: 4). She points out that while the actual *content* of the sphere of 'objectivation-in-itself' is highly variable, both historically and with respect to different sub-groups, all societies must out of necessity utilize language, tools and norms as the basis for material production and practical forms of human intersubjectivity. However – and here Heller agrees strongly with social theorists like Schütz – this sphere is typically taken for granted by social actors. It is part of their 'stock knowledge' of the world: everyday objectivations are strongly 'indexical', to use the ethnomethodological term, in that they are linked to practical, ongoing accomplishments and linked inextricably to the minutiae of social context. In taking this position, Heller eschews the structuralist view of social agents as automatons. Actors do not necessarily adhere to these norms and procedures in a blind or mechanical fashion. Rather, norms are best understood as a bundle of rules and resources that are creatively and reflexively employed by actors in the course of their day-to-day lives, although of course they set broad limits on the range of options that an individual can pursue effectively. As Heller explains, the human being 'is not a puppet pulled by the strings of custom. Norms need to be inter-preted in ever new contexts, persons need to take initiatives in unforeseeable situations; they must also cope with the catastrophes of everyday life. Against the backdrop of mere routine [the] unique-ness of persons comes literally into relief' (1987: 305). 'Objectivation-in-itself' is properly understood as a framework or guide to action that is mastered and internalized by the individual actor. By way of mastering these skills and competencies, the individual appropriates the external world and engages in an 'objectivation' of the self, whereby a sense of unique personhood is formulated. 'In everyday life the person . . . shapes his world (his immediate environment) and in this way he shapes himself', Heller observes. '[In] my relationship with the everyday datum, in the affects connected with this relationship, in my reactions to it, in the possible "breakdown" of everyday activity – in all of this we are dealing with objectivized processes' (1984a: 6).

However, activities located within the sphere of 'objectivation-for-itself' are heterogeneous and fragmented. After all, Heller writes, there is 'no systemic connection between saying "hello" to one another, cooking a meal, having an argument about family expenditures, riding a bus, making a pass and so much else' (1987: 305). Generally speaking, human praxis in the context of everyday life is highly *particularistic* – that is, oriented toward the task at hand and designed to fulfil the basic needs of a given person. In comparison to more formalized or specialized knowledges, everyday knowledge and practice is marked by the following characteristics: it is ruled by emotion and affect; it is highly repetitive, prone to analogical forms of reasoning and over-generalization; and it is very pragmatic, based upon immediate perceptions and experiences and subordinated to the requirements of mundane tasks. In Marxist terminology, everyday thinking and action is typically fetishized and habitualized, in the sense that it accepts reified appearances at face value and rarely attempts to delve beneath the surface of things. Everyday knowledge is a form of *doxa*, based upon commonsensical opinion; it does not rely on 'certainty' in any scientific sense (Heller 1975). As such, because its scope is limited and oriented towards multifarious ends and means, there is little impetus to transcend the immediate environment and develop 'generic' or species-specific human powers and capacities. Everyday activities are performed in a largely unconscious and custom-bound fashion. From a subjective point of view, practical accomplishments within everyday life tend to be centred around the existential and material requirements of the self, and are therefore 'anthropocentric' in nature. If there is a 'we-awareness', it is rudimentary and tribalistic, usually concerned with the immediate in-group (especially the family unit), or else embraces a xenophobic nationalism. What this encourages, according to Heller, is a highly egocentric and solipsistic outlook, one that is dominated by the concerns of self-preservation.

Yet Heller also insists that the particularistic nature of everyday life is not eternal or immutable. Its reified and habitualized form can be explained by contingent social and historical factors. Specifically, it is capitalism as a socioeconomic formation that supports this particularistic and 'person-centred' form of existence. The paradox is that by destroying the traditionalism and parochialism of premodern societies, capitalism and modernity hold out the possibility of a universalization of certain values regarding human rights and freedoms. Under capitalism – and to a certain extent in any class-based society – the person is a representative of humanity only insofar as he or she 'partakes in class possibilities, class values, class tendencies, and relays these in correlated form' (Heller 1984a: 28). In other words, the person in a capitalist society can only be the bearer of species-essential qualities within the limits of the division

135

of labour fostered by the reigning system of production. Moreover, bourgeois liberalism has encouraged a rapacious egoism and the unencumbered accumulation of wealth and commodities, on the dubious assumption that this selfish pursuit of personal interests ultimately benefits all society. This is the ideological core of Adam Smith's quasi-religious belief in the 'hidden hand' that regulates the marketplace. Finally, the fetishized character of everyday thinking is reinforced by the fact that capitalism is dominated by the production and exchange of commodities, wherein the forms of appearance of capitalist economic relationships present themselves spontaneously to consciousness as natural and eternal.

> As long as an immediate identification with the self and an equally immediate identification with we-awareness characterizes man – average man, civilization will nourish and foster particularity. According to Marx, the human essence develops via an 'emptying-out' of individual existence, the efflorescence of human wealth proceeds *pari passu* with the impoverishment of persons. It is this process of alienation which has nourished particularity. Particularity is the subject of alienated everyday life.
>
> It is a tough world into which we are born and in which we have to make our way. In this tough world, people work, eat, drink (usually less than they need) and make love (usually by the rules); people rear their children to play a part in this tough world and timorously guard the nook they have managed to corner for themselves; the order of priorities, the scale of values in our everyday life is largely taken over ready-made, it is calibrated in accordance with position in society, and little in it is movable. There is little opportunity to 'cultivate' our abilities beyond, at best, very narrow confines.
>
> (Heller 1984a: 15)

But again, the everyday lifeworld is not irredeemably corrupted, and remains open to change. In attempting to combat the fetishized and reified character of daily life, Heller fully subscribes to the Marxian goal of *ideologiekritik*. Such an ideological criticism, as practised by the Frankfurt School and others, does not disregard the surface appearances or the experiential dimension of everyday life, but rather attempts to show how the immediate lifeworld is *alienated* or separated from conscious human control and understanding.

Heller asserts that daily activities do involve the participation of what Lukács called the 'total man' or the 'all-sided personality'. However mundane or trivial they might appear at first glance (which is why they are so often ignored or denigrated), the objectivations within daily life must be understood as enduring accomplishments that transcend their creators and the immediate needs they are designed to satisfy. As Heller explains, they represent 'externalized human capabilities [that] proceed to live their own lives detached from their human source; wavelike, they undulate onwards in such a way that, if only at second-hand, they merge into and blend with the current of history, and thus take on objective value-content' (1984a: 47). The sphere of 'objectivation-in-itself' constitutes the foundation for 'higher' forms of objectivation. Heller's basic argument is that everyday life is not *ipso facto* inauthentic or trivial. In this, she remains faithful to the notion that however degraded and reified it might be under specific sociohistorical conditions, pragmatic human life does contain valid forms of knowledge and suppressed potentialities that need to be identified and encouraged. For example, Heller suggests that everyday life harbours imaginative and creative practices that cannot be fully utilized by the essentially repetitive and habitualized character of mundane activities as they exist within capitalist social relations. Daily life generates a 'cognitive' or 'cultural surplus' that can be translated into less heterodox and hence more 'generic' forms of human activity that concern the enrichment of species-being. The transition from heterogeneous to 'homogeneous' objectivations constitutes a transcendence of the taken-for-granted character of everyday existence, and the cultivation of 'higher' human powers and capacities. Moreover, it marks a transformation of particularity (a preoccupation with selfish needs) into generality (a concern with the human species in general), and of the egoistic 'person' into an autonomous and responsible 'individual'. Only the latter, suggests Heller, is capable of surmounting the crippling effects of human alienation and realizing a generic human potential. It is the 'individualities who have most successfully absorbed the value-substances, to whom we shall refer as "representative individuals" – who individually incorporate the evolutionary generic maxima of a given society' (1984a: 16).

But how does 'individuality', as Heller defines it, genuinely represent generic human enrichment? The answer, not surprisingly, hinges on the concept of individuality itself. Again, the early Marx is the main inspiration. In the *1844 Manuscripts*, Marx argued that insofar as the development of society contributed to an enhancement of the species essence, an individual could become a genuine representative of humanity. As a conscious 'species-being', a person's life constitutes an 'object' for him or her; consequently, one's activity could be, at least under ideal circumstances, a free and creative endeavour. Alienation denies the individual access to his or her own species-essence by making that essence a means to an end, which is exemplified by the sacrifice of creative work in exchange for a living wage. But even under capitalism, this inversion of means and ends is not irreversible: no matter how exploited and manipulated we are, some individuals will be able to see beyond alienated appearances, and can relate to themselves and others as a species-being as opposed to a particularistic person. The genuine 'individual' is a 'person for whom his own life is consciously an object, since he is a conscious species-being' (Heller 1984a: 17). The generic essence represents the 'all-sided personality', the integrity of which is threatened by capitalism, mainly because under such a socioeconomic system all of the physical and intellectual capacities of human beings 'have been replaced by the simple estrangement of all these senses – the sense of having' (1984a: 18). Communism, as Marx understood it, represented the reintegration of the total human being and the realization of species-essence. Generations of Marxists have since reaffirmed this as the supreme goal of social emancipation. However, Heller's specific innovation lies in her suggestion that it is within the terrain of everyday life that flesh-and-blood men and women must pursue the unrestricted development and enrichment of species-specific or generic potentialities.

What Heller implies strongly is that the Marxist theory of alienation is most productively understood as a critique of daily life, as it is experienced within the existing division of labour and capitalist social relations. As Marx was keenly aware, the irony of capitalism is that although it allows humanity to develop enormous powers, particularly on the level of productive technique, these potentials are developed in a manner antithetical to our species-essence, and hence our concrete needs are subordinated to the requirements of the technological apparatus. In order to understand fully the way in which a given society impedes or facilitates the absorption of species-essential values, we have to examine the social system in its entirety, and relate this totality to wider historical changes. For instance, Heller argues that the capacity for individual human beings to reflect species-essential values is not historically uniform. There is a qualitative change from one epoch to the next, which involves a greater enhancement of rationality over time. For all of its faults, and these are considerable, modernity constitutes an era that holds the greatest promise for the realization of generic human values. Heller asserts that the modern period has encouraged the development of certain knowledge-forms that have shed light on the nature of the human essence, as in the universalistic discourses of morality, politics and the arts, even though these objectivations continue to be alienated.

I shall return to Heller's views on modernity and rationality in due course, but the central thrust of her argument is that generic objectivations – i.e. objectivations for the species, which emerge from collective social needs rather than from purely individual desires – provide each human being with the opportunity 'to transcend his particularity, to formulate his conscious relationship with the species, to become an individuality. [It] is not obligatory for every person to receive the world in its concretely given existence; it is not necessary for every person to identify himself with the alienated attitudes' (1984a: 19–20). This coming-to-be of individuality can only begin when self-preservation as an overriding concern is suspended; it concerns an 'opening out' to the world, a cultivation of reciprocity between self and world and between self and others. It also involves the enhancement of reflexivity or self-consciousness, by which Heller does not mean a subjectivistic or inward-looking awareness, but rather a consciousness of species-essence, which involves some distanciation from 'self', narrowly understood. Rather than be satisfied with mere preservation, the Hellerian 'individual' is concerned with a more substantial index of values. This value system implies a capacity for autonomous judgement and the *prima facie* acceptance of responsibility for one's deeds. Kant once defined Enlightenment as an awakening from self-imposed immaturity, and Heller finds much of value in this maxim. Yet in adopting the generic perspective, the individual does not abandon his or her unique qualities. The generic essence finds a different manifestation in each and every human being, and hence the particular is not subsumed under the general. In any event, Heller feels that our capacity to distance ourselves from immediate wants and to consider the needs and viewpoints of others involves 'prudence', a concept derived from Aristotle's notion of *phronesis*, meaning 'practical wisdom'. Furthermore, the exercise of prudent and autonomous judgement necessarily takes place within everyday life, within practical social intercourse.

139

Reproduction of the person is a unified process. But it is a process in which choice between the interests and needs of particularity and the needs and values of individuality has often to be made. [Everyday] life is the aggregate of activities belonging to the self-reproduction of the person – the human being born into the given conditions of a given world. [In] history up to the present, particularity has been the subject of everyday life in the great majority of social orders and social relations. . . . Exceptionally, however, integrations have come about in which individual reproduction has been more or less typically equivalent the maturation of the individual – at times and in settings where the existence of the community itself demanded a personal relation to integration, that is to say, in democratic communities.

(Heller 1984a: 27)

In ontological terms, the shift from a particularistic to a species-generic outlook marks a transition from 'objectivation-in-itself' to what Heller terms 'objectivation-for-itself'. The former does involve the 'all-sided personality', but there is no real refinement of any given practice, no cultivation of special talents or capacities. Heller makes it clear that everyday life is not hermetically sealed off from other structures and activities; rather, it is possible to reach beyond daily life to embrace such higher objectivations as philosophy, art or science, which can then act back on the everyday realm and transform it. According to Heller, the primary function of the sphere of 'objectivation-for-itself' is to provide 'men and women with meanings, as a complex of rules, norms, signs and contextual signification, cross-significations. It is precisely meanings (in the plural) that it provides' (1987: 303). This provision of meanings is a precondition for the reproduction of any society. They cannot be generated from within the sphere of 'objectivation-in-itself', which is custom-bound and taken for granted. 'Objectivation-for-itself' performs this task by establishing a unity between the hetero-geneous activities of everyday life, and by absorbing the cultural and cognitive surpluses generated by individuals and groups in the course of their daily lives which cannot be exhausted in mundane forms of action and thought. As with 'objectivation-in-itself', the sphere of 'objectivation-for-itself' is an empirical universal. More-over, it often surpasses the here and now: a particularly rich set of higher objectivations (as found in, for example, Greco-Roman philosophy or Elizabethan drama) can persist for extended periods of time and be continuously reinterpreted in very different cultural and historical contexts. The appropriation of the complex cultural meanings generated within the sphere of 'objectivation-for-itself' involves a 'suspension' of narrowly utilitarian everyday activities and the rigorous concentration on one task. In so doing, the human-as-a-whole is transformed into 'human wholeness'. Innovative and creative thoughts and actions are more predominant here than in the sphere of 'objectivation-in-itself', because in undertaking such higher objectivations, one 'concentrates all of one's abilities, endowments, emotional dispositions, [and] judgmental powers' (1987: 306).

> All of the subject's mental, spiritual and manual abilities developed and *practised* in pursuing several distinct activities are thus unified, expressed and objectified in and through a homogeneous medium. This objectivation is simultaneously a new form the subject 'in itself' that existed prior to the experience, the subject 'for itself' is born from the subject 'in itself'.
>
> (Heller 1985a: 110–11)

This leaves a third primary ontological sphere: what Heller designates as 'objectivation-for-and-in-itself'. This consists of various institutions and formal organizations that together conform to 'the *identity* of a *particular social structure*' (1985a: 104). According to Heller, the sphere of 'objectivation-for-and-in-itself' is a specialized and institutionalized sphere that, unlike 'objectivation-for-itself', does not concern the human-being-as-a-whole. Indeed, for Heller the progressive bureaucratization or 'rationalization' of modern society – Max Weber's 'iron cage' – represents a distinct threat to the fulfilment of human potential, because such institutional structures actively exclude vital human capacities, particularly as expressed through artistic and philosophical objectivations. At the same time, Heller argues against the pervasive thesis of 'one-dimensionality' – that is, the idea that the critical impulses contained within art and philosophy have been entirely co-opted and institutionalized, absorbed into the prevailing system of power. Her basic argument is that everyday life has always been 'colonized' *à la* Habermas; it has always been subject to the hegemony of 'a particular institutionalized, meaningful world-view' (1985a: 129).[3] Despite this, however, the Weberian process of rationalization

cannot wholly absorb or supplant everyday life, or else the reproduction of the individual, and hence society itself, would be under
threat of extinction. Science, which remains the dominant worldview of modernity, is simply incapable of binding together the
heterogeneous 'norms-and-rules' of everyday life into a meaningful
whole. Because of this, science 'can only *technically, not morally
legitimate* domination', which means that its capacity to successfully
induce 'one- dimensionality' is limited (1985a: 137). Objectivation-
in-itself remains a human universal, and the primary sphere
responsible for the socialization of the individual and the formulation of fundamental human needs, values and identities. 'Obviously',
Heller asserts, 'without everyday socialization of a certain kind,
without at least the preserved vestiges of the human person as a
whole, the human condition would inevitably collapse. The model
of complete institutionalization seems to be the model of chaos, for
a total manipulative order *is* chaos' (1987: 311). In this, Heller
subscribes to a dialectical view of modernity, one that remains
cognizant of both its repressive and emancipatory qualities.
Nonetheless, she does concede that under the conditions of late
modernity, modes of human intersubjectivity and creativity lose a
certain degree of richness and intensity, primarily because human
thought and action is more and more constrained by formalized
institutions. People often act as bearers of highly specialized functions, and not as 'whole human beings'. As such, intersubjectivity is
increasingly reduced to a means to an end, and human beings
remain alienated and deprived of species-essential qualities:

> Knowledge is decreasingly mediated in personal human
> interaction. Face-to-face interaction (everyday communic-
> ation) is no longer the basic source of information, of
> advice, of know-how and know-what. The tension, richness
> and density of primary human contact is thus imperilled.
> Some contend that emotional intensity might redress this
> loss, yet this can only be true if human contact is sought as
> an end in itself.
>
> (Heller 1985a: 134)

RATIONALITY AND ETHICS

As a critical social theorist, Heller is not satisfied with simply
describing these sociohistorical processes. She is equally concerned

to outline concrete ways to overcome the subordination of everyday life to the functionalist logic of the technological apparatus and the division of labour, and to reverse the positivist denigration of issues pertaining to moral worth and qualitative value (Heller 1996). In so doing, Heller advances a series of powerful arguments regarding the nature of human agency and rationality, the centrality of ethics in social life, and the inviolate status of subjective and objective human needs. In a highly compressed and programmatic essay entitled 'Everyday Life, Rationality of Reason, Rationality of Intellect', Heller sets out to clarify the relationship between rationality and everyday life. She begins by arguing that all known societies evince a 'value-orientation'; that is, they distinguish between right and wrong, or valid and invalid norms. The desire to construct a coherent axiology, or system of values, and to attribute meaning to the world around us, is therefore a central human inclination. Indeed, Heller defines 'reason' as 'the faculty of discriminating between good and bad', and 'rationality' as 'action according to reason' (1985a: 74). Rationality concerns our ability to comprehend and internalize the value-system of a particular society and culture, and to act consistently on behalf of positive values. The human capacity for rationality is to be contrasted with mere 'thinking', which for Heller is valuationally neutral. According to Heller, human rationality is essentially *practical*: it is pre-eminently oriented towards the performance of pragmatic tasks and activities within the sphere of everyday life. Historically speaking, most human societies have displayed a monolithic value-system – Durkheim's *conscience collective* – and the social delineation of right and wrong and the enactment of 'correct' behaviour has been a relatively straightforward process. Modernity, however, is marked by the collapse of such homogeneous value-orientations and the ethical pluralization of the lifeworld. The result, bluntly stated, is a 'crisis of rationality'. Inasmuch as the task of value-discrimination, involving hermeneutical interpretation and pragmatic action, devolves on the individual, morality and intersubjective relations become existential problems, for which there are no obvious collective solutions (Heller 1991). Modernity signals the birth of radical *contingency*, and the contemporary *Zeitgeist* is marked by an acute awareness of the implications of this indeterminacy for the human condition (Heller 1990a). Modernity might well be an 'unfinished project', as Habermas puts it, but in Heller's opinion it is one that is incapable of ultimate completion. If anything, postmodernity further deepens this consciousness of contingency, because it represents a demise of the 'grand narratives' that used to legitimate the dominant worldview.

In Heller's opinion, 'reason' primarily concerns the faculty of discrimination. However, this can be understood in two distinct ways. First, reason can represent an uncritical and unquestioning adherence to extant norms and values; that is, values can be internalized and followed in a largely unconscious and automatic fashion. Heller refers to this as 'rationality of reason', which is typical of many patterns of thought and action within the sphere of 'objectivation-in-itself'. The habitualization of action is to a certain extent necessary and desirable; as Schütz pointed out in his theory of 'typification', social intercourse and practical activities would be well-nigh impossible if every act, no matter how trivial, had to be scrutinized and consciously planned and executed. Tying one's shoes, for instance, requires a relatively complex series of psycho-motor movements. However, once mastered, it is an act that involves little in the way of conscious thought. Yet the full automatization of our actions would spell disaster, for it would imply the death of the subject as an autonomous and rational entity. So there are repetitive and quasi-instinctive elements within everyday life that will never disappear, but there are also imaginative, problem-solving and intuitive aspects. If we are capable of utilizing and cultivating these creative propensities in a conscious manner, we can make the transition from 'rationality of reason' to what Heller calls 'rationality of intellect'. The latter concerns the reflexive capacity to utilize a particular value-system in order to critically evaluate the habit-bound norms within the sphere of 'objectivation-in-itself', and to act in a reasoned and autonomous manner. 'Rationality of intellect', put differently, functions to unleash the reflexive, critical potential of the sphere of 'objectivation-in-itself', by articulating new needs and liberating repressed human impulses and inclinations. It is a 'pleasurable release', because it allows us to live to our fullest potential, to indulge all of our abilities and propensities, whether bodily, intellectual or affective. It generates what Heller calls 'radical needs' – by which she means needs that cannot be satisfied within society as it is currently organized, not least because our needs are ever-evolving. This explains why she describes modernity as the 'dissatisfied society', although she denies that some kind of ultimate satisfaction of needs is possible. Hence, radical needs express a Habermasian 'emancipatory interest' that cannot be ignored.[4] In acquiring 'rationality of intellect', moreover, the individual seeks to place his or her stamp on the situation, to realize fully one's personality. However, Heller is at pains to point out that all autonomy must be conceived of as *relative*. We are not free to construct a world of meaning just as we please; this is pure Nietzschean voluntarism, as exemplified by his concept of the *Übermensch*. We are not 'beyond' good and evil, but must take into account existing value-hierarchies and moral considerations. Moreover, in undertaking a project of value-creation, we must always be cognizant of the needs and requirements of the concrete other. Yet we can still modify such hierarchies, appropriate certain elements at the expense of others, and in general strive to articulate a personal vision of the world.

The achievement of 'rationality of intellect' is never easy; rather, it is a continuous, life-long process. For one thing, it involves maintaining some degree of distance from the time/space of everyday life. We must forsake an exclusive preoccupation with immediate needs and desires in favour of a more imaginative and reflective approach to life and to our status as moral beings. We need to engage in what the utopian philosopher Ernst Bloch has called 'anticipatory thinking', which Heller characterizes as a '"free," uncommitted play of the human spirit' (1984a: 199). In developing such a 'theoretical attitude', we can break through the reified appearances and taken-for-granted routines of daily existence. 'Reflective thinking and praxis', Heller writes, 'can be seen as disengagement in that our capabilities are thus liberated so that they can be applied to the solution of tasks which can only be tackled via inventive praxis (or thinking)' (1984a: 129–30). 'Rationality of intellect' therefore indicates a move from 'rationality' as such (which is a universal human capacity) to a historically specific but generalizable *culture of critical rationalism*. The ability to develop the latter is enhanced by the conditions of modernity, partly because of the dissolution of mythopoetic forms of legitimation, and also by the fact that social life ceases to be regulated by a centralized and homogeneous value-system. So while both repetitive and innovative modes of thought and action must be present if the reproduction of the individual and society is to be successfully achieved, Heller seeks to tip the balance away from ingrained habit and blind determinism towards freedom and spontaneity, so as to attain a 'heightened feeling of satisfaction, pleasure or happiness' (1985a: 171). Such an enriched experience, whether emotional or intellectual, can be re-directed back into everyday life in order to transform it. *Contra* Heidegger, therefore, Heller does not advocate a pure transcendence of the particularism of everyday life. This would represent a futile project, a seduction by what Adorno (1973) once called the 'jargon of authenticity'. Rather, we should seek a transformation of daily life into a richer and more fruitful realm of human endeavour. This, in turn, would encourage the reintegration and efflorescence of the 'all-sided personality', the fulfilment of the liberatory promise of human rationality, and the full development of a multiplicity of human needs and propensities. The maturation of the 'human-being-as-a-whole' involves the cultivation of all of the individual's affective, emotional, sensory and intellectual qualities; however, according to Heller, this must occur within the framework of an enhanced 'rationality of intellect'.

> Rational character 'for itself' is familiar with dreams and hopes, fears and pleasures, playfulness, imagination, intuition, mystical contemplation, unrestricted self-expression. It does not relinquish the right to weeping, crying, to touch, to shut the eyes when the light is harsh, nor does it resign the ability of self-abandon, of excitement, of nirvana, of idiosyncratic (if not private) speech, of the language of gestures, of being-together, of listening to 'purposeless' voices and embracing 'purposeless beauty,' and so on. Only the 'when' and 'where' and 'how' is regulated by the personality in order that the non-rational does not impede the observance of norms and of 'norms-and-rules,' the hierarchy of which constitutes the hallmark of personality.
>
> (Heller 1985a: 227)

For Heller, modernity signals a differentiation between *practical* and *theoretical* reason, and she highlights the importance of the former. Moreover, it is in the modern world where morality in the true sense of the word makes its appearance, because acting in a good or ethical fashion is now dependent upon an individual's *'conscious and practical relation to their world of normative customs'* (1985a: 75). Heller goes against the grain of conventional moral philosophy by arguing that morality is not about the construction of ethical systems or abstract codes, but rather concerns how concrete moral conceptions impinge on day-to-day social behaviour. As such, Heller adopts a broad conception of morality. It is not a specialized topic or a separate domain of social life, but rather a 'human relationship that is immanent in all spheres' (1984a: 70). An ethical community, or *Sittlichkeit*, implies a total form of life. To the modern individual, the pursuit of 'truth' as a guide to correct action becomes a central preoccupation, which concerns the attainment of a delicate balance between one's inner conscience and a plurality of competing normative and valuational systems located in the social world. The faculty of prudent or wise judgement (*phronesis*) becomes paramount, in terms of the regulation of intersubjective relations and the pursuit of moral conduct under the regime of modernity. For Heller, *phronesis* is primarily a moral propensity, one that requires 'intuitive and inventive thinking and praxis if it is to be effective' (1984a: 181). She asserts that Kant's categorical imperative – an absolutist moral doctrine that unequivocally states 'do not treat others as a means to an end' – is a worthy notion in theory, but in practice, as fallible individuals we have to utilize prudent judgement, and interpret the Kantian imperative with respect to complex and conflict-ridden real-life circumstances. In mundane social intercourse, nothing is morally self-evident, and there are no guarantees, not only because of the sheer range of divergent value-orientations, but also because of the distinct possibility of failure or the causing of unintended and undesirable consequences. We need practical reason in order to *translate* abstract ethical norms into guidelines for action that are appropriate to everyday life. In this, Heller seeks to resurrect the Aristotlean tradition of practical philosophy, with its stress on the cultivation of personal goodness and virtue.

Again, this capacity for hermeneutical value-interpretation and pragmatic action is enhanced under the conditions of modernity. In the modern era, Heller argues, the 'individual is capable of greater pliancy in the adaptation of the overall demand structure to the individual case, his choice among conflicting demands and values is better informed, and he is more readily disposed towards the formation of an individual hierarchy of values' (1984a: 78–9). Paradoxically, the fact that individuals are now the primary authors of moral actions encourages a transcendence of particularism and the formation of an ethical model that is amenable to generalization. 'The acknowledgment of authorship', she writes, 'is *the attitude of authenticity*' (1993: 112). 'Authenticity', in the Heideggerian sense of the concept, can therefore only be achieved through *moral autonomy*. This explains why Heller stresses the limits of theoretical reason and the primacy of practical reason, defining the latter as a 'philosophical construct (an idea) which encompasses, and in a few philosophies also explains, the major personal and impersonal constituents of moral practice and attitude' (1988: 404). However, our ability to utilize *phronesis* is dependent on the wider social context; it is enhanced by an open, dynamic society, and negated by

147

a rigid and authoritarian one. This is an important element of Heller's argument: that the liberation of the hidden potentialities within everyday life is contingent upon a radical democratization of society, which parallels Aristotle's view that virtuous behaviour can only be fully realized within a 'good society'.

However, there remains a dialectical twist in Heller's generally optimistic account. Under the conditions of modernity, rationality is not attributed to the 'human-being-as-a-whole', but rather the 'specialized human who acts within rationalized institutions' (1985a: 206). 'Goodness' is now equated with purely instrumental or utilitarian success, and practical reason has been gradually transformed into 'calculative reason'. This fostering of a particularly narrow side of rationality at the expense of the 'all-sided personality' – what Max Weber characterized as the subordination of *value* to *purposive* rationality – forcefully excludes or represses such non-instrumental human powers and capacities as fantasies, dreams, the imagination, and uncommodified bodily and intellectual pleasures. Everyday life cannot be shaped by a free, purposive activity, because it is dominated by an ethos of 'calculation and rationalization'. The wholesale adoption and internalization of bureaucratized roles means a retreat into particularism, an uncritical worship of the 'facts', and an abrogation of human responsibility. With the con-solidation of modernity, writes Heller, 'the human reason at work is *minima ratio*: it is rationality that resembles a dry leaf; it is cut off from the totality of life, from the personality, from the prerational and postrational aura of action' (1985a: 209). The most extreme irrationality masquerades as pure rationality, leading to a 'trivializ-ation of human personality' (Heller 1984a: 223). The manifest failure on the part of many people to translate everyday forms of human creativity into 'higher' objectivations has all manner of malevolent and destructive consequences. For Heller, this is the Faustian bargain that modernity has paid for the alienation and repression of dialectical rationality: 'The disenchanted world of modernity is the world of alienated rationality' (1985a: 212). Science, understood as both a pervasive worldview and a powerful social institution, is the most visible representative of this techno-logical rationality in contemporary society; as such, its hegemonic and manipulative tendencies must be resisted strenuously. In a particularly illuminating passage, Heller writes:

'Scientific-technological' manipulation, as it is today, has taken over all the negative functions of religion, without its

148

compensating positive aspects. It 'fattens up' particularity and particularistic motivations, but promotes, or indeed, permits, only those particularistic qualities to flower which go to serve the interests of a given 'organization'. It prevents the person from taking a moral decision in ideological or political questions; it forms attitudes and ideologies which serve the *status quo,* without making it in any way questionable. It replaces the ancient myths with new ones – the myth of technology, the myth of the leader, the myth of the 'qualified professional'. It keeps an eye on our private lives, and either abolishes the 'private' sphere or subjects it to social supervision. Demands and expectations in whose interest certain sectors of particularity may be suppressed (so that particularity as a whole may be nourished) no longer represent, in any sense whatever, generic development, and are totally devoid of the species-essential values they could and did retain in the case of religion.

(1984a: 106–7)

The task of a critical social philosophy, as Heller sees it, is to combat this technocratic domination and to defend and foster individuality, 'felt' human needs, and species-essential values. In particular, she refers to art, philosophy, and the non-instrumentalized qualities of daily life as exemplars of liberated human thought and action. These represent human activities that resist commodification and alienation, and they hold out the possibility of the fulfilment of 'rationality of intellect' and generic human values. Regarding art, Heller rejects the 'cult of aestheticism' that has found favour with many postmodernists. Art, she argues, cannot in and of itself transform or humanize life. The quest to live life as an artwork, which was essentially Nietzsche's main goal, is premised upon an extreme individualism, in which everything is subordinated to the task of aestheticizing life (Nemas 1985). 'Being-for-oneself' is present in the Nietzschean project, but not 'being-for-others'; for Heller, the latter is an indispensable component of a moral society. Yet she acknowledges that art is a vital human pursuit, because it provides us with a vision of a transfigured social existence, in which the construction of a meaningful life is everyone's prerogative. Art can give the project of social transformation badly needed emotional and intellectual support. Hence, Heller advocates the pursuit of a meaningful life, which is inherently democratic, as opposed to an aesthetic life, which is elitist and aristocratic: 'The guiding norm in the meaningful life is always generalizability, extensibility of the meaningful life to others: in the long run, to the whole of humanity' (1984a: 268). Art provides us with a model of a free and unalienated activity that inculcates a feeling of 'sensuous pleasure', as against a utilitarian outlook that denigrates bodily and affective human needs. It is not governed by instrumental logic; its only purpose is to provide us with enjoyment and delight. 'Beauty of any kind partakes in art', writes Heller, 'in so far as it transcends the category of direct utility, even when the object or institution in which it is manifested is "employable"' (1984a: 110; Heller and Fehér 1986b). However, art provides us with more than a fleeting glimpse of a non-alienated and 'humanized' world. Following Kant, Heller asserts that artistic creations can provide us with concrete norms for 'rationality of intellect', of the sort that contradict a reified everyday existence:

> art works too can provide actors with norms to be observed and critically employed, opposed to the 'norms-and-rules' of the regular routine of institutions and everyday life. The attitude of rationality of intellect is to adopt the position of norms provided by art works, and *to devalue* 'norms-and-rules' as void and meaningless if measured with the yard-stick of these norms.
>
> (1985a: 175–6)

Similarly, Heller conceives of philosophy as a species-essential endeavour that effectively unites the properties of science and art, a synthesis of non-dogmatic, critical inquiry with a desire for creative expression and the pursuit of sensuous beauty. Its chief function is to de-fetishize the taken-for-granted and challenge received truths, and to provide us with a worldview and a set of ethical standards that must be adhered to in our daily life if we are to fulfil the injunction to act as moral creatures. Moreover, Heller suggests that the utilization of a creative, unrepressed imagination is central to the philosophical project. This ability to articulate utopian alternatives to the *status quo*, or what philosophers call 'counterfactuals', makes philosophy a crucial resource in subverting both the commonsensical norms and rules of daily life and the unquestioned authority of the apparatus of bureaucratic power. Whereas positivism makes a fetish of the 'facts', and thereby sanctions 'what is' as the only possible horizon for human thought and action, genuine philosophy delves beneath immediate empirical reality in order to formulate a set of 'value ideals' that express humanity's species-character. For the philosopher, nothing is obvious or self-evident; the validity of any norm must always be subjected to rational debate and argumentation, a process in which 'truth' is equated with 'goodness'. Philosophy, she writes, 'demystifies what is from the perspective of what ought-to-be – the unity of the good and the true' (1984b: 24). Hence, philosophy, which is an exemplification of 'rationality of intellect', is primarily concerned with overcoming self-deception through a Habermasian unconstrained dialogue; as such, it aims to enhance the self-knowledge of all interlocutors who partake in value-discussion. Here, Heller subscribes to the idea, developed originally by the classical German idealists, that reflexive self-understanding promotes human freedom by expanding the scope of human action and perception. This explains her suggestion that reason 'is the remedy against self-deception' (1993: 24), and not inherently oppressive, dominating or totalitarian, as many postmodernists hold. In this, Heller believes that the philosophical endeavour is, or should be, a universal enterprise with practical or everyday ramifications, and not the sole prerogative of professional philosophers or educated elites:

> What hitherto has happened only in philosophy can and does now happen in political practice and life. Men and women constantly juxtapose Ought, that is, universal values, to Is, to their political and social institutions, which fail to match or live up to Ought. Men and women interpret and reinterpret those values in their daily practice and they go about using them as vehicles of critique and refutation, of realizing philosophy, or philosophy's ultimate end.
>
> (1990b: 120)

After art and philosophy, the third domain of human activity that Heller identifies as capable of resisting the logic of the commodity and instrumentalized reason concerns the non-utilitarian experiences of private life. Heller mentions silence, quiet moments of reflection and insight, fleeting and spontaneous joys and pleasures, highly personalized memories and reminiscences, and, above all, the experience of shared intimacy. In her opinion, all of these things embody 'possibilities which are available for the free assertion and development of human capabilities within a person's lifetime' (1985a: 264). Love, in particular, remains the sole refuge of qualitative experience for many people: in essence, it is a recognition of human wholeness. 'The great moments of love', writes Heller, 'are *utopia*' (1985a: 215). However, this becomes problematic if love becomes the *only* way we can relate to human wholeness; moreover, it is highly susceptible to commodification by the culture industry. Nonetheless, the feeling of familiarity, security and emotional support nurtured within everyday life is of paramount importance, particularly in the face of an impersonal, bureaucratized lifeworld. For Heller, these highly subjective emotions and feelings should not be blithely written off as woolly-minded sentimentalism, or equated with a reactionary ideology of domesticity. However manipulated they might be under consumer capitalism, the experiences of private life still express essential needs and values, and it is where human intersubjectivity exists in its most immediate and passionate form:

> 'Home' is not simply house, roof, family. There are people who have houses and families but no 'homes'. For this reason, familiarity is not in itself equivalent to 'feeling at home' though familiarity is, of course, an indispensable ingredient in any definition of 'home'. Over and above this, we need the feeling of confidence: 'home' protects us. We also need the intensity and density of human relationships – the 'warmth' of the home. 'Going home' should mean returning to that firm position which we know, to which we are accustomed, where we feel safe, and where our emotional relationships are at their most intense.
>
> (1985a: 239; Heller 1979)

A NOTE ON UTOPIA

All of the thinkers discussed in the present study implicitly or explicitly combine a preoccupation with everyday life with a utopian perspective. Heller is no exception. In fact, she has written extensively on the topic of utopianism and its implications for our understanding of daily life. Essentially, she follows Marx and Engels's original critique of utopian socialism, and rejects the latter's attempt to construct detailed blueprints of a possible future society. She does not wish to discard the utopian dimension completely, but seeks to locate transcendental or utopian propensities within actual social and historical tendencies. In attempting to uncover traces of a liberated human consciousness within the most banal and prosaic moments of social existence, Heller would seem to subscribe to an 'immanent utopia', one that is 'within' everyday life and yet desperately at odds with the social world as it currently exists. Hence, Heller rejects the postmodernist position that the utopian impulse *per se* is identical with the modernist predilection for constructing 'grand narratives'. Indeed, she makes it clear that in eschewing the 'counterfactual' or defetishizing role of utopia, certain postmodernists wholly abandon any attempt to develop alternative visions of social life, and thereby abrogate any pretence to radical social critique. Establishment postmodernists, in short, admonish us to accept the prevailing social and historical horizon as inescapable, and to be satisfied with cultivating a playful and ironic cynicism *vis-à-vis* the *status quo*. Heller and Fehér succinctly sum up the prevailing attitude of postmodernism toward utopia as follows: 'the postmodern political condition is tremendously ill at ease with Utopianism, which makes it vulnerable to easy compromises with the present as well as susceptible to "doomsday myths" and collective fears stemming from the loss of future' (1988: 4). It is this sense of a 'loss of future', one that seems to be endemic in contemporary society as we begin the third millennium, that Heller seeks to avoid at all costs. We need to continue to articulate alternative visions, to enrich and enliven what Castoriadis has termed the 'social imaginary', and to be cognizant of the open possibilities that modernity has to offer us. At the same time, however, she has come to reject the Marxian version of utopia as untenable. For one thing, Marxism (or 'radical universalism') provides humankind with a rigid 'philosophy of praxis' understood as a categorical imperative. By identifying an inherent *telos* in history operating 'behind the backs' of actual social agents, radical universalism makes a mockery of individual will, initiative and responsibility. Moreover, she claims that the utopia envisaged by Marxism represents a desire for a simplified social world, an erasure of difference, and it adheres to the untenable ideal of completely transparent social relations undistorted by ideology or commodity fetishism. By contrast, Heller seeks to encourage the inherent differentiation and pluralization of society that is part of the dynamic of late modernity.

In essence, Heller repudiates the 'redemptive' or messianic elements contained within many Marxian utopias, such as those envisaged by such figures as Walter Benjamin or Georg Lukács (Gardiner 1997). Such utopias, which foresee a total, even apocalyptic transfiguration of society, are essentially theological in inspiration, and as such must be resisted. As an Absolute Idea in the Hegelian sense, the messianic utopia evinces a profound nostalgia for a lost totality. What postmodernism has forced us to confront is the impossibility of ever reconstructing such a totality; a radical pluralism has, at least for the foreseeable future, supplanted the unified and homogeneous social world of the past. There is no possibility of ultimate reconciliation or salvation, a realization that is part and parcel of the postmodern condition. 'A fragmented world lives with fragmented utopias', writes Heller, 'and unless the Messiah descends from Heaven, these fragments will remain here unredeemed' (1993: 60). Nonetheless, the utopian impulse remains valid. It is the major animating force behind the social imaginary, and expresses genuine human needs and desires that continue to call out for actualization.

> [Utopias] are not mere figments of human imagination. They draw their strength from actuality; they exist, insofar as they exist, in the present. Utopia is lived, practised, maintained by men and women as a form of life. [The] utopian form of life is, for those who live it, the rose on the cross of the present.
>
> (Heller 1993: 58)

If Heller abandons the Marxian goal of total dis-alienation as unrealistic, she continues to maintain a certain degree of faith in emancipatory possibilities, however fragile or constrained these might be. The utopian imagination will not die; however, we must accept that utopianism has definite limits that are primarily of an *ethical* nature. Specifically, each 'major' utopia, understood as a projection of a total form of life that foresees a successful fusion of goodness and human happiness, is (at least in the postmodern context) inherently particularistic. Simply put, given the radical pluralization of the lifeworld, one person's utopia is another's idea of hell, as the essayist Max Beerbohm once put it. Consequently, instead of striving to develop a utopia with a specific *content*, and which aims at some kind of spurious normative consensus, Heller favours the 'open' utopia. Such a utopia would strive to uphold a multiplicity of value-systems, by enshrining a few core or universalistic values necessary to protect this pluralistic pursuit of value-orientations. These would include (i) an ideal of domination-free communication, as articulated by Habermas in his notion of the 'ideal speech situation';[5] (ii) the unconditional recognition and acceptance of all human needs, which excludes the use of people as a means to an end; and (iii) the full development of all the

individual's physical, psychical and intellectual abilities in a free
and unconstrained manner (1984b: 157–74). In an interview conducted in 1985, Heller clarified her conception of the open utopia:

> The utopian is not the impossible; it is the 'counterfactual',
> conceived as a realisable alternative to present realities. My
> suggestion about the acceptance of universal political
> principles is utopian but I am convinced that it is not a
> pipedream. Utopia is one of the constituents of an alter-
> native 'imaginary institution' which should be contrasted
> to the *dominant* 'imaginary institution' of the present. But
> utopias are in the present, not in the future. The more a
> utopia captures the imagination of people in the present,
> the more it is transformed into a new utopian mentality
> which can transcend the dominant social imagination. In a
> future-oriented and future-directed society such as ours,
> utopias are always at work. . . . In the simplest possible
> terms, the universal utopia that I propose is that of a
> society in which the norms and rules of justice are set by all
> members of society through rational discourse, whereas all
> other norms, among them the purely moral ones, remain
> diverse and pluralistic.
>
> (1985b: 39; Heller 1982b)

CONCLUSION

In seeking to combat the power of the technocratic stratum under late
modernity and the pervasiveness of an instrumentalized rationality,
Heller argues that any social theory which claims to be animated by
an 'emancipatory interest', and hence critical of the *status quo*, must
be sensitized to the qualitative needs, emotions and feelings of actual
men and women. In other words, it must be grounded in a thorough
understanding of the everyday lifeworld, and of those hidden
potentialities within daily life that can give rise to higher human
accomplishments, including philosophy, art and morality. If social
theory is not so attuned, its critical thrust will be blunted, and the
abstractions it generates will merely reinforce the alienated character
of the lifeworld as it currently exists, in which case even the most
ostensibly radical theory will dovetail with the most conservative
positivism, and end up sanctioning 'what is' at the expense of what
'ought to be'. Meaningful social change does not simply concern

large-scale institutions and structures; it must equally involve a transformation of the everyday lifeworld and an injection of the 'ethics of care' into the most basic forms of human intersubjectivity. At the same time, Heller affirms the necessity for critical thought to go beyond the reified appearances of everyday life under capitalism, in order to grasp fundamental human values and proclivities that only exist today *in potentia* – that is, in a suppressed or distorted form, which requires the exercise of a utopian imagination.

As such, Heller would argue that postmodernist talk of the 'death of the subject' is misguided, if by this is meant an abandonment of such values as responsibility and autonomy. Subjecthood is not simply given to us; we must *create ourselves* as subjects, as purposive, responsible and self-reliant entities. If we do not make this existential 'leap', we become passive and conformist, and hence subject to external powers (1990b: 61–78). This is essentially a wager of the Pascalian sort; deprived of the cosmological and existential certainties of the premodern lifeworld, the only viable option left to us is actively to transform 'givenness' into an existence that has meaning for us. Furthermore, a fulfilment of the rational personality, or 'Being-for-itself', requires a commitment to the open utopia of radical democracy, and to the unquestioned needs of the other. Only then can we witness a genuine 'homecoming of reason', and realize the 'good life'. In this, Heller shows her dissatisfaction with a currently fashionable cynicism and pessimism characteristic of many postmodernists. But given that these things only exist in the present in a distorted form, as an unfulfilled promise, we are saddled with insoluble moral dilemmas in the here and now. To ease this burden, Heller advocates a return to the tenets of Classical and Hellenistic philosophy, particularly the Stoic and Epicurean traditions. We must cultivate what she terms a 'Stoic-Epicurean attitude', because it is primarily concerned with a desire to live a rational and virtuous life to the fullest extent possible under current circumstances. Like Brecht's character Shen Teh in his play *The Good Person of Szechwan*, we must face the paradox of striving to be moral within the confines of an immoral society. This requires a resoluteness of character and a determination to transform one's life from an inherited 'bundle of possibilities' into *destiny*, within the terrain of everyday life. To conclude with Heller's thoughts on this subject: 'We have only one life and if this life does not turn out the way we wanted it, we can still enjoy everything it offers. If "history" plays a dirty trick on our hopes, we can still do better than despair: even in dark times, we can maintain the hopes of humanity' (1985b: 39).

7

MICHEL DE CERTEAU: THE CUNNING OF UNREASON

The surfeit of possibilities available to us far exceeds what we can effectively cope with and utilize, and our everyday life is choked with opportunities which we are unable to seize.

Alberto Melucci

INTRODUCTION

Before his premature death in 1986, the French social theorist and historian Michel de Certeau had authored nearly twenty books on numerous topics. Born in Chambéry in 1925, Certeau acquired degrees in classics and philosophy and then a doctorate in theology from the Sorbonne in 1960. He became an ordained member of the Jesuit order in 1956. From then until the late 1960s, his writings were confined primarily to fairly mainstream excurses into religious and intellectual history, which were published in a variety of Catholic publications. After this, however, Certeau's work became increasingly preoccupied by a remarkably broad range of topics, including psychoanalysis (he participated in Jacques Lacan's famous seminars at the École Freudienne), the philosophy of history, contemporary issues in politics and education, as well as what would today be described as cultural studies (Certeau 1988, 1997a, 1997b).[1] His work came to prominence outside France after the translation into English of his 1980 book *L'Invention du Quotidian*, rendered as *The Practice of Everyday Life*. This study, later supplemented by a second, collaborative volume (Certeau *et al*. 1998), has had a demonstrable impact on Anglo-American cultural studies (Buchanan 1997).

In the context of the present study, Certeau is of interest for several reasons. First, his discussion of the everyday extends and deepens the original insights developed by Surrealism, Lefebvre and the Situationists. With an ethnographer and historian's eye for detail, Certeau's analyses of concrete daily practices contribute a specificity to the theory and critique of 'everyday life' that is sometimes lacking in his predecessors' work. Secondly, because he went against the French predilection for abstract theorizing, Certeau has few analogues in his homeland, at least until recently. In many ways, his approach to popular culture and everyday life has more parallels with postwar British social history and the sociology of culture, as evinced by the writings of Richard Hoggart, Raymond Williams, E. P. Thompson, and others. Indeed, Certeau's orientation is largely faithful to Williams's (1989) stricture that 'culture is ordinary', and not the sole prerogative of elites, artists or intellectuals. Finally, many of Certeau's arguments about language, representation and 'otherness', which contain a substantial ethical component, anticipated later developments in French poststructuralist and postmodernist thought. At the same time, however, he rejected the more extreme formulations of postmodernism. For instance, Certeau articulated a trenchant critique of Foucault's ideas about discourse and power. In so doing, he retained a critical and utopian perspective that emphasized the centrality of human agency and the possibility of resistance to the dictates of bureaucratic reason, whilst at the same time distancing himself from the more grandiose revolutionary schemes of Lefebvre or Debord. This chapter will discuss the dominant themes within Certeau's work as they bear on the central concerns of the present study, concentrating on *The Practice of Everyday Life* and related texts.

THE POPULAR CULTURE DEBATE

It might be useful to begin by examining the commonalities and differences between Certeau and Lefebvre and the Situationists regarding the topic of everyday life. For the latter, daily life under modernity was thoroughly routinized and degraded. Colonized by the commodity and the instrumentalized needs of state and capital, everyday existence could no longer provide the framework through which the human requirement for creativity and interhuman dialogue could be fulfilled. The promise of human plenitude had been replaced by the passive and manipulated consumption of endless signs and images, designed to provide a surrogate form of gratification and to negate any potential social discontent. In *Everyday Life in the Modern World*, for example, Lefebvre argues that daily life under late capitalism has become irredeemably corrupted. Echoing Bataille, he contends that a viable cultural revolution must 'put an end to the everyday by shattering all constraints, and by investing the everyday, immediately or gradually, with the values of prodigality and waste' (1984: 73). If society constitutes a totality, and all facets of human existence are now dominated by the repressive logic of capital and exchange-value, then the only possible solution is total social transformation, and the inauguration of a completely different set of cultural, economic and political relations. As Brian Rigby points out in his perceptive study *Popular Culture in Modern France* (1991), the position advanced by Lefebvre and the SI was part of a wider controversy in postwar French intellectual life regarding the relative merits of 'popular' versus 'high' culture. The notion that popular or 'mass' culture was puerile, formulaic and aesthetically bankrupt, and that it had a detrimental effect on the values and beliefs of the general population, was an idea that commanded a broad consensus in France across the political spectrum in the three decades following World War Two. The ire of the French intelligentsia was especially directed against American popular culture, which was widely felt to constitute a serious threat to the purity and high standard of French language and culture (Mathy 1993).

It is important to realize, however, that this French debate was part of an ongoing preoccupation within Western societies concerning the deleterious effects of modernity and mass culture. This controversy can be traced back as far as the eighteenth century, and it attracted the attention of thinkers as diverse as de Tocqueville, Nietzsche, and T. S. Eliot. On the left, the analysis of mass culture developed by Adorno and Horkheimer in their well-known essay 'The Culture Industry: Enlightenment as Mass Deception', included in *Dialectic of Enlightenment* (1979), has become paradigmatic of this approach. It therefore warrants a brief summary here. In essence, Adorno and Horkheimer suggested that the arrival of modernity signalled the manipulation of culture for political and economic ends. With the continuous interlocking of state, economy and polity, as well as the extension of exchange-value into every sphere of social life, the production and distribution of art and culture were now almost entirely dependent on finance and industrial capital. Moreover, the advertising and mass media monopolies created 'false needs' in order to realize the exchange-value of these commodities.

Hence, culture had become fully integrated into and subordinated to the needs of capital: the culture industry produced and distributed cultural artefacts for the express purpose of mass consumption and maximum profitability. The continuous drive for maximum profit and efficiency entailed the endless repetition and imitation of standardized popular works. However, in order to preserve what Walter Benjamin (1969) called the 'auratic' qualities of premodern art, the culture industry had to project the appearance of novelty and originality. This was what Adorno and Horkheimer called 'pseudo-individualization' – the attempt to imbue each product or artist with the air of individuality and authenticity, mainly through advertising. Despite the essential sameness of popular cultural artefacts, this procedure was generally successful in preserving the illusion of spontaneity and free choice in the act of consumption. Yet despite the fact that artistic and cultural objects had become cheap and accessible, these artefacts could no longer manifest any semblance of a critical or emancipatory impulse. What is new about modernity is not that culture *is* a commodity, but that 'today it deliberately admits it is one; that art renounces its own autonomy and proudly takes its place among consumption goods constitutes the charm of novelty' (Adorno and Horkheimer 1979: 157).

Not only did the culture industry provide an irresistible impetus towards the commodification and standardization of all cultural forms, it aimed at the solicitation of standardized responses as well. Pre-designed modes of interpretation were embedded in cultural commodities and endlessly repeated, leading to the automatization of psychological and bodily reactions. This process served to weaken individual resistance to the dominant ideology, and ensured passivity and compliance by supplying a 'substitute gratification' in the form of distraction and amusement. In reality, the promise of spontaneity, meaning and pleasure proffered by the commodity only allowed for a cathartic adjustment to existing social conditions. Thus, mass culture was, in Leo Lowenthal's phrase, 'psychoanalysis in reverse', because it created rather than cured authoritarian personalities (albeit 'well-adjusted' ones). By providing fleeting relief from the drudgery of everyday life, mass culture helped to sustain the capacity for wage-labour on the part of the working masses. People were reduced to 'objects of contrivance', and the ideology that made this calculation possible no longer represented the universal revolutionary aspirations of the rising bourgeois class, but rather a 'manipulative contrivance' designed to fulfil the naked self-interest of capital.

Culture as a common denominator already contains in embryo that schematization and process of cataloguing and classification which brings culture within the sphere of administration. And it is precisely the industrialized, the consequent subsumption which entirely accords with this notion of culture. By subordinating in the same way and to the same end all areas of intellectual creation, by occupying men's senses from the time they leave the factory in the evening to the time they clock in again the next morning with matter that bears the impress of the labour process they themselves have to sustain throughout the day, this subsumption mockingly satisfies the concept of a unified culture which the philosophers of personality contrasted with mass culture.

(Adorno and Horkheimer 1979: 131)

Again, this position attracted considerable support amongst leftist culture critics and Marxist theoreticians in the postwar era. Ironically, as Alan Swingewood points out in *The Myth of Mass Culture* (1977), it also mirrored the conservative rejection of mass culture and liberal democracy. Beginning in the late 1960s, however, Certeau decisively challenged this position, and initiated the 'rehabilitation' of popular culture that was later to become a hallmark of British cultural studies. He did so by stressing the emancipatory and creative nature of consumption and popular culture, rather than dwelling on its manipulative qualities. As Jeremy Ahearne puts it, Certeau's approach to contemporary culture is 'designed precisely to drive a wedge between [proffered cultural] representations and the multiple practices through which they are appropriated' (1995: 157). For instance, in his 1974 essay 'The Beauty of the Dead' (co-written with Dominique Julia and Jacques Revel), Certeau argues (*pace* Bourdieu) that debating the aesthetic merits of popular as opposed to high culture gives us little understanding of how a cultural formation actually functions in relation to the prevailing dynamics of power and domination. Specifically, we must take into account how particular cultural practices are construed as *objects of knowledge* by elite social groups that have donned the mantle of science and objectivity. The characteristic rhetorics and metaphors used by technocratic elites to characterize popular culture are not examples of a 'neutral' or purely descriptive terminology. Rather, such discourses are mobilized to legitimate projects of a hegemonic, political nature. In the mid-nineteenth century in France, for example, an idealized version of rural folk culture was lauded as a model of simplicity and 'natural-ness', which served to justify the imposition of a standardized version of French language and culture on the general population. During other periods, when faced with the growing militancy and rebelliousness of the labouring urban poor, popular culture was demonized by the French intelligentsia and bourgeoisie and sup-pressed accordingly. The issue at stake, according to Certeau, does not simply concern the use of unsuitable methods of investigation or inappropriate nomenclatures. It involves the 'internal' connection between power and knowledge, a linkage that can only be chal-lenged through concerted political action. In other words, the battle against the illegitimate exercise of institutionalized power cannot be fought wholly on the technocrat's 'home turf', the terrain of functionalist, bureaucratic rationality itself. Countering this hege-mony is a matter of circumventing the incorporation of popular culture and everyday practices into formalized discourses and instrumentalized practices, and by giving such popular activities, including specific acts of cultural consumption and the appropri-ation of meaning, a legitimacy they lacked hitherto. Certeau's attempt to develop a 'heterology', a plurality of meaning-constitu-tive practices, as against the official practice of historiography and sociological analysis, is intended to highlight and preserve the irreducible multiplicity of human social and cultural forms. He sought to demonstrate to intellectuals that 'social mechanisms of selection, critique, and repression are everywhere present' in his-torical research, and remind them 'that it is violence that invariably founds a system of knowledge'. But whilst affirming the importance of sociocultural criticism, Certeau also warns us about its limits. He remains sceptical that we can expect a complete 'emancipation of cultures, a finally liberated outpouring, an unchained spontaneity to result from a political critique' (1986: 136). The possibilities of social transformation cannot be determined in advance, by theor-etical or ideological fiat; rather, an understanding of the limits and potentialities for change can only emerge out of direct experience and the concrete options available to us at a particular moment.

Certeau's nuanced argument has certain affinities with the earlier positions sketched out by Lefebvre and the SI. At the same time, however, there are significant and telling differences between them. As previously indicated, Lefebvre and the Situationists were also concerned to uncover and criticize the repressive function of special-ized and reified knowledges in contemporary society. Vaneigem, for instance, argued that any form of mediation or specialization reinforced human alienation and led to a further loss of control over everyday life, and was therefore the handmaiden of social control, a bulwark of the society of the spectacle. Such a rationality emptied subjectivity of any real content, because it utilized 'categories ready to condemn to incomprehensibility and nonsense anything which they can't contain, or summon into existence-for-Power that which slumbers in nothingness because it has no place as yet in the system of Order' (1983: 75). For his part, Lefebvre contrasted 'abstract reason', which was idealist, dogmatic, and insulated from concrete existence, with 'dialectical reason', which was materialist and critical yet still open to creative and imaginative human activities, including the imperatives of desire, collective celebration and the body.

Neither Lefebvre nor the Situationists would, however, have accepted the argument that the theoretical attempt to understand contemporary society as a totality was indicative of a domineering and destructive 'will to knowledge'. The postmodernist position is that such a desire is both epistemologically suspect and guilty of perpetrating a form of 'symbolic violence' on the object of inquiry. Indeed, both Lefebvre and the SI would have defended such a theoretical knowledge as intrinsic to the project of social transformation. In this, they remained faithful to the basic tenets of Hegelian philosophy. Hegel, as is well known, suggested that history evinced a growth of reason over time, a progressive correspondence between the 'real' and the 'rational', which meant that the potential for human self-actualization increased markedly in the modern era. For Hegelian Marxists like Debord and Lefebvre, this meant that despite the negative features of modernity, such as alienation and commodification, this period also represented the best hope for human emancipation, mainly because it laid the technological and material foundation for a genuinely free and democratic society. This implied that the spontaneous culture of everyday life, despite its latently resistant and liberatory qualities, could not in and of itself provide the impetus for sociocultural revolution. Everyday life was overly fragile and ephemeral, too vulnerable to the imperialism of the commodity form. As Sadie Plant (1992: 4) has observed, for all of its anti-elitist rhetoric, the SI resolutely defended the necessity of a theoretical understanding of consumer capitalism that was superior to both unreflexive everyday knowledge and competing idealist social theories. The Situationists poured scorn on both high and popular culture (especially television and the cinema), suggesting they were milksops for a spectacularized economy and displayed few if any emancipatory characteristics.

In essence, or so Certeau would argue, Lefebvre and the Situationists continued to cling to the modernist conceit that theory could accurately 'represent' the totality of social relations, and that this form of knowledge was in some way superior to the non-formalized knowledges generated by everyday cultural practices. Certeau therefore draws attention to the limits of rationality, dialectical or otherwise, and raises provocative questions about our desire and ability to capture the 'real' in language and thought. This orientation is at least in part based on his affinity with psycho-analysis, with its stress on the irrational and non-discursive components of human thought and behaviour, but also with poststructuralism, which calls into question the straightforward distinction between 'fact' and 'fiction' in historiographic or socio-logical descriptions (Frow 1991; Poster 1992; Schirato 1993). In particular, Certeau would no doubt charge that his predecessors failed to analyse everyday life as it was actually lived in the context of consumer society, as opposed to some idealized conception of the everyday. What cannot be denied is that Lefebvre and the SI were less concerned with everyday life as such than with dramatic, celebratory ruptures from a routinized and degraded daily existence, as this occurred during periods of sociopolitical unrest (industrial militancy, student occupations, etc.), or in such non-Western or premodern practices as the potlatch or the festival, which they held up as exemplars of non-alienated social practices. Certeau, by contrast, sought to locate more subtle moments of creativity and festivity within the delicate skein of everyday life as it was actually experienced, which included mundane acts of consumption, cultural or otherwise. In taking this position, Certeau gave up the pretence to 'total critique', and virtually abandoned the goal of complete revolution espoused by the May 1968 activists, whether inspired by Mao, Marcuse or the Situationists.[2] Consumer capitalism is certainly oppressive and domineering, suggests Certeau, but ultimately it cannot fully contain the spontaneous and imaginative energies of the people (Rigby 1991: 162). The ubiquity of the commodity form, and the apparent solidity of capitalist social relations, means that traces of resistance and a critical imagination can be detected in the here and now. This anonymous creativity is evinced in marginal-ized practices and rituals largely ignored by both technocratic reason and leftist cultural criticism, which, in Certeau's opinion, includes 'houses, clothes, do-it-yourself, cooking, the thousand things that people do in the town and in the country, that families and friends do together, the multifarious forms of professional work – all these are spheres in which creativity can be seen on all sides' (cited in Rigby 1991: 19). Accordingly, Certeau's interpretation of creativity is very different from Lefebvre and the Situationists, insofar as the latter advocated a ceaseless creation and re-creation of lived time and space based on the principle of *autogestion*, or self-management, which they felt was inseparable from the Marxian project of subordinating history to conscious human will and desire. Finally, both Lefebvre and the SI bemoaned the fragmented and utilitarian nature of culture under late capitalism, and looked forward to a time when a common, unified culture would again emerge. To Certeau's way of thinking, this endorsement of an integrated culture is, ironically, part of the technocratic rationality that dominates contemporary society, because it seeks to reduce the inherent complexity and diversity of the world to homogeneity or sameness, thereby denying the right of 'otherness' to exist. Hence, Certeau is more interested in the unsystematic and pluralistic qualities of culture, and with life on the margins as lived by the 'anonymous' masses, rather than with Lefebvre's more Promethean concept of the 'total man'.

THE PANOPTICAL SOCIETY AND ITS DISCONTENTS

Given these differences with Lefebvre and the Situationists, how does Certeau actually conceptualize the resistant qualities of everyday life and cultural consumption? A useful way of answering this question might be to examine Certeau's critical assessment of the work of Michel Foucault, especially the latter's ideas about power, resistance and disciplinary practices. In *Discipline and Punish* (1977), a study that neatly encapsulates his central themes and preoccupations, Foucault postulates that there has been a qualitative shift in the nature of power corresponding to the emergence of Western industrial society. During the period of the *ancien régime*, absolute power was embodied in the personage of the king. Individuals who transgressed the king's authority were not categorized as 'criminals' in the modern sense, but were defined as a threat to the continued stability of a highly elaborated and complexly stratified cosmic order. Punishment was not designed to rehabilitate the individual in question, or to compensate the victims of wrongful acts, but to re-establish this cosmic balance. Accordingly, the punishment of wrong-doers took the form of spectacular and (to our eyes) brutal public displays of torture and execution, exemplified by the description Foucault provides of the execution of Damiens the regicide in 1757 in the opening pages of *Discipline and Punish*. These public rituals had the effect of reasserting the sanctity of the existing legal code and, more generally, of the legitimacy of the king to preside over his subjects. Yet, Foucault argues, the exercise of power through such spectacular displays of violence eventually became too unwieldy and costly for effective social control, and unsuited to the demands of an increasingly complex socioeconomic system and the demographic pressures of a rapidly expanding population. Consequently, power is increasingly organized and administered by a massive, impersonal bureaucracy that commands both the resources and the knowledges capable of observing the masses, and of developing the necessary corrective procedures to be able to control and manipulate individual behaviour. The goal is now the production of subjects who internalize power, in the process becoming 'regimented, isolated, and self-policing'. According to Foucault, these 'micro-techniques' of observation and control eventually became encoded into a standardized, 'global' set of techniques and practices, which were extended to all major sectors of society (education, medicine, industrial production). Another of Foucault's key suppositions is that the 'normalization' of both individuals and populations has historically been associated with the emergence of the human sciences – especially demographics, psychology and criminology – which seek to create unitary knowledges involving the measurement and classification of modern individuals now defined as 'objects' of study. The constitution of self-monitoring beings is effected through the operation of these external disciplines and procedures, the paradigmatic example being the surveillance techniques pioneered by Jeremy Bentham in his eighteenth-century plans for the Panopticon, a circular prison structure with a central watch tower designed to observe and record the activities of inmates. The result, asserts Foucault, is the development of a modern form of domination he designates by a series of ominous neologisms: the 'disciplinary society', the 'age of bio-power', the 'carceral archipelago', and others.

> 'Discipline' may be identified neither with an institution
> nor with an apparatus; it is a type of power, a modality for
> its exercise, comprising a whole series of instruments,

techniques, procedures, levels of application, targets; it is a physics or an anatomy of power, a technology. And it may be taken over by a 'specialized' institution [or] finally by state apparatuses whose major, if not exclusive, function is to assure that discipline reigns over society as a whole.

(Foucault 1977: 215–16)

According to Certeau, Foucault's account of power and modernity is important and insightful, mainly because it focuses less on the obvious manifestations of power (the state, army and judiciary) than with the 'microphysics of power', or with how power actually functions on the level of day-to-day existence. Certeau's main objection to this Foucauldian narrative, which chronicles the birth and consolidation of this carceral society, is that it tends to 'reduce the functioning of a whole society to a single, dominant type of procedure', in this case the panoptical or the disciplinary (1986: 188). Certainly, he would agree with Foucault that the goal of such disciplinary apparatuses is the effective surveillance and control of heterogeneous practices. Recalling the argument developed by Adorno and Horkheimer in *Dialectic of Enlightenment*, Certeau asserts that modernist forms of knowledge have actively encouraged the manipulation of objects and events. These knowledges have a 'totalizing' function: they seek the containment of both the natural and social worlds within an immutable, unified system of concepts and categories, for the purpose of pragmatic control. Technocratic reason seeks to construct a totally controlled space that prohibits all physical, mental and political 'contamination', a site where everything can be rationally calculated and ordered. In practice, the exercise of technocratic reason excludes practices and discourses that fail to conform to this model of abstract rationality, thereby expunging difference or otherness. While this rise of instrumental or technological rationality created the economic and technical infrastructure necessary for the generation of greater productive wealth, it also raised the spectre of the complete enslavement of human beings and the alienation of humankind from nature, leading to what Max Weber called the 'disenchantment' of the world.

Nonetheless, Certeau is adamant that the apparent success of the technologies of power that Foucault analyses – 'instrumental rationality', in Adorno and Horkheimer's terminology – can be traced to specific historical conditions. As such, the simple presence of these technologies cannot guarantee their coherence, or their automatic success in the effacement of otherness. There continue to persist less visible or 'minor' practices that, under different conditions, could have become equally efficacious. As Certeau put it, 'behind the "monotheism" of the dominant panoptical procedures, we might suspect the existence and survival of a "polytheism" of concealed or *disseminated practices,* dominated but not obliterated by the historical triumph of one of their number' (1986: 188). Foucault, or for that matter Adorno and Horkheimer, can tell us little or nothing about such unofficial practices, which also have an intrinsic structure and logic. These minor practices, suggests Certeau, have remained 'unprivileged by history', yet they 'continue to flourish in the interstices of the institutional technologies' (1986: 189). Whereas the procedures and techniques (or what Certeau terms 'strategies') that Foucault describes are visible manifestations of power, and occupy an identifiable physical space (the academy, the clinic, the prison), unofficial or marginal practices ('tactics') operate without such a fixed locus. Unlike strategies, which are the hallmark of institutionalized power, tactics represent 'clandestine forms taken by the dispersed, tactical, and makeshift creativity of groups or individuals already caught in the nets of "discipline"' (Certeau 1984: xiv). By focusing on strategies of official power rather than the rhetorical tactics utilized by the weak to undermine them, Foucault's own theories, despite their subversive intent, are unwittingly panoptical and function to shore up disciplinary apparatuses and discourses. In contradistinction to Foucault, who wants to establish a genealogy of disciplines, Certeau wants to understand 'anti-disciplines', the silent and unacknowledged forms of resistance that 'break through the grid of the established order and accepted disciplines' (1986: 197). Certeau is virtually unique amongst postmodern and poststructuralist theorists in that he concentrates mainly on issues of resistance and agency, rather than upon extant systems of power and dissimulation. This orientation makes him one of the least pessimistic and most politically astute of contemporary French thinkers.

TACTICS VERSUS STRATEGIES

Inasmuch as Certeau's work on everyday life revolves primarily around the distinction between tactics and strategies (Ahearne 1995: 157–89), it is incumbent upon us to investigate these two concepts in more detail. His central premise, one he broadly shares with Pierre

Bourdieu, is that the investigation of any sociocultural field requires an understanding of the complex of *practices* that constitute that field. A practice conforms to a particular logic, a characteristic way of thinking and acting. In the context of late capitalism, given the general shift from production to consumption, it is not surprising that the activity of consumption itself acquires a heightened significance. The maintenance of social hierarchy and inequality, however, requires that the mass of the population be prevented from having any effective control over what goods and artefacts are actually available in the marketplace, or indeed how the socioeconomic system itself operates. On the surface, it would therefore appear that the powerless are subject to the repressive and alienating dictates of consumer capitalism. Consumers are forced to move about, work, eat and sleep in a series of technocratically constructed and utilitarian spaces within which nothing is left to chance. In so doing, they passively consume the cultural objects proffered by the marketplace, which augments the accumulation of power and capital. More controversially, it is frequently suggested that consumers internalize the values and attitudes promoted by the system alongside the commodities themselves, through the acquisition of what Bourdieu (1977) has called cultural, symbolic and economic capital. Indeed, as discussed previously, this has been the general position adopted by many left critiques of consumer capitalism, including Adorno and Horkheimer's concept of the 'culture industry', Lefebvre's 'bureaucratic society of controlled consumption', and Debord's 'society of the spectacle'. The central premise behind these theories is that the symbolic value invested in the commodity by the dominant ideology is automatically consumed along with the physical object or image itself, leading to an alienated and pacified population. The following quotation from an early text by Jean Baudrillard entitled 'The System of Objects' is symptomatic of this point of view: 'objects are *categories of objects* which quite tyrannically induce *categories of persons*. They undertake the policing of social meanings, and the significations they engender are controlled. Their proliferation, simultaneously arbitrary and coherent, is the best vehicle for a social order, equally arbitrary and coherent, to materialize itself effectively under the sign of affluence' (1988: 16–17).

Certeau agrees that 'marginality' now defines the mass of the population, and that this process of marginalization is central to the reproduction of consumer capitalism itself. However, he parts company with those who suggest that the 'system' is largely self-sustaining, and that reproduction takes place 'behind the backs' of

169

social agents, as structuralists like Althusser used to argue.[3] While
the scope of manoeuvrability of consumers is highly constrained, they
can still utilize the resources available to them in a host of inventive
and creative ways. In other words, we have to be highly attentive to
the concrete situation: to the social groups doing the consuming, the
nature of the commodity (it is more difficult to be inventive with an
ironing board than, say, a home computer), and the forces at play
during the activity of consumption itself (for example, what is the
specific site of consumption – public, private, or semi-public?). In
order to explore such a cultural field properly, we must focus on the
types of operations that characterize consumption within the framework of the economy, so as to ascertain hidden moments of creativity
and self-expression. Although the cultural activity of the non-
producers of culture is largely 'unsigned, unreadable, and unsym-
bolized', because it is not governed by formalized logic and escapes
the gaze of official power, it is nonetheless present. Again, this is
because non-producers seek to appropriate, use, and attribute meaning to cultural artefacts in a myriad of unexpected and surprising
ways. This is where Certeau differs substantially from Bourdieu.
Whereas Bourdieu seems to suggest that practice is regulated by an
explicit principle of administration located in a particular space
(especially the educational sphere), Certeau counters that there is no
single logic of practice at work in contemporary society, but a series of
contradictory and multiple logics, some hidden, other explicit. As
such, argues Certeau, 'the tactics of consumption, the ingenious ways
in which the weak make use of the strong, thus lend a political
dimension to everyday practices' (1984: xvii), but are neither as
deterministic nor as rooted in social class as Bourdieu tends to assert.
Consumers 'produce' through the adoption of 'errant' or non-formalized practices, which obey internal logics that are often unintelligible
to an outsider. Although these practices must ultimately utilize the
vocabularies and resources proffered by elites, the actual trajectories
adopted reflect the 'ruses of other interests and desires that are neither
determined nor captured by the systems in which they develop'
(1984: xviii). This process of creative appropriation or non-predeter-
mined usage represents, in Certeau's terminology, a 'transcription',
because it transforms the original symbolic and physical materials
contained in the commodity into something quite different:

> In reality, a rationalized, expansionist, centralized, spectac-
> ular and clamorous production is confronted by an entirely
> different kind of production, called 'consumption' and

characterized by its ruses, fragmentation (the result of the circumstances), its poaching, its clandestine nature, its tireless but quiet activity, in short by its quasi-invisibility, since it shows itself not in its own products (where would it place them?) but in an art of using those imposed on it.

(1984: 31)

In taking this line, Certeau explicitly challenges a host of more orthodox Marxist assumptions regarding the nature of production, needs and ideology. To begin with, he jettisons much of the Marxian 'metaphysics of labour', which upheld the notion that the self-actualization of each human being was rooted in the production and reproduction of the material conditions of existence. Certeau, by contrast, wants to assert that it is primarily through consumption that the individual acquires a sense of identity and selfhood – or, to be more precise, consumption *is* the locus of production under the conditions of late capitalism. (We might term this gambit 'Weber's revenge'.) Moreover, since needs are now defined in and through the everyday practices and desires of consumers themselves, rather than by intellectuals, Certeau calls into question the validity of the distinction between 'true' and 'false' needs, or indeed between use-value and exchange-value (Marcuse 1964; Leiss 1978). This contrast, which some theorists have characterized as ahistorical and elitist, has been the cornerstone of much leftist cultural criticism, especially that of the Frankfurt School. Finally, Certeau would reject what has come to be known as the 'dominant ideology thesis' (Abercrombie *et al.* 1980; Gardiner 1992: 59–98). The popular masses, he would hold, are not victims of 'false consciousness'; they do not straightforwardly internalize the values and beliefs supplied to them by elites. On the contrary, although they cannot or do not always articulate their dissent, few non-elites would accord any real legitimacy to the prevailing regime. They act to subvert the structures of power in the less visible and non-confrontational ways that are available to them. In taking this stance, Certeau would deny Baudrillard's suggestion that the symbolic contents attached to commodities by advertising and other media are automatically absorbed by the consumer along with the commodity itself. Whereas, for example, a critical theorist like W. F. Haug (1986, 1987) sees in the fantasies and desires that accompany acts of consumption only evidence of a mystified consciousness, Certeau claims to have located what Umberto Eco has called 'semiotic guerilla warfare' and the exercise of an unfettered imagination.

In essence, Certeau's central presumption is that most everyday activities of consumption are 'tactical' in character; like the trickster of premodern mythology, they incorporate cunning, manoeuvres, clever tricks, simulations, feints of weakness, and poetic as well as warlike elements (in Greek, *mētis*). He speculates that these techniques may even be biological or evolutionary in origin, as in the obfuscatory colouration of the chameleon or the spots that resemble large, intimidating eyes on the wings of an otherwise defenceless species of butterfly. For Certeau, tactics are to be sharply contrasted with strategies. Strategies seek to colonize a visible, specific space that will serve as a 'home base' for the exercise of power and domination, in order 'to delimit one's own place in a world bewitched by the invisible powers of the Other' (1984: 36). They master space through a combination of tried and tested panoptic practices which surveil and quantify a particular site. Historicity itself is perceived as a threat to this power, because it introduces a degree of temporal indeterminacy. As such, strategies attempt to negate time and memory, by reducing them to elements within an observable and readable system. Tactics, by contrast, are dispersed, hidden and ephemeral, and improvised in response to the concrete demands of the situation at hand. They are also temporal in nature, and reliant on the art of collective memory, on a tradition of popular resistance and subversion passed on from generation to generation since time immemorial. Tactics, like the ancient art of rhetorics initially developed by the Sophists, are intended to make the 'weaker appear stronger', to gain for the powerless every advantage they can, given that they cannot directly challenge or confront the existing structures of power. To use the terminology developed by James C. Scott in his book *Domination and the Arts of Resistance* (1990), public assent to the legitimacy of power on the part of dispossessed social groups is matched by a 'hidden transcript' of popular resistance, which relies on stealth, guile and anonymity. The following quotation should clarify the distinction between tactics and strategies:

> I call a 'strategy' the calculus of force-relationships which becomes possible when a subject of will and power (a proprietor, an enterprise, a city, a scientific institution) can be isolated from an 'environment'. A strategy assumes a place that can be circumscribed as *proper* (*propre*) and thus serve as the basis for generating relations with an exterior distinct from it (competitors, adversaries, 'clienteles', 'targets', or

'objects' of research). Political, economic, and scientific rationality has been constructed on this strategic model.

I call a 'tactic', on the other hand, a calculus which cannot count on a 'proper' (a spatial or institutional localization), nor thus on a borderline distinguishing the other as a visible totality. The place of a tactic belongs to the other. A tactic insinuates itself into the other's place, fragmentarily, without taking it over in its entirety, without being able to keep it at a distance. It has at its disposal no base where it can capitalize on its advantages, prepare its expansions, and secure independence with respect to circumstances. The 'proper' is a victory of space over time. On the contrary, because it does not have a place, a tactic depends on time – it is always on the watch for opportunities that may be seized 'on the wing'. Whatever it wins, it does not keep. It must constantly manipulate events in order to turn them into 'opportunities'. The weak must continually turn to their own ends forces alien to them.

(Certeau 1984: xix)

It is important to realize that in making these pronouncements, Certeau is not relying on a conception of the perfectly rational, autonomous subject. Like Foucault and Derrida, he wants to discard this model as an illegitimate vestige of Enlightenment rationalism and individualism. That is, Certeau is not so much interested in the activities, intentions or self-interests of the individual social actor so much as the underlying 'operational logic' of the practice that is involved, a logic that is collective or structural in nature. For example, the individual speaker is not free to disregard entirely the extant rules of grammatical construction or intonation, so long as some form of communication is desired. As Wittgenstein argued long ago, the notion of a 'private language' is an oxymoron. Any language that is subject to actual usage – or language understood as a form of *discourse* – is irreducibly social, a point that Bakhtin also emphasizes continually; it transcends the subjective intentions of its users, and is inseparable from the 'form of life' contained within a particular society and culture. Nonetheless, the scope that Certeau accords to agency is far greater than someone like Foucault. Foucault, of course, wants to assert that people are not self-directed, autonomous agents, but are 'produced' by the matrix of power/ knowledge relations within which they inextricably find themselves. In other words, subjects are entities that are constituted by the discursive and disciplinary configurations that have accompanied the emergence of the carceral society. As such, it is difficult to conceive of how social actors could possibly engage in alternative forms of action or formulate 'counter-disciplines'. This problem arises because of an over-hasty poststructuralist desire to dispense with the subject *tout court*, combined with a pronounced tendency to reify the notion of 'discourse'. Human agency, as Anthony Giddens (1987) has convincingly argued, is not mechanistically determined by sign-systems or power/knowledge relations, insofar as human beings have the intrinsic capacity to reflexively monitor their actions, a phenomenon that primarily occurs in the non-discursive realm of 'practical consciousness'. Foucault's rejection of the agent or subject entails the *de facto* acknowledgement that the enforcement of a dominant system of norms and disciplines can never be resisted effectively. Certeau's alternative conception of agency and resistance provides us with a way out of this poststructuralist aporia.

THE 'GRAMMAR' OF EVERYDAY PRACTICE

For Certeau, the paradigmatic instance of the process of appropriation described above is reading, or the apprehension and interpretation of visual symbols. Reading is a tactical enterprise *par excellence*, and an extremely important one, insofar as our media-saturated society is increasingly reliant on signs and visually encoded information. In common with what is today called 'reader-reception theory', Certeau argues that whereas reading appears to be passive, it is in fact a form of 'silent production'. A purely literal reading of a text is a rare achievement, and indeed a very difficult one. In fact, he suggests that the ability to enforce a literal reading or decoding of a text is the perennial dream of technocratic power, and a central aspect of what he calls the 'scriptural economy'. More commonly, the reader roams over the surface of the text, appropriating or 'poaching' certain images, words or passages whilst ignoring others. In so doing, the reader constructs what Paul Ricoeur (1985) has termed a 'world of the text', an imaginary landscape that the author may never have envisaged or intended. 'By its very nature available to a plural reading', writes Certeau, 'the text becomes a cultural weapon, a private hunting reserve, the pretext for a law that legitimizes as "literal" the interpretation given by *socially* authorized professionals and intellectuals' (1984: 171). How many times has each of us formed a distinct mental image of what a particular text 'means', only to discover upon re-reading that we had mistaken certain key words or phrases and subconsciously insinuated our own meanings? For Certeau, this does not represent an illegitimate 'misreading' of a text, but rather indicates the pervasive desire on the part of readers not to accept passively the 'authority' of the text, but to find pleasures and personal significances wherever they can be located. When a reader approaches a text, writes Certeau, 'he poaches on it, is transported into it, pluralizes himself in it like the internal rumblings of one's body. Ruse, metaphor, arrangement, this production is also an "invention" of the memory. Words become the outlet or product of silent histories' (1984: xxi). Just as a renter turns an empty apartment into something liveable, imbuing this space with subjective meanings and resonances through the arrangement of furniture, the placement of photographs, plants, and decorative bric-à-brac, readers and speakers insert into the text their own narratives, images and desires.[4] If modernity 'owns' the text through the construction of a dominant discourse that introjects a preferred set of meanings (scientific, medical, academic), the 'procedures of contemporary consumption appear to constitute a subtle art of "renters" who know how to insinuate their countless differences into the dominant text' (1984: xxii).

It is no different with verbal speech. Echoing Mikhail Bakhtin's notion of 'dialogism', as discussed in Chapter 3, Certeau asserts that ordinary conversation consists of a complex of practices that appropriate and transform an inherited system of language – Saussure's *langue* – into an 'oral fabric' binding speakers together to produce meanings that are unique to the concrete context of verbal production. As such, speech is essentially rhetorical and tactical in nature. 'Conversation', observes Certeau, 'is a provisional and collective effect of competence in the art of manipulating "commonplaces" and the inevitability of events in such a way as to make them "habitable"' (1984: xxii). Although structuralism attempts to de-contextualize the practice of verbal production and 'eliminate the *operation* of speakers in particular situations of time, place and competition' – which, in Certeau's opinion, is symptomatic of the modernist tendency to reduce the logic of ordinary practice to an artificial metalanguage – speech-acts are in fact indissociable from an everyday historicity and spatiality and the concrete interlocutors that enunciate and interpret given words and phrases. Discourses, to quote Certeau,

> are *marked by* uses; they offer to analysis the *imprints* of acts
> or of processes of enunciation; they signify the *operations*

whose object they have been, operations which are relative
to situations and which can be thought of as the
conjunctural *generalizations* of statements or of practices;
[they] indicate a social *historicity* in which systems of
. representations or processes of fabrication no longer appear
only as normative frameworks but also as *tools manipulated
by users*.

(1984: 21)

One of the central claims that Certeau makes in *The Practice of
Everyday Life* is that the operations of reading and speech can be
extended to other practices, that there is a correspondence or
homology between certain enunciative procedures that regulate
action in both the field of language and the wider network of social
practices. For instance, he provides detailed analyses of the appropriation of space (walking, living, etc.), the consumption of images
(televisual, cinematic), the more literal consumption of food and
drink, as in techniques of cooking, and many other everyday
procedures. These investigations have had a significant impact on
contemporary cultural studies, as evinced by the work of John Fiske
(1989, 1991), for instance. Although this metaphorical extension of
the practice of reading is essentially semiological in inspiration,
there are some important differences. In particular, Certeau suggests
that the linguistic model utilized by semioticians like Barthes or
Lévi-Strauss cannot really account for the mechanisms of power,
domination and resistance. As such, he advocates the replacement of
a purely linguistic paradigm with what he calls a 'polemological'
one. The problem with the structuralist model is that it takes too
much from de Saussure's original formulations about the nature of
language. In essence, the Saussurean model conceived of language as
a static and abstract system comprised of phonetic differences,
which was disconnected from history and social conflicts. By contrast,
a polemological approach is primarily concerned with the analysis of
'battles or games between the strong and the weak, and with the
"actions" which remain possible for the latter' (Certeau 1984: 34).
In all such practices, unrecognized producers – or, more poetically,
what Certeau calls 'trailblazers in the jungles of functionalist
rationality' – are able to develop 'indeterminate trajectories' at odds
with the dominant rationality visibly inscribed in the given text,
object or space. Such idiosyncratic trajectories 'remain heterogeneous to the systems they infiltrate and in which they sketch out
the guileful ruses of *different* interests and desires' (1984: 31). For

Certeau, this complex of practices and modes of appropriation are in some sense 'internal' to the particular form of life within which a culture is embedded, or what Raymond Williams (1977) has called a 'structure of feeling'. As such, popular culture is at some remove from the sociocultural location of intellectuals, and any attempt to transcribe such practices into some pre-existing theoretical discourse will represent a coercive and manipulative act. Indeed, writing itself is for Certeau an imperialist medium that has always been allied to the interests of the powerful. Not surprisingly, therefore, he asserts that traditional forms of sociological analysis, especially those reliant on quantitative methods, can tell us very little about these practices. As a specialist armed with an authoritative discourse, the sociologist is always tempted to translate the procedures of everyday life into categories and taxonomies that are synonymous with the logic of rationalized production and bureaucratic control. For Certeau, what is important is not so much the actual materials utilized in consumer practices, but rather the process of appropriation or 'making do' associated with their usage. This is why, for example, the proliferation of studies of television violence that concentrate solely on the overt content of such programming will tell us next to nothing about what is actually going on. According to Certeau, 'making do' represents a set of rules and procedures that 'have their own formality and inventiveness and that discretely organize the multiform labor of consumption' (1984: 30). Again, this logic of practice is invisible to the 'universe of codification and generalized transparency. [The] practices of consumption are the ghosts of the society that carries their name. Like the "spirits" of former times, they constitute the multiform and occult postulate of productive activity' (1984: 35).

This helps to explain why everyday practices are highly resistant to translation and codification into a formalized, authoritative language, and why the basic grammar of tactics can be traced back many thousands of years. Indeed, their very incomprehensibility in the face of an instrumentalized rationality is a continuing source of strength and vitality. Despite the concerted attempt on the part of technocratic power to suppress or expunge otherness, and to isolate and control individuals as subjects of power/knowledge, such 'ghostly' voices can still be detected in the 'night-side of societies'. They are heard in 'rambling, wily everyday stories' told by women, children and other social marginals, and glimpsed furtively in the creative practices of daily life that rely on the logic of the 'gift' rather than of exchange. These excluded voices have managed to escape from the 'domination of a sociocultural economy, from the organization of reason, from the grasp of education, from the power of an elite and, finally, from the control of the enlightened consciousness' (1984: 158). However, Certeau warns us against attributing some kind of abstract unity to these micro-narratives, which is the cardinal error of traditional Marxist and socialist historiography. Such voices are always impure, heterodox and idiosyncratic. As he writes: 'we must give up the fiction that collects all these sounds under the sign of a "Voice," of a "Culture" of its own – or of the great Other's. Rather, orality insinuates itself, like one of the threads of which it is composed, into the network – an endless tapestry – of a scriptural economy' (1984: 136). Of course, institutionalized power responds to these resistances by mobilizing a whole series of technical discourses and procedures (psychiatric, pedagogic, and so on), which are designed to bring such heretical voices back into the fold and to re-establish the authoritative word. Nonetheless, Certeau insists that the popular imagination is capable of creating and sustaining a 'utopian space' that resists total assimilation or incorporation, and within which justice is done and the powerful de-throned, at least symbolically. In the inexhaustible narratives contained within such utopian moments, suggests Certeau,

> can thus be revealed, dressed as gods or heros, the models of good or bad ruses that can be used every day. [The] formality of everyday practices is indicated in these tales, which frequently reverse the relationships of power and, like the stories of miracles, ensure the victory of the unfortunate in a fabulous utopian space. This space protects the weapons of the weak against the reality of the established order. It also hides them from the social categories which 'make history' because they dominate it. And whereas historiography recounts in the past tense the strategies of instituted powers, these 'fabulous' stories offer their audience a repertory.
>
> (1984: 23)

CONCLUSION

In his various writings, Michel de Certeau has fashioned a distinctive and insightful approach to the critical analysis of everyday life.

With his suspicion of modernist theory, he draws our attention to the 'symbolic violence' that can be done to the integrity of daily practices and to 'otherness' under the guise of a systematic theoretical understanding of social reality. As such, his writing retains a strong ethical quality that is sometimes lacking in other accounts of the everyday examined in the present study, and in mainstream social theorizing more generally. Moreover, his ethnographic dissection of the alternative logics inscribed in such mundane practices advances our understanding of how they actually work 'on the ground', and with how forms of resistance function concretely. Finally, his arguments regarding the nature of consumption, the formation and satisfaction of human needs, the role of desire and poesis, and the operation of ideology, to name but a few, have effectively challenged a range of orthodoxies on the left, and have already helped to generate a very productive debate regarding these and related issues (Lee 1993). If at times he seems to overemphasize the resistant and 'utopian' qualities of popular consumption and everyday practices, thereby giving short shrift to what Zygmunt Bauman (1992: 222–5) has identified as the 'seductive', integrative qualities of (post)modern consumerism, Certeau's work still manages to provide a powerful corrective to Foucault's highly pessimistic and one-dimensional analysis of our present-day 'disciplinary society'. In the final analysis, perhaps what is required, as Samuel Kinser (1992: 82) cleverly puts it, is a way of synthesizing the 'paranoia of Foucault and the idealism of Certeau'.

8

DOROTHY E. SMITH:
A SOCIOLOGY FOR PEOPLE

There is no hell against which we must fight, nor a heaven
we must buttress: there is no unique god with a necessary
counterpart. We are confronted by a pantheon which
incarnates the plurality of our lived experience. In this is all
the tragedy and all the uncertainty of social existence. Here
indeed we find what we might call confrontation with
destiny.

Michel Maffesoli

INTRODUCTION

Dorothy E. Smith has, over the last several decades, fashioned a
distinctive and avowedly feminist critique of existing sociological
methods, theories and practices, one that concentrates especially on
the character of everyday life and its relationship to gendered social
experiences and practices. Born in the north of England in 1929,
Smith studied at the London School of Economics in the early 1950s,
where she developed an enduring interest in the discipline of
sociology. She moved to the United States to attend graduate school
at the University of California at Berkeley in 1955, and it was here
she acquired her doctorate. As she describes it in 'A Berkeley
Education' (1994), the environs of Berkeley proved to be decisive to
her intellectual development in a number of crucial respects. In
terms of theoretical influences, Berkeley first exposed Smith to the
work of such micro-oriented social thinkers as the American
symbolic interactionist George Herbert Mead, the French Marxist
and phenomenologist Maurice Merleau-Ponty, and the progenitor of
'dramaturgical' sociology, the Canadian-born Erving Goffman. From
the standpoint of her political sensibilities, Berkeley was between the

late 1950s and the early 1970s a hot-bed of American student activism and radical politics. Although not being a US citizen limited her direct involvement in leftist organizations and activities, Smith attended many anti-war demonstrations, lectures and 'teach-ins'. At this point in her career, she turned to the writings of Karl Marx as a primary source of political and intellectual inspiration. Her growing radicalization brought with it a certain sense of frustration, as Smith came to the realization that existing institutional structures, or what she was later to term the 'relations of ruling', curtailed meaningful social change. In particular, *de facto* male control of important organizations – educational, medical, political and economic – functioned to effectively de-legitimate and marginalize women's interests and aspirations. This insight precipitated a life-long involvement with the women's movement, which, in her words, represented 'a total transformation of consciousness at multiple levels, which led me into the strange paths I'm still pursuing of undoing, among other things, the sociology I'd learned so hard to practice' (1996a). This statement is revealing, because it demonstrates that Smith came to the conclusion at a very early stage of her career that orthodox academic sociology plays a significant role in maintaining the existing structure of masculine power and privilege. Sociology is complicit with the relations of ruling, at least in part because it studies the social world at considerable distance from the actual realities of day-to-day existence. In constructing elaborate models and theories to explain society, sociology abstracts from the ground of daily life and substitutes highly formalistic and intellectualized accounts that bear little resemblance to the former. The discipline provides us with a 'surrogate' account of the social world that dovetails with and reinforces established patterns of power and authority. In 'A Berkeley Education', Smith observes that, during this period, 'I wanted sociology to tell the truth, but I came to think that it didn't know how. The realities of people's daily lives were beyond anything sociology could speak of. [I] became preoccupied with sociology's strange divorce from the local actuality of people's lives' (1994: 54). In her opinion, sociology should be engaged with the moral and political task of challenging such distortions and telling uncomfortable truths about existing asymmetries of power, with how ingrained hierarchies of gender, class or race are perpetrated by established institutions that pay lip service to liberal ideals of freedom and equality of opportunity. With respect to women, insofar as they have, in the modern context, been largely relegated to a private sphere external to the activities of academe, politics and business, the abstracting and distorting character of sociological discourse has been especially pronounced in terms of misrepresenting the minutiae of women's everyday experiences, which are qualitatively distinct from those of men.

After graduating from Berkeley in 1963, Smith briefly taught at Berkeley and Essex, England, and then took up a full-time position at the University of British Columbia. Teaching and working in Canada added another dimension to Smith's theoretical direction. It fostered a heightened awareness of the process of ideological hegemony at the geopolitical level, insofar as Canadian sociology was at the time 'a colony of the American sociology establishment' (Smith 1992: 126). In combating this marginalization and coloniz-ation, Smith has made a considerable contribution to the develop-ment of a distinctive Canadian sociology that was more attuned to local conditions, attitudes and histories. In 1977, she moved to the Department of Sociology at the Ontario Institute for Studies in Education, which is affiliated with the University of Toronto, and she has more recently become Adjunct Professor at the University of Victoria, Canada. In a half-dozen major monographs, including *The Everyday World as Problematic*, *The Conceptual Practices of Power* and most recently *Writing the Social*, as well as innumerable articles, reviews and shorter pieces, Smith has assembled the building blocks of what she terms a 'sociology for women'. Her work also represents an influence that has been felt in women's studies more generally (Campbell and Manicom 1995). Smith's approach has, in essence, a tripartite character: first, a critical interrogation of the relationship between knowledge and institutionalized forms of power, especially as reflected in mainstream sociology; secondly, an attempt to forge the lineaments of a sociology for women, which in turn necessitates a critique of the gender biases within establishment sociology; and thirdly, to inquire into the practices of daily life, so as to supersede what she characterizes as the 'lack of connection between the everyday world and the sociology of the classrooms and the books' (1994: 54). A consideration of these three themes will constitute the major focus of the present chapter.

SOCIOLOGY AND THE 'RELATIONS OF RULING'

I shall begin with Smith's investigation into the role that sociology and other institutionalized discourses have played in the suppression and distortion of everyday life, particularly its gender component. This involves an analysis of what she terms the 'social organization of the objectified knowledges that are essential constituents of the relations of ruling of contemporary capitalism' (1990a: 1). The central tenet here is that existing apparatuses of power and authority have a vested interest in portraying the social world in a way that is congruent with their sociopolitical interests. Knowledge about society has an intrinsic connection to control over social processes, and hence with the phenomenon of power itself. In taking this stance, as Seidman (1994: 305) has perceptively noted, Smith's work has numerous affinities with the poststructuralist argument that there exists a close, even necessary connection between power and knowledge, an orientation that is especially marked in the work of Michel Foucault (1980). The discipline of sociology typically claims access to an objective knowledge of social life, and asserts that it is concerned with the investigation of real social events and processes. It has even arrogated to itself a kind of 'underdog ethos'. However, Smith claims, this ostensive identification with relatively marginalized and dispossessed segments of the population is belied by the fact that sociology is actually concerned, not with the domain of actual social experience, but with second-order textual constructions that are at a considerable remove from the delicate and largely hidden texture of everyday social relations. In this sense, overt political or moral commitments are largely irrelevant. 'The objectified knowledge of social science does not connect up with immediate realities', writes Smith. 'An intelligentsia that works within the objectified forms of knowledge of the relations of ruling does nothing to change that problem, no matter what its politics' (1992: 131). Sociologists, generally speaking, only 'know' the lifeworld in a vicarious sense. This gulf is actively perpetuated by the institutional character of sociology itself, which is engaged in a process of abstraction and hypostatization by virtue of its very history, organizational status, and commitment to what Bauman (1987) terms 'legislative reason'.

How does this procedure work? As has been often observed, sociology as an academic discipline is largely a product of the European Enlightenment and the nineteenth-century infatuation with objective, positivistic science (Seidman 1983). According to this historical scenario, social thought has traditionally ignored or denigrated everyday life and the 'private sphere' as trivial and inconsequential. As such, it was widely felt that the inchoate characteristics of profane social life had to be supplanted by a rigorous, abstract model of social structure and linear historical progression that displayed an intrinsic order, logical consistency and predictability, a view that sees the world as 'an essentially ordered totality' and allows for a 'sort of explanation of events which – if correct – is simultaneously a tool of prediction and (if required resources are available) of control' (Bauman 1987: 3). Such a model is, in Smith's terminology, 'extralocal', in the sense that it is removed from 'local and particular settings and relationships' (1990a: 2). General and universalistic concepts are substituted for the dense and rough-hewn particularities of daily social life. Moreover, these 'official' accounts do a considerable disservice to the actual lives and relationships as experienced by people on a first-hand basis. Sociology has usually assumed that such nomothetic models and explanations are isomorphic to, or congruent with, given social processes. Smith, however, differs strongly on this point. She contends that mainstream, institutionalized forms of sociology present us with versions of the social world that are systematically exclusionary and distorting. Smith is adamant that there is always the potential for multiple inter-pretations of social practices, not least those proffered by the actual participants themselves. Formalized accounts of these practices operate to suppress and de-legitimate unofficial or non-expert narratives, simply because they do not coincide with official interests, purposes and requirements. 'Repression', Smith observes, 'operates in part through the management of ignorance' (1992: 131). The indexical system of spatial and temporal coordinates, normative expectations and informal interpretive procedures that social actors utilize habitually in the course of their everyday lives and through which they construct a shared social world – what Smith terms the 'deictic order' – is replaced by a quite different referential and interpretive matrix. Biographical factors and pragmatic, action-oriented references are 'bracketed', or pushed to one side, by an abstract and essentially bureaucratic indexical system. Actual subjects are 'positioned' within this prescribed representational order, and construed as entities internal to the textual domain so constructed. Social actors are therefore transformed into objects of a formalized knowledge, and are drained of any real agency. This procedure conforms to what Smith labels 'textualization', which she describes as a 'detached and objectified mode' (1990a: 3) that locates actors outside the everyday lifeworld. In this manner, embodied, active subjects are deleted from the sociological gaze, and replaced by a system of abstract concepts and logical relationships that aim at a fully objective, detached, 'God's eye' perspective of the social world.

'Texts create their own internal ordering of subjectivity independent of the local setting in which the embodied subject reads, hears, or looks yet no deictic order or locking procedure is completed in the text or document', writes Smith. 'It remains to be completed in the relation between that and where the reader or hearer stands already' (1990a: 58).

Perhaps a concrete example might clarify Smith's approach. One of her main substantive interests concerns how the phenomenon of mental illness is constructed in and through official discourses of psychiatry, medicine and social work. Although aware of Foucault's (1973) existing work in this area, she is critical of his reluctance to move analysis beyond the level of the text, and of his tendency to ignore the role played by unequal gender relations within psychiatric and medical institutional practices and discourses (Smith 1990b: 108). The central essay in this context is 'K is Mentally Ill: The Anatomy of a Factual Account', originally published in the late 1970s. Here, Smith argues that all formal institutions, whether private or state-sponsored, have developed various techniques and procedures for the accumulation and interpretation of data regarding the 'correct' versus 'aberrant' behaviour of individuals. Institutions like mental hospitals, although they have an ostensive therapeutic function in society, are no exception to this. Doctors, nurses and administrators learn and reproduce a particular set of bureaucratic and professional practices and terminologies that become part of their essential frame of reference, particularly when they treat patients and make crucial diagnostic and administrative decisions. Through the application of this system of reference, 'local' events and phenomena – for instance, the subjective plight of particular disturbed or distressed individuals – are transformed into a set of neutral 'facts' which can then be effectively categorized and 'dealt with' by the organizational apparatus concerned that are empowered to handle such cases. The initial step in this process of institutionalization involves the identification of a given individual as suffering from a form of mental illness, which in turn requires that someone in the patient's immediate sphere of activity – a member of the family, legal guardian, or friend – engages in an informal process of labelling by which this person's behaviour is interpreted as erratic, unpredictable or self-destructive. So there is a complex and highly mediated process occurring here – a person's actions are identified as 'abnormal' by others close to them, who then approach professionals with this non-expert diagnosis. Medical professionals scrutinize this information, and/or interview the individual already labelled as deviant or abnormal, and make their own diagnosis about possible mental illness. The potential consequences are, of course, very serious for all parties concerned, and can lead to pharmacological intervention, involuntary detainment, and worse.

In the essay 'K is Mentally Ill', Smith focuses on a young woman, designated 'K' for the purpose of this study, whom her new roommates initially saw as a well-adjusted, physically active and intelligent individual. Over time, however, K's actions appeared increasingly irrational and bizarre: she would develop inconsistent likes and dislikes *vis-à-vis* food, seemed unable to plan or budget household expenses suitably, was uncomfortable in group situations and cut off conversations abruptly. Eventually, K's roommates decided that she was mentally ill, and contacted the appropriate authorities. In a detailed textual analysis of the roommate's accounts of K's allegedly problematic behaviour, Smith attempts to demonstrate the actual procedure by which such accounts are constructed and how they present themselves as 'authoritative', factual versions of the events they claim to describe. What is actually happening is a process of exclusion and objectification, whereby the volition, and indeed the very *presence* of the subject under scrutiny, is progressively marginalized and de-legitimated by the discourse in question, and quite literally 'written out' of the textual account. In particular, events and actions are torn out of their appropriate context, yoked together with abstract categories and labels, and presented as a neutral set of irrefutable facts to the reader of the sanctioned narrative. By so intervening between the reader and the object of knowledge, individuals in positions of power and authority within official institutions substitute their textually mediated version of events for the actor's own experiences and explanations of the same occurrences. 'Authority bleeds from the institutional relations of ruling to the relations of authority at the surface of media', as Smith puts it (1990b: 101). As non-experts, we are conditioned to accept such authoritative accounts as isomorphic with actual events, and hence as 'truthful' and 'convincing', at least rhetorically.

Smith asserts that there is always the possibility of multiple accounts of such occurrences; official versions merely utilize a given set of 'authorization procedures' to sanction its perspective and to undermine or efface the subject's own account. It is quite possible, with the appropriate context uppermost in mind, to interpret K's actions as not especially bizarre or anomalous, as mere idiosyncrasies rather than unambiguous evidence of 'mental illness'. The essential point is that all accounts of social reality, including authoritative ones, must rely on a process of creative interpretation, by which we exclude certain factors, highlight others, and use rhetorical figures or tropes to authorize a given version of events. (This is not to say that all versions are equally truthful or acceptable, according to Smith; such a postmodernist relativism is something that she seeks to avoid, as we shall see in due course.) Again, however, what is distinctive about official, authoritative accounts is that they engage in the systematic occlusion of appropriate contextual information and strive to discredit, implicitly or explicitly, the subject's own version of events, and suppress their own experience of time and space, activities and relationships, personal values and biases – in short, to circumscribe a person's very subjectivity. When authoritative accounts do make use of a social agent's knowledge, they generally do so in a selective and distorting fashion, by 'framing' such understandings within pre-existing formalized categories and explanatory modes. Official discourses now constitute the essential referential matrix of interpretation, rather than the subject's own experiential sphere of action.

It is instructive to view Smith's critical strategy here as a version of ideological criticism, or *ideologiekritik*, as it has been taken up and practiced by the tradition of Western Marxism (Eagleton 1991; Geuss 1981). Smith's own writings tend to reinforce this perspective, insofar as she is highly sympathetic to Marx's materialist method and such twentieth-century Marxists as Merleau-Ponty, who also sought to combat the abstractions of scientific positivism and return us to the terrain of embodied, lived experience (Smith 1974, 1981). Although commentators have isolated several quite different meanings of the concept of ideology in Marx's writings, one consistent account that emerges turns on the notion that ideology is a representational system that substitutes abstract ideas and concepts for a properly materialist understanding of social relations and historical processes (Larrain 1983). Ideology is not to be understood as 'false consciousness' (a term Marx never actually used), a wholly imaginary or illusory picture of reality. But because it is abstracted from the actual ground of social relationships, and substitutes fixed concepts for events-in-process, ideological accounts present us with a distorting view of events, in a manner that validates the existing organization of society instead of what might be possible, or by deflecting our attention away from immanent tendencies towards sociocultural change. Through this process of reification and 'naturalization', ideology must be understood as symptomatic of human alienation and the hegemonic status of philosophical idealism in the modern period, and hence of the supersession of lived reality by ideas that project themselves as eternal and irrefutable truths. Ideology consists of 'ideas and images through which the class that rules society by virtue of its domination of the means of production, orders, organizes, and sanctions the social relations that sustain its domination', suggests Smith. It 'directs us to look for and at the actual practical organization of the production of images, ideas, symbols, concepts, vocabularies, as means for us to think about our world' (1987: 54). So ideology is not simply a neutral belief system; it is inscribed within the matrix of social activities that structure our relationship to the world and helps to generate a particular knowledge of it. Accounts or explanations of the social world are therefore 'ideological' in Smith's sense if they bypass the world of lived experience and proffer an abstract, idealized model that is constructed *within* discourse, and that represents a form of encoding and textual organization conforming to a pre-existing form of what Alvin Gouldner (1976) has called 'ideological grammar'. For Smith, there is no fast and easy line to be drawn between truth and falsity, bias and objectivity. Rather, the distinction lies primarily between *different modes* of narrating and interpreting events and the nature of their correspondence to the relations of ruling. The alternative to such ideological accounts involves the articulation of what Smith terms 'primary narratives' (1990b: 157). These are commentaries that are expressive of social conditions as they are actually lived and experienced by the social actors themselves, and that attempt to delimit this process of textualization and abstraction, or at least make us reflexively aware that such an ideological process is at work (Thompson 1984). The ideological procedure is

> a method of producing an account [that] selects from the primary narrative an array of particulars intending the ideological schema. The selection and assembly procedure discards competing reasons (*her* reasons) and permits the insertion of ideological connectives. The resulting collection of particulars will intend the ideological schema as its 'underlying' pattern. [The] resulting factual account may be entirely accurate, but the order that provides its grammar, its logic, and the connectives sequencing its clauses will be provided by schemata originating in the discourse rather than by an explication of actual social relations.
>
> (Smith 1990b: 171)

It is important to realize that Smith is not simply addressing an arcane philosophical issue here, or ruminating about the manner in which we go about constructing narratives about our world. Ideological practices are structured in such a way as to reinforce existing patterns of power and authority, and therefore provide an essential bulwark for the maintenance of systems of domination in Western societies. Ideologies are *practical* – they motivate people, reinforce patterns of action, and legitimate existing institutions and ways of doing things. The evacuation of subjectivity and agency and the naturalization of existing power structures that are an inherent part of the 'grammar' of ideology operate to legitimate official, bureaucratic versions of the truth, as opposed to marginalized and unofficial ones. As Smith writes, 'ideological practices are not only in texts, they are functional constituents of a ruling apparatus. Ideological circles transpose actual events, located in specific places and performed by real individuals, into the generalized forms in which they can be known, knowable and actionable within an abstracted conceptual mode of ruling and organization' (1990b: 172). And, as intimated earlier, sociology as an academic discipline is not entirely innocent of this 'ideological effect'. For much of its history, sociology has sought to identify with the so-called 'hard' sciences, and has enthusiastically adopted positivistic and objectivistic methodologies, forms of explanation, and approaches to theory construction. In practice, what this has entailed is a tacit acceptance of a Cartesian epistemology, in which a solitary mind reflects on an independently existing object-world, through which it derives 'correct' ideas that are felt to be isomorphic with this reality. There is a dual strategy occurring here: first, the active knower is banished from the production of sociological knowledge, because objectivity demands the suppression of individual and social influences, biases and values. What is expressly denied is that the knower is necessarily an embodied entity, situated in a particular time and place, and irrevocably part of the world that is under investigation. This account suggests that knowledge is value-free, and phenomena like reflexivity, corporeality and subjectivity are irrelevances. Secondly, Cartesianism (in the guise of mainstream social science) disavows the notion that the objects of knowledge – in this case, the social actors who are being studied – have an entirely legitimate and wholly independent perspective into their own practices, beliefs and activities. Sociological explanations typically circumvent this experiential realm and assert that social behaviour is rigidly determined by the underlying structural properties of a given

189

sociocultural system, the most notorious example being the functionalist paradigm (which can take on a liberal or Marxian hue), in
which the actions of subjects, or 'cultural dopes', blindly follow
existing norms and merely reproduce existing social structures. In
short, sociological models often simply bypass the everyday
lifeworld, and, in so doing, play an important role in legitimating
elite knowledges and upholding the relations of ruling. 'Sociological
methods of thinking and research write over and interpret the site
of experience', asserts Smith. Its 'methods of analyzing experience
and of writing society produce an objectified version that subsumes
people's actual speech and what they have to tell about themselves;
its statements eliminate the presence of subjects as agents in
sociological texts; it converts people from subjects to objects of
investigation' (1990b: 31).

A WOMAN'S POINT OF VIEW

Given Smith's strongly pro-feminist leanings, it is important to
understand more precisely how the relations of ruling are bound up
with the phenomenon of gender. In tandem with many other
feminist writers, she argues that the abstracting and reifying
tendencies of official textual accounts of the world, especially as
reflected in the discipline of sociology, are part and parcel of a
pronounced asymmetry of power between men and women in
contemporary society. Simply put, it is men who, as a distinct social
category, are primarily in charge of the construction and regulation
of the relations of ruling, at both the organizational and discursive
levels. It is therefore no accident that official discourses operate in
such a way to abstract from everyday and 'everynight' social
practices. In taking this stance, Smith follows a well-established
line of feminist argumentation that men tend to occupy (at least on
the ideological plane) the terrain of the formal, the incorporeal and
the hyperrational, whereby women generally partake of the unofficial, the embodied and the affective. Feminists have, for instance,
analysed in great detail how Western rationality is structured by
expressions of gender in a manner that reinforces stereotypical male
identities of autonomous self-control and emotional detachment,
whilst at the same time devaluing feminine qualities (Harding
1986, 1990; Keller 1985; Rose 1983). Whatever their theoretical
differences, radical feminists generally agree that the blind
commitment of modern science to standards of objectivity and

formalized method – what Mary O'Brien (1989) aptly calls the 'tyranny of the abstract' – serves to marginalize the human body and its connectedness to others and to the wider environment, debase woman-centred values, and denigrate the sphere of the qualitative and the informal.

Historically speaking, what cannot be disputed is that sociology has been mainly conducted by men, and it has tended to investigate those manifestations of the social world that are connected to extant power structures – such as the state apparatus, economic systems, or movements rooted in social class (Oakley 1981). This is a world created by and for men, using a vocabulary and a descriptive idiom that is congruent with the characteristics of this domain. Since early modern times, women have been largely excluded from the public sphere. Lacking full access to this world and the language that it habitually utilizes, women have, in the main, been relegated to what are generally viewed as trivial domestic concerns. With certain exceptions (such as ethnomethodology), from the perspective of mainstream sociology the sphere of everyday practices is of limited interest, or when it is a topic of investigation, the activities and forms of consciousness typical of this world are transcribed into rarefied textual constructs that bear little relation to their real nature. Since sociological descriptions have been unduly influenced by the male point of view, reflecting an overly formalized stand-point, the result has been that women's experiences are 'organized extra-locally, abstracted, grounded in universal forms, and objectified' (Smith 1990a: 6). So-called 'malestream' sociological accounts of the everyday world effectively rob women of any real agency, of any meaningful capacity to understand and transform their world. The discursive images that sociology constructs are then proffered back to the very subjects and their experiential world from which they have been removed. Sociology therefore constitutes an idealized and homogenized world of textual representations that real human behaviour is supposed to approximate, regardless of whether it actually does so in reality. In her essay 'Femininity as Discourse', Smith argues that received notions of gender, such as commonplace ideals of femininity, are constructed discursively and projected as already-constituted entities, rather than what they really are: a series of social practices embedded in concrete socio-historical activities and relations and that are undergoing constant change and transformation.

Under these conditions, the viewpoint of women tends to remain concrete, localized and particularistic in nature. As such, the essential challenge, as Smith sees it, is to develop a woman-centred sociology that respects the integrity of everyday life, and hence the 'lived' character of female experience, but without translating this experiential realm into abstracted textual forms that dovetail with the requirements of bureaucratic power and control. It has been suggested that Smith's stance here is vulnerable to arguments often marshalled against 'essentialism' or 'feminist standpoint theory', in which women's penchant for the concrete and the particular is felt to be both an inherent component of their subjectivity or even biology, as well as in some sense epistemologically superior. This is a position that certain approaches, especially ecofeminism, are prone to (Clough 1993; Hekman 1997; Longino 1993). In responding to this charge, Smith (1993, 1997) does assert that women as a group do tend to have a distinctive outlook, but that this is a perspective rooted in particular sociohistorical circumstances, in terms of both the institutional or structural context of action and the more mundane forms of social intercourse. What this means is that we cannot talk about gender as a general, all-embracing category, but only in relation to 'particular local historical sites of women's experience[,] as multiple and sometimes contradictory relations' (Smith 1990a: 159). For Smith, it must be understood that capitalism as an economic system has encouraged a general process of abstraction and idealization, especially through the growing importance of the commodity-form and what Habermas refers to as the 'colonization' of the lifeworld by the imperatives of bureaucratic systems. As discussed earlier, such critical theorists as Adorno and Marcuse felt the extension of the commodity into virtually every aspect of life under late capitalism is correlated with a process of intensive quantification, in which the lived, subjective aspects of human existence are reduced to universal, abstract units of value that facilitate the exchange of commodities through the medium of money. And because men are largely in control of the mechanisms of capitalist production, distribution and exchange, their worldview tends to take on a hyperrational and reified character. 'Capitalism creates a wholly new terrain of social relations external to the local terrain and the particularities of personally mediated economic and social relations', writes Smith. 'These extralocal, impersonal, universalized forms of action became the exclusive terrain of men, while women became correspondingly confined to a reduced local sphere of action organized by particularistic relationships' (1987: 5). In malestream sociological discourse, the body – especially the female body – is marginalized and commodified, separated from the functioning of wider institutions and the abstract knowledges used to operate them. Any consideration of embodiment is generally restricted to women's role in biological reproduction and the maintenance of the domestic sphere. 'Men's daily environment had to be brought into line with the practices of an existence out of this world', observes Smith (1987: 213), which means that male control of the public sphere tends to reinforce a conception of social existence in which corporeality is not considered significant. In taking this position, Smith follows Simone de Beauvoir's suggestion in *The Second Sex* (1984) that immanence is characteristic of women's lives, whereas transcendence is more typical of the world of men. Hence, the relations of ruling have a strongly gendered character. The central conclusion that emerges from this discussion is that there is nothing 'essential' about men that encourages the reified character of the masculinist worldview; it is a by-product of their location in a specific set of social and cultural practices that reinforces a certain ideological perspective on the world, or what Pierre Bourdieu (1977) has termed *doxa*: schemas of thought and knowledge that are unquestioned and viewed as natural. It also means that men, by virtue of their membership in a distinct social category and set of sociohistorical relations (rather than as individuals), are invested with a certain degree of authority in both the public and private spheres, and enjoy the lion's share of institutionalized power over women. In the context of late capitalism, extant forms of power are, in Smith's words, reflected in the 'application of systematically rational modes of theorizing and inquiry in a wide variety of settings, bringing politics, literature, art, and warfare under their dominion. These expansions of men's powers in the elaboration and expansion of the relations of ruling in this mode were built first on women's exclusion from the extralocal organization of market relations' (1987: 213).

By adopting this stance, Smith wants to abandon a certain line of feminist thinking that strives to identify 'gender differences' as inherent qualities that are fixed, immutable and universal. This would be to confuse something that is constructed in discourse – in this case, idealized textual images of 'men' versus 'women', understood as a simple binary opposition – as opposed to grasping gender as a *social practice*, as an historical phenomenon that must be understood in a processual sense, as contradictory sets of social relations that are always open to further transformation. A more promising line of inquiry is to 'take up "gender" from within, exploring social relations gendering the particular local historical

193

sites of women's experience[,] attending to specificities, not gender in the abstract, not as total, but as multiple and sometimes contradictory relations' (Smith 1990a: 159). As Smith herself notes, this move recapitulates Marx and Engels's critique of Ludwig Feuerbach's speculative philosophical anthropology. Although Feuerbach was correct to repudiate Hegelian idealism, he failed to go beyond simplified and abstract concepts of 'humanity in general' or 'species-being'. Such purely metaphysical notions must be re-placed by an investigation into the concrete social relations that regulate and organize people's everyday lives. However, Marx and Engels themselves failed to extend this insight into the realm of phenomenological analysis, or the experience of gendered social differences. These are oversights that Smith seeks to remedy. Her goal is to explore gender as a 'distinctive effect of a complex of social relations specifically defining femininity and organizing, in and across actual local sites of people's lives, the homogeny of gender difference' (1990a: 160). The investigative model that she envisages is roughly as follows: women are involved actively in the construction of particular social patterns and relationships, especially concerning the domestic sphere and the world of everyday life – biological reproduction and child-rearing, shopping, cleaning, preparing meals, and engaging in informal modes of communic-ation. However, discourses about 'femininity' that circulate through-out society are also influenced strongly by the wider structural and institutional context, particularly images generated by the mass media regarding what constitutes ideal examples of feminine behaviour (dress, demeanour, bodily deportment, idiomatic language-use), what Bourdieu calls the 'habitus'. These iconic images are linked to capitalist imperatives, and act back on women's social relationships and self-conceptions in a constraining and exclusionary fashion. Smith's essential point is that virtually all social relations are textually mediated – and increasingly so, as our society becomes increasingly media- and image-saturated. As such, we must understand the complex dialectic between the gendered nature of everyday social practices and broader sociocultural images and discourses that are produced within the public sphere. This dual sociological focus – actual practices sustained by embodied subjects occurring in real times and places, and more generalized images and textual constructions that transcend specific temporal and spatial locations – is the key to understanding how gender as a social practice is constituted within the context of late capitalist societies. The textual mediation of gender is something that gives norms of masculinity and femininity (including the formation of desire and bodily appearance) a relative coherence and uniformity across widely separated geographical and temporal settings, because they provide people with ubiquitous reference points that do the 'work' of interpretation for specific individuals. These phenomena are ultimately 'overdetermined' by market forces which, as has been widely observed, are increasingly global in character. 'The ideological circle locks a fixed relation between the textually given and interpretive schemata established in the discourse' (Smith 1990a: 179), in a manner that provides an authoritative interpretive schema injecting specific gendered meanings into local practices, relationships and events.

In the previous discussion, Smith would seem to be adhering to a familiar poststructuralist line: that human consciousness is constructed in and through extant discursive formations, and that subjects are really 'effects' of pre-existing systems of power/ knowledge, as Foucault has argued. This would, however, imply that any sociopolitical agency we have is largely illusory, and that the possibility of wholesale structural change within late capitalist society is a remote possibility. This is a scenario that Smith seeks to avoid. She insists that this 'ideological circle' can be disrupted: that women can gain a greater critical awareness of how the process of textual determination works and they can then act on the basis of this knowledge, especially in a collective sense, to transform their circumstances in the direction of increased autonomy. Women, she asserts, are 'active, skilled, make choices, consider, are not fooled or foolish. With discourse there is play and interplay' (1990a: 203). In other words, systems, discursive or otherwise, are not immune to change, and a critical reason still has a central role to play in exposing the nature of such systems and highlighting points of vulnerability. Even women who conform on the surface to proffered gender stereotypes and appear to defer to male authority can do so in an ironic, double-edged fashion, in a manner that does not necessarily signal passive compliance, but rather what Michel de Certeau identifies as 'tactics', as discussed in Chapter 7. These stereotypes can be reversed or creatively manipulated, as Judith Butler has demonstrated in *Gender Trouble* (1991). At the same time, there still remains a definite asymmetry of power in place, inasmuch as media-generated images of gender continue to reflect and ultimately reinforce the prerogatives of male power and the reproduction of capitalism. As such, we must go beyond postmodernist notions of 'play' or ironic reversal in order to grasp the underlying socioeconomic mechanisms of exploitation and domination that generate such stereotypical images – which means that Marxist political economy still has a crucial role to play in understanding the contours of late capitalist societies (Smith 1989). We cannot be satisfied wholly with remaining at the level of discursive or cultural analysis alone, mainly because the 'inequities of the economic burdens born by women and their access to wealth and power are real'. Bluntly put, the 'mass media and its increasingly concentrated and global ownership by capital, the slippage of our societies towards new forms of totalitarianism [are] not combated by resorting to a politics of theory that denies the very possibility of investigating, describing, and seeking to understand what is going on so that people could know' (Smith 1993: 198).

The preceding discussion helps to explain why Smith does not want to abandon the notion of socioeconomic and political analysis and critique. Her position is that feminist theory needs to pursue a critical interrogation into the interrelationship between the structural organization of late capitalism and the specific forms that patriarchy has taken in contemporary society. The knowledge generated by such an investigation can facilitate the construction of a specifically women's point of view on social reality, 'an experience of being, of society, of social and personal process that must be given form and expression in the culture, whether as knowledge, as art, or as literature or political action' (Smith 1987: 36). Ideological critique in the form of a female-centred social theory can give women the intellectual resources to participate more fully in the political and cultural life of their societies, to articulate forms of thought and self- expression that are congruent with their own lived experiences, aspirations and hopes. The point of Smith's approach is therefore to 'make visible and to analyze the relations of ruling that create the phenomena that traditional sociology mystifies as natural kinds' (Longino 1993: 203). To control the means of intellectual production, as Marx noted, is also to have enormous influence over the way consciousness itself is shaped, and so the production of social knowledge from a women's perspective has a crucial role to play in any viable emancipatory project. To reverse women's oppression and their exclusion from the epicentres of power requires a 'deliberate remaking of our relations with others and of these the relations of our knowledge must be key, for the dimensions of our oppression are only fully revealed in discoveries that go beyond what direct experience will teach us' (Smith 1987: 107). To give voice to the silenced requires that women become knowers rather than known, active subjects rather than passive objects of scientific discourse. In this, Smith would appear to adhere to a Habermasian 'strong programme' of reason, albeit an expanded, 'corporeal' rationality that reminds one strongly of Lefebvre's 'dialectical reason'. But to adopt such a point of view is to abandon the pretense of the 'God's eye' point of view encouraged by malestream social science, a universalizing and implicitly normative perspective masquerading as a value-neutral stance, one that is blithely unaware of the conditions of its own existence and of its embeddedness within specific sets of social practices and historical circumstances. By contrast, the central focus of a sociology for women must be represented by the standpoint of the situated, embodied and reflexive subject.

> A sociology for women preserves the presence of subjects as knowers and as actors. It does not transform subjects into the objects of study or make use of conceptual devices for eliminating the active presence of subjects. Its methods of thinking and its analytic procedures must preserve the presence of the active and experiencing subject. A sociology is a systematically developed knowledge of society and social relations. [We] go further than Marx in insisting that both subject matter and the 'head' that theorizes it as well as its theorizing are enfolded in the existence of our subject matter. A sociology for women must be conscious of its necessary indexicality and hence that its meaning remains to be completed by a reader who is situated just as she is – a particular woman reading somewhere at a particular time amid the particularities of her everyday world – and that it is the capacity of our sociological texts as she enlivens them, to reflect upon, to expand, and to enlarge her grasp of the world she reads in, and that is the world that completes the meaning of the text as she reads.
>
> (Smith 1987: 105–6)

THE EVERYDAY/EVERYNIGHT WORLD

According to Smith, the everyday world must be the main focus of a sociology for women, rather than a textually mediated discourse that reflects the material interests of privileged groups and bolsters the relations of ruling. The everyday lifeworld is produced through mundane but highly skilled practices and accomplishments on the part of specific social actors. However, we remain largely ignorant of daily life and how it operates, particularly with 'how people are knitted into the extended social relations of a contemporary capitalist economy and society and not discoverable with them' (Smith 1987: 110). To elucidate this nexus must be one of the paramount concerns of a critical feminist sociology. This is because the standpoint of women is generally 'situated outside textually mediated discourse, and hence exists within the actuality of our everyday lives. We must direct our attention to an embodied subject located in a particular actual historical setting' (Smith 1987: 108). Even textually mediated images and relations are ultimately played out in the locale of the everyday world, and it is precisely this domain that has been more or less ignored by orthodox sociology. Whereas traditional social science has typically suppressed the presence of the (female) subject, a feminist sociology must reverse this, and bring the active subject back into the picture. In this approach, Smith demonstrates her appreciation for such micro-oriented sociologies as ethnomethodology and symbolic interactionism, because these help us to articulate an 'insider's knowledge' of language and other sociocultural practices. Her writings are peppered with references to such social thinkers as Harold Garfinkel, Erving Goffman, George Herbert Mead, Alfred Schütz, and more recently Mikhail Bakhtin (Smith 1998). At the same time, however, her fidelity to the political cause of the feminist movement has sensitized her to the limitations of such approaches. Although the writings of Schütz and others do operate quite effectively to draw our attention towards the subject's own practices and the relevant biographical and pragmatic setting of his or her activities, and to demonstrate the inherent limitations of structuralist-type explanations, there is no real motivation in such approaches to go beyond a surface description of these practices, so as to grasp the underlying mechanisms of domination, and to provide a moral critique of existing social arrangements with an eye to transforming them. What is lacking in established forms of microsociology is a utopian vision of a transfigured social landscape, a belief in the possibility of a society with a more equitable distribution of power and resources and more closely attuned to the possibilities of human self-realization, community and solidarity. Any sociology worth pursuing must combine an intimate understanding of real individuals and the material conditions of their existence, including how our activities are jointly co-ordered in time and space, with an insight into how these conditions operate to suppress the legitimate aspirations of marginalized groups towards greater autonomy and self-organization. The problem with theories like ethnomethodology is that, although they acknowledge that sociological accounts are creative interpretations in which there is an active relation between knower and known, and that all such descriptions are in an important sense context-dependent, they tend to assume that the Schützian 'natural attitude' is the only possible one, that there is no real potential for transforming consciousness into a more intensively reflexive form, what Paul Ricoeur (1981) refers to as a 'depth hermeneutics'. The latter requires an understanding of how everyday practices are connected to wider social institutions and processes that are themselves historically situated, and a heightened awareness of our own locatedness in these activities and organizations, as subjects with particular gender, class and racial affiliations and experiences. 'Located in the actualities of our everyday life, we cannot grasp how it is put together', writes Smith (1992: 131). Hence, there is no appeal in her work to 'raw', unmediated experience as some sort of privileged site of authenticity or superior knowledge.

Critique, as Smith understands it, is therefore a form of inquiry into the nature of everyday life that involves 'explicating our practices of doing, hearing, and reading descriptions to identify how these practices interpose between us and that of which we speak. It identifies a problem in how these practices structure our relation to what is described' (1990a: 91). It is imperative that we go beyond the lay social actor's account of their own practices, inasmuch as these may be ideologically circumscribed, but without denigrating these accounts or transcribing them into formalized and distanciated sociological categories. There is a delicate balancing act involved here. On the one hand, we must respect the integrity of the experiences of actual human subjects and remain highly cognizant of the proximate settings involved, particularly the somatic aspects, our 'bodily being and activities of looking, touching, smelling, hearing, etc.' (Smith 1996b: 194). Yet, on the other hand, we must not be satisfied with remaining at the level of such 'naive' accounts, if we want to grasp underlying structures and processes that reinforce relations of domination in ways that agents may not be fully cognizant of. 'The everyday world is not fully understandable within its own scope', suggests Smith. 'It is organized by social relations not fully apparent in it nor contained in it' (1987: 176). So we require the services of Mead and Garfinkel,

but we need to supplement this with a Marxian-inspired institutional analysis. The 'phenomenological deficit' in Marx's own
writings does not mean that political economy should be abandoned
in critical feminist inquiry, because the microsociological processes
of everyday life must be related to the wider, and increasingly global
mechanisms of capital accumulation. By restricting sociological
investigation to the formal structure of conversational exchanges,
for instance, ethnomethodology collapses into a kind of solipsism
that takes members' own narratives as the only real object of
analysis, whilst at the same time appealing to the language of a self-
legitimating ideology masquerading as descriptive, value-neutral
social science. Although they claim to examine the everyday
lifeworld and aspire to understand the practices contained therein as
practical, indexical accomplishments, theories like ethnomethodology have in reality operated with an atrophied notion of what
constitutes 'context' that excludes arbitrarily such phenomena as
history, structural inequities of power, or ideology (Chua 1977;
Freund and Abrams 1976). In eschewing the path of normative
engagement and *ideologiekritik*, the result, as Tim May usefully puts
it, has been the development of an 'idealist and empiricist social
theory, which is inevitably conservative in orientation and has
achieved little in the way of advancing an understanding and
explanation of the dynamics of social relations' (1996: 92). So for
Smith the 'natural attitude' has a specific history and a gendered,
ideological character, and it tends to operate in such a way so as to
uphold existing asymmetries of power. The problem is essentially
one of a lack of critical reflexivity: ethnomethodologists suppose
that there can be a more or less direct correspondence between
actor's categories and sociological descriptions, and that there is no
essential tension between them. They remain mired within the
perspective of mainstream sociology, because they fail to consider
that the extant relations of ruling can affect radically how social
phenomena are constructed and interpreted at the discursive level.
Put differently, they do not consider that sociologists and the
individuals and groups they study do not have an equal capacity to
construct accounts of their own practices in a manner that reflects
faithfully their first-hand experiences of the lifeworld. 'Universities
suck knowledge out of people outside the university, put it through
a special filtering procedure provided by social science, and confine
it to specialists', asserts Smith. 'It serves the organization of ruling
people, rather than serving people' (1992: 130). Even in interpretive
microsociologies, it would seem, it is only the (generally male)

sociologist who is privileged to speak. Relations of ruling always intervene between formalist textual accounts and a social agent's actual practices, and ethnomethodology is blind to this process of mediation. The absence of reflexive critique and an inattentiveness to how the relations of ruling function with respect to sociological descriptions in approaches like symbolic interactionism or ethnomethodology means that 'textual surfaces presuppose an organization of power as the concerting of people's activities and the uses of organization to enforce processes producing a version of the world that is peculiarly one-sided, that is known only from within the modes of ruling, and that defines the objects of its power' (Smith 1987: 84).

In rejecting mainstream sociological approaches, whether functionalist or micro-oriented, a currently fashionable alternative is to embrace a postmodernist relativism, to accept the intrinsically pluralistic nature of all accounts of the social world and their epistemic equivalence. However, this is not a path that Smith chooses to follow. She proposes to move the focus away from arcane and obstructive epistemological debates about what 'truth' really means, towards what she takes to be a more productive consideration of 'how our everyday worlds are organized and how they are shaped and determined by relations that extend beyond them' (1987: 121). Smith seeks to recapitulate the trajectory followed by earlier existential phenomenologists, from the realm of epistemology – the *idée fixe* of Western philosophy at least since Descartes – towards a reflection on the nature of social ontology, particularly the existential fabric of the everyday world. This does not mean that Smith advocates the abandonment of any notion of truth, but she does caution us that any epistemological claims we advance must be tentative, fallibalistic and pragmatic in nature, and rooted in our shared participation in, and joint construction of, the everyday lifeworld. Our knowledge of the social world must be 'an ontology, a method of thinking (a theory if you like) about how the social can be said to exist so that we can describe it in ways the can be checked back to how it actually is. The very character of the social itself that lies in the ongoing active recreation of a world in common, this possibility exists' (Smith 1987: 122). Yet not all accounts of the lifeworld are equally valid: *some are relatively more ideological than others*, if only because the powerful have a vested interest in projecting a doxic version of the social world that is congruent with their material interests, thereby maintaining the relations of ruling. Oppressed and marginalized groups, by contrast, are motivated to expose such obfuscations and advance a more complete and multifaceted image of the world. In arguing this, Smith (1993) rejects the Althusserian argument that all subjects are inextricably mired in ideology, and that there is no escape, even partial, from its effects. She acknowledges that, in an important sense, there are multiple social worlds and viewpoints. However, this recognition is not tantamount to the acceptance of a radical relativism, in which there is no possibility of dialogue across such language games, mainly because we are jointly interwoven into a shared lifeworld through our mundane, corporeal activities. As Ian Burkitt suggests, we have to understand that at the heart of the everyday lifeworld is a 'group of interrelated, interacting beings, and also an environment of objects with which the active, communicating beings in the group are engaged' (1994: 14). The current preoccupation with epistemology and the 'problem' of relativism proves to be a *non sequitur* if we shift our focus away from the level of the text toward the material quality of lived social relations, and of human embodiment itself. Hence, Smith is not making foundationalist claims of a modernist sort, but she is arguing that we need to be more aware of a situated and embodied form of knowledge that has largely escaped the attention of sociology.

Marx and Engels, insists Smith, have already shown us the rudiments of such an approach. We must, as they argued in *The German Ideology* and elsewhere, start from real individuals and the material conditions of their activities. If we adhere to this imperative, our accounts of social relations can be more or less faithful to the contours of the everyday lifeworld, in the same sense that a map is a faithful (if not exact) rendering of the layout of streets in a given town or a network of highways, a resource through which we tacitly 'make sense' of the experiential world. At the same time, we must abandon the desire to construct a singular, universalistic and objectively 'certain' account of such relations, or what Lyotard calls a 'metanarrative'. So the pluralistic nature of such sites of experience is only a problem for sociology if we aspire to construct a meta-discourse that supersedes all such particularities. 'A sociology beginning in people's everyday/everynight experience takes for granted that experience is as various as people are. It does not seek to supersede this variety by constructing a version that overrides all others', suggests Smith. 'The project is to explore concerting and co-ordering and hence the organization and relations that generate the varieties of lived experience' (1996b: 172). Once we accept the existence of an ontology of actual activities located in particular sociohistorical settings, the problem of relativism effectively disappears. But to do this consistently, we need to go beyond textually mediated accounts of society that are intertwined with the organizational needs of the relations of ruling, in order to develop a 'knowledge of the social relations within which we work and struggle as subjects' (Smith 1987: 140–1). We must begin with individuals as active subjects, engaged pragmatically in an endless series of everyday projects and accomplishments, that are located in the same lifeworld that we inhabit. We are active in this world, not only as 'knowers', but as 'doers', as skilled and accomplished members in tandem with others. Hence, we co-participate in the construction of a shared lifeworld. Since sociologists are part of the everyday world they study, in a very real and embodied sense, they can 'know' this world in the sense that Vico envisaged. In short, the sociology that Smith envisages 'insists that its grasp of the world be constrained not by a discourse organized for the theoretical subject tucking his own life out of sight, but for subjects situated outside discourse in the actualities of their everyday' (1987: 142).

In exploring the indexical accomplishments and social relations that are immanent in the everyday, such a sociology must be concerned to develop new 'methods of thinking and writing texts that will relate us to each other in ways that preserve the presence of subjects in the text as knowers' (Smith 1987: 211). By this, she means an inquiry into social relations that starts from a point outside textually mediated accounts, and that acknowledges that the standpoint of women undermines the authority of official knowledges as these are constructed in various institutional domains. But the perspective of women is not the only one that is potentially subversive of the relations of ruling. Smith recognizes this, which explains why in more recent works she talks more about a 'sociology for people', as opposed to a 'sociology for women', and begins to align herself more explicitly with the so-called 'new social movements', including gay rights activism or radical ecology. Whereas official knowledges are concerned primarily with the functioning and continued existence of established institutions, a sociology for people would be more fully sensitized to the 'felt' needs and experiences of individuals and groups, and which can give marginalized groups the intellectual tools necessary to expose and understand their own oppression. Specifically, Smith proposes an 'alternative, reflexive, and materialist method of developing a systematic consciousness of our own society through which we can become conscious both of the social organization and relations of the objectified knowledges of the ruling institutions and of our tacit and unconscious complicity in them' (1990b: 7). Part of the process of constructing an alternative sociology involves circumventing the 'ideological circle' mentioned above, in which 'facts' are constructed by an authoritative interpretive community in a manner that is co-terminous with the relations of ruling. Since the role that asymmetrical power relations play in organizing the textual forms of official accounts of the social world is generally occluded, through a process that Michel Pêcheux (1982) has labelled 'misrecognition', we must bring these ideological determinants to consciousness. This, in turn, involves recourse to 'primary' rather than textually mediated narratives. Without supposing that there can be a version of the social world that can be totally 'ideology-free', Smith would argue that there are accounts that are relatively less compromised by their relationship to the relations of ruling, and that serve the goal of sociopolitical critique and human emancipation better than others. Primary narratives, because they are more attuned to the rhythms and exigencies of everyday life, are to be preferred to formalized, bureaucratic accounts.

> In identifying ideological methods, the contrast drawn is not between ideological and scientific, between biased and unbiased (objective), procedures for generating or reading accounts. We do not suppose that there is one objective account of 'what actually happened' against which other accounts may be measured. The lived actuality remains a resource in memory in a relation of reflection through which 'what actually happened' arises. Here ideological practices in encoding and constituting 'what actually happened' will be contrasted with procedures which are directly expressive of the lived actuality in experience. The latter we will call 'primary narrative' modes of expression. The difference is not one of accuracy, completeness, or truth. It is one of methods of telling and interpreting. [Ideological accounts] originate in a textual discourse (a 'conversation' mediated by texts) rather than being constrained by connections arising as expressions of the lived actuality.
>
> (Smith 1990b: 157)

So whereas primary narratives empower readers to use their own experiences in order to draw conclusions regarding the veracity of particular sociological descriptions or interpretations, free from the weight of what Mikhail Bakhtin calls 'second-hand' definitions, ideological accounts never proceed beyond the level of formalized knowledges, and are hence self-validating and immune to criticism. Smith advocates what she terms an 'insider's feminist materialism', one that 'takes concepts, ideas, ideology, and schemata as dimensions and organizers of the ongoing social process that we can grasp only as insiders, only by considering our own practices' (1990b: 202). In so doing, sociological inquiry must be construed as a form of reflexive critique, in which the everyday world is 'known' only insofar are we ourselves participate in it. By exploring these relations, and reflecting on the nature of 'primordial' existence as well as second-order sociological descriptions of the lifeworld, we can 'bring into view not just our actual practices of thinking, reasoning, reading, making sense of accounts, and so forth, but the social relations we participate in by doing so' (Smith 1990b: 204). Hence, what Smith envisages by a feminist social theory is in most respects antithetical to the current gamut of postmodernist feminisms. The problem with postmodernist approaches is that they fail to consider the role of subjects other than as 'positions' within particular discourses. A materialist insider's feminism, by contrast, insists that ideological criticism remains of relevance and that there are relatively more and less accurate accounts of the social world; that marginalized groups, especially women, have shared material interests (though largely for socioeconomic rather than metaphysical reasons); and that there always remains the possibility of transformative agency, particularly in a collective sense. Postmodernism must be subjected to critical scrutiny because it tends to deny

> the possibility of speaking of a world beyond discourse; theory itself legitimates the speaker's claim for theory's authority. [In] a phenomenal universe of discourse without people and activity, nothing even happens; nobody does anything, there is no history; there is no work; there is no economy; there are no wars, no misery, no violence, no rape, no watching your children starve. If there is a lived world, we may not speak of it. [But] of course we've learned in practice that women speaking as such (in our sexed bodies) have things to tell us of their lives, of how things happen to them, of their work and struggles that we don't already know, that discourse hasn't already previsaged. Speaking from experience has the power to disrupt discourse, not simply because the feminine speaks and when it speaks it

disrupts, but because women speaking their experience as women, speak from where they are in their sexed bodies as they live.

(Smith 1993: 189)

CONCLUSION

In reading Dorothy Smith, we are privy to the work of a theorist engaged passionately in an ambitious project, one that involves nothing less that the rethinking and re-invigoration of the socio-logical enterprise. She seeks to jettison the positivist tendencies and objectivistic pretenses of orthodox sociology, moving the discipline towards a position of moral engagement and institutional critique, but at the same time resisting the siren call of fashionable post-modernisms. All of her writings bespeak of the need to challenge existing hierarchies of power and authority, by exposing their intrinsic connection to expert knowledges which are implicated in perpetuating a form of 'symbolic violence' upon the everyday lifeworld, and by extension the marginalized groups that tend to occupy this sphere. In taking this position, she refuses to write off Marxism as an intellectual anachronism, for which she has been criticized vigorously (Doran 1993). At the same time, however, Smith opens up Marxism to a variety of invigorating influences, especially feminism, dialogism, existential phenomenology and micro-oriented sociologies. Out of these diverse influences there emerges an unconventional social theory that is far more than the sum of its parts, and that occupies an important position in the critical analysis of everyday life. As Steven Seidman puts it in *Contested Knowledge*, Smith's goal 'has been to craft a sociology by and for women that looks to women's experiences, interests and values as the basis of social knowledge and politics. [She] offers a powerful, imaginative moral vision of a sociology and a society in which knowledge is both the dominating power and our social hope' (1994: 304, 305).

9

CONCLUSION

[T]he effort of the philosopher does not and cannot stay on
an isolated philosophical level, in a separate consciousness,
sphere or dimension; the source of his theories is social
practice, and he must direct them back towards life, be it
through his teaching or by other means (poetry? Literature?).
Dialectical thought can and must transform itself into
dialectical consciousness of life, in life: unity of the mediate
and the immediate, of the abstract and the concrete, of
culture and natural spontaneity. In this way it will pass from
ideology and specific knowledge into culture, language,
perhaps into direct perception of the world – in any event,
into everyday life.

Henri Lefebvre

In this book I have sketched out the main elements of a critical
'everyday life' paradigm, focusing on certain thinkers and traditions
I felt to be most representative of such an approach. Less a unified
'theory' than a general sensibility or ethos connected by a series of
overlapping themes, it represents a mode of cultural, social and
historiographic investigation that is, in the best and most productive sense of the word, interdisciplinary. Drawing inspiration from
anthropology, sociology, geography, literary and cultural theory,
political studies, and philosophy, it is fraught with possibilities that
extend well beyond these disciplines. Although the tone of my
commentary has been occasionally critical, even the casual reader
will recognize an overarching sense of empathy and enthusiasm for
this project – mainly because the perspective outlined here sets out
to supersede many of the debilitating dualisms, philosophical blindspots and ethico-political compromises of mainstream social science.
It argues that everyday life deserves to be taken seriously and is
worthy of intensive study in its own right. Yet it is not satisfied
with the mere documentation or neutral description of mundane

social practices, as practised by ethnomethodology or symbolic interactionism. It is also concerned with the transformation of daily life into something quite different, because the latter is held to contain 'redemptive' moments that point towards a transfigured and liberated social existence, and that must be realized fully. Established forms of social theorizing have occluded rather than facilitated a proper understanding of this sphere because they have transcribed the embodied, affective and experiential qualities of profane social life into rarefied abstractions that dovetail with the requirements of technocratic power. This denigration of the everyday is both symptom and bulwark of the alienated, reified character of society under the regime of modernity, and its tendency to hypostatize the phenomenally 'given' at the expense of deeper, underlying processes and potentialities. By concentrating on such apparent trivialities as the 'culinary act, festive moments, daily walks, leisure activities and the like', the everyday life standpoint effectively side-steps such static sociological abstractions as 'roles' or 'structures'. We are therefore able to bear more accurate witness to the pluralistic, collective energies that constitute the minutiae of lived social relations, generate new forms of personal identity and express our corporeal needs and desires, and that might even denote a 'new form of sedition', as Michel Maffesoli characterizes it (1990: 90, 92). The everyday life paradigm seeks to relate the particular to the general, locate the concrete in the universal, and to grasp the wider sociohistorical context within which everyday practices are necessarily inscribed. It evinces certain affinities with the postmodernist predilection for the peripheral and the de-centred, and its imperative to give a voice to the silenced, but it declines to make a fetish of marginality for its own sake. It does not shirk from the difficult task of social and ideological critique, and articulates an ethics of alterity or 'otherness'. In so doing, it adheres to a more synoptic and dialectical (or 'dialogical') perspective than 'establishment' postmodernism would ever contemplate. The critical approach to the study of everyday life therefore conforms to what Rob Shields (1999: 188) has usefully termed a 'utopian humanism': it is an outlook that celebrates the intrinsic but oft-hidden promises and possibilities of ordinary human beings and the inherent value of commonsensical forms of thought, but that recognizes limitations in the prosaic world as it is currently constituted, and that is attuned to the transgressive, sensual and incandescent qualities of everyday existence, whereby the entire fabric of daily life can take on a festive hue and be considered akin to a 'work of art'.

NOTES

1 INTRODUCTION

1 Maffesoli contrasts what he calls the *social* ('mechanical solidarity, instrumentality, projects, rationality and goal orientation') with *sociality* ('organic solidarity, the symbolic dimension (communication), the non-logical (Pareto), and a concern for the present') (1989: 1). Traditionally, Maffesoli suggests, sociology has analysed the social using scientistic notions of economic or political determinism, which turn on the belief that social behaviour has fully predictable, rational, logical qualities. The concept of sociality, by contrast, suggests to us that the largely taken-for-granted world of everyday life is one of ceaseless, intersubjective interaction and has an irreducibly *ethical* character that positivistic approaches cannot comprehend.

2 The following quote from Kaplan and Ross helps to clarify this point: 'everyday life is situated somewhere between the subjective, phenomenological sensory apparatus of the individual and reified institutions. Its starting point is neither the intentional subject dear to humanistic thinking nor the determining paradigms that bracket lived experience' (1987: 3–4).

3 This selection may appear somewhat arbitrary, and indeed to a certain extent it is, although there is enough thematic overlap to justify the inclusion of each of them. One might counter that I have overlooked the important work of such critically minded social theorists as Pierre Bourdieu, Anthony Giddens or Jürgen Habermas *vis-à-vis* everyday life. Although I do allude in passing to all of them, they constitute three of the most widely read, discussed and cited living theorists. As such, I am more concerned here to elucidate a lesser-known strain of critical thinking about everyday life. I have also generally overlooked Freud's notion of a 'psychopathology of everyday life' and the various attempts to wed this approach to Marxism, although this has been covered adequately in Brown (1973).

4 To illustrate the sensibility of the mainstream interpretive approach, Jack Douglas writes in the preface to the well-known anthology *Understanding Everyday Life* that the sociological analysis of human life begins with 'an understanding of everyday life gained from a systematic and objective study of the common-sense meanings and actions of everyday life. We must begin by studying these meaningful social phenomena on their own grounds, but, true to our goal of creating a science of man's existence, *we must then seek an ever more general, trans-situational (objective) understanding of everyday life*' (1970: x; my emphasis).

5 This point is expressed clearly in Kosík's *Dialectics of the Concrete*: 'The everyday has its experience and wisdom, its sophistication, its forecasting. It has its replicability but also its special occasions, its routine but also its festivity. The everyday is thus not meant as a contrast to the unusual, the festive, the special, or to History: hypostatizing the everyday as a routine over History, as the exceptional, is itself the *result of* a certain mystification' (1976: 43).

6 It is worth mentioning that the work of the French theorists discussed in this book represents in part a reaction against Althusser's version of Marxist structuralism and his denunciation of the themes of the early Marx (alienation, sensuous embodiment, etc.) in favour of quasi-scientific notions of 'structural causality' and his binary distinction between ideology (which he equates with everyday life) and science (Kurzweil 1980: 75).

7 According to Ben Agger (1992: 294–302), there is a distinction to be made between what could be termed a 'critical' postmodernism, one that is aware of the limitations of absolute Reason and the aporias of modernity, but which continues to hold out the possibility of a progressive political praxis and non-dogmatic critique, and 'establishment' postmodernism, which favours a purely ironic or satirical relationship to the *status quo* and has thus made its peace with consumer capitalism. It might be possible to refer to most of the thinkers discussed in the present study as 'critical postmodernists' according to Agger's definition, at least in certain respects.

8 In the space of everyday life, however, resistance does not take the form of a direct clash with the powers that be, with heroic or grand revolutionary gestures, but takes a more subtle and evasive form, what Certeau calls the tactics of the weak (1984; Scott 1990). Gouldner (1975) and Featherstone (1992) suggest that the politics of everyday life is an 'unofficial' type that seeks primarily a transformation in the quality of daily living. As such, it has an explicitly anti-heroic orientation, which is to be contrasted with the public, institutionalized political activities that modernist social theorists have typically been concerned with. It is worth noting that the issue of bringing everyday life directly into the heart of political discourse has been one of the hallmarks of the so-called 'new social movements' that have emerged out of the great sociopolitical upheavals of the 1960s and 1970s

(Katsiaficas 1997; Melucci 1989), especially the demand for *autogestion*, or self-management.

9 It should be noted in passing, however, that postmodernists generally argue that the process of differentiation that has characterized modernity is now being reversed, and that we are now entering a phase of implosive *de*-differentiation, marked by an increasing dissolution of institutional and symbolic boundaries (especially between the domains of science, culture, and law and morality) that at one time were rigidly compartmentalized (Crook *et al.* 1992; Maffesoli 1996). As Lash puts it, 'if modernization is the phase of cultural differentiation, [then] '*post*modernization is a process of de-differentiation' (1990: 5).

10 Parenthetically, this close (though not necessary) connection between the forms of power/knowledge characteristic of modernity and the visual mode, or what Martin Jay (1993) calls 'ocularcentrism', might explain why most of the thinkers discussed herein tend to evoke the aural register over the ocular (although, admittedly, Lefebvre does talk about spatial dialectics). Blanchot notes, for instance, that everyday life at least partially escapes the gaze of power: it cannot 'be introduced into a whole or "reviewed," that is to say, enclosed within a panoramic vision; for, by another trait, the everyday is what we never see for a first time, but only see again, having always already seen it by an illusion that is, as it happens, constitutive of the everyday' (1987: 14). For more on this, see Gardiner (1999); Levin (1995).

11 It would seem pertinent at this juncture to mention the influential Italian Marxist Antonio Gramsci. In his *Prison Notebooks* (1971), Gramsci analysed at length the nature of 'common sense' in contemporary society and the role it played *vis-à-vis* ideological hegemony. He argued that the very essence of hegemony lay in the ability of the dominant class to sponsor the development of a systematic and coherent ideological viewpoint (which he called its 'philosophy') and to portray its perspective as the most natural, all-embracing and universal one possible. Generally, under 'normal' circumstances, the perspective of the subordinate classes remained 'corporate' – that is, restricted to immediate and self-interested concerns – and lacked the capacity and the conceptual tools necessary to generate a distinctive, coherent socio-political viewpoint. Common sense was a 'diffuse and unco-ordinated' form of thought, one that was unsystematic and did not 'make explicit its own mode of reasoning'. Thus, common sense was not simply the sedimented deposits of dominant philosophies and worldviews; to an important extent it also consisted of experiences and ideas generated by the everyday experience of class solidarity. The common sense of oppressed social groups, in the context of their daily lives, retained a 'healthy nucleus' of 'good sense' and a nascent oppositional consciousness. As with the theorists discussed in the present study, therefore, everyday life for Gramsci is dialectical and contradictory, containing both liberating and repressive elements.

12 Mark Gottdiener makes the important point that for the Frankfurt
    School, mass consciousness under late modernity effectively becomes
    'false consciousness', to the extent that alienation is no longer
    recognized as such by the majority of individuals in society. Fetishism
    and reification had so mystified the social relations of capitalist society
    that the oppressed could no longer comprehend the experience of
    alienation, and hence had become 'socially impotent'. If alienation is
    unrecognized and there is no real possibility of a radical, collective
    project of superseding it, then the reification of social relations and
    consciousness becomes permanent, and evoking the possibility of a
    non-alienated existence as the basis for social critique loses its *raison
    d'être*. What is most interesting about this is that it dovetails
    remarkably with numerous postmodernist theories, particularly those
    of Jean Baudrillard, wherein the masses are so manipulated and docile
    that effective resistance to the commodification of daily life is all but
    impossible. The everyday life tradition discussed in this book is
    therefore marked, in Gottdiener's words, by an adherence to an
    ' "alienation" problematic rather than the postmodern problematic of
    "simulation," depthless culture, and behavior in an image-driven
    society' (1996: 145).

13 Foucault often talked about resisting the effects of power/knowledge,
    but it remained a purely abstract, metaphysical possibility. Although
    he claimed to side with what he called *savoir* (unsystematic, practical
    knowledge) over *connaissance* (formal, technical knowledge), he concen-
    trated almost exclusively on how the latter was inscribed within
    disciplinary practices. Indeed, Lefebvre felt that Foucault's researches
    never went beyond the theory of the system, and hence hindered rather
    than facilitated everyday struggles against instrumentalized power
    (Kofman and Lebas 1996: 25). For the thinkers discussed here, by
    contrast, resistance is rooted in the daily struggles and embodied,
    intersubjective activities of everyday life. This stress on individual and
    collective agency, in which subjectivity and personal identity are not
    merely 'effects' of power/knowledge, parallels a sociological critique of
    poststructuralism and postmodernism that has been gathering force in
    recent years (see Burkitt 1994; Dunn 1998; O'Neill 1995).

14 For Bloch, the utopian impulse was an inherent (if historically
    mediated) component of the human condition, an unfulfilled and
    irrepressible longing for the realization of authentic human com-
    munity. Bloch's philosophy has been described as an 'ontology of not-
    yet-being', insofar as he felt that all things (including nature and the
    physical universe) existed in a state of dialectical tension, suspended
    between present and future, 'was is' and 'what could be'. Insofar as
    history and nature alike are embedded in a perpetual process of
    'becoming', nothing is static or unchangeable: 'the world is full of
    propensity towards something, tendency towards something, latency of
    something, and this intended something means fulfillment of

intending' (Bloch 1986: 18). Bloch posits that this 'latency of being-to-come' can be glimpsed most clearly in great art and literature, but also in a myriad of traces, signs and ciphers from fairy stories to architectural designs to advertising slogans as well as the reveries, dreams and fantasies that pervade our everyday lives. These signs are a kind of 'pre-cognition', an anticipatory illumination of the promise of transformed sociopolitical conditions.

15 In this sense, the utopianism sketched out here conforms to what Bloch calls the 'concrete utopia' (a term, incidently, that Lefebvre also uses), as opposed to the 'abstract' utopia. Whereas the latter is based on a wholly voluntarist and idealist view of the future, the former is rooted in daily life and evinces a structural isomorphism between what Bloch calls the 'potency of human hope' and the actual potentialities of change in the natural and social worlds (see Hudson 1982: 100; Gardiner 1993a; Levitas 1997).

16 It is important to point out that when the theorists examined here invoke everyday life, they are not essentializing immediate or direct experience. Lefebvre, for instance, warns us that

it has always been possible to erect the *immediate* as a barrier to wider and more far-reaching ways of seeing. It is in the name of the immediate (immediate demands, immediate needs, etc.) that people have opposed and continued to oppose wider visions, wider solutions to their problems. [Thus] the task facing a constructive, critical thought becomes clear: to penetrate ever deeper into human raw material, into the immediate which is a fact of everyday life, and to resolve their ambiguities.
(1991a: 189–90)

17 Smith's work can be said to be indicative of a general shift in the critical everyday life tradition away from a focus on production and the public sphere to social reproduction, broadly understood. Interestingly, the relationship between gender and everyday life was anticipated by Lefebvre when he wrote that the everyday 'weighs heaviest on women. [They] are the subjects of everyday life and its victims and objects and substitutes' (1984: 73; also Gouldner 1975: 421–2).

2 DADA AND SURREALISM: POETICS OF EVERYDAY LIFE

1 Dada and Surrealism have not only spawned a distinct intellectual heritage; their anarchic and utopian impulses can be traced back in history many hundreds of years, from medieval heresies through de Sade, Fourier, and Futurism (see Home 1988; Marcus 1989).

2 In his essay 'On the Affirmative Character of Culture', Marcuse suggested that although bourgeois high culture expressed 'moments' of transcendence or deliverance from the grubby realities of an increas-

ingly manipulated and totalitarian modernity, it reconciled real social contradictions only at the level of ideas or consciousness, in the realm of cultural consumption. So although affirmative culture held out the promise of human fulfilment, inasmuch as this only took place through the cultivation of 'spiritual' or intellectual qualities without a corresponding transformation of existing social conditions, this promise was ultimately a false and escapist one (Marcuse 1968: 195; also Arato and Gebhardt 1982).

3 It is important to note that although the original Dada movement eventually ran its course, many Dadaist-inspired notions and techniques eventually found their way, not only into Surrealism, but also a host of neo-Dada and Pop Art forms in the post-World War Two era (see Home 1988).

4 It is worth pointing out that, for Adorno, this stress on the 'collective unconscious' was Surrealism's chief defect, which helped to render it unrecuperable for a progressive politics. On this point, he and Benjamin disagreed strenuously. A useful overview of this discussion can be found in Lunn (1982: 56–8); also Jameson (1977).

5 To quote Breton on utopia:

Perhaps some people use the word utopia, accompanied by a shrug of the shoulders, as the most poisonous weapon of all. Like it or not, we've had to admit that this word required more careful use. Provided we not insist on utopias in the strict sense – dreams that to all appearances are impracticable – I believe that many predictions hastily branded with the same discredit should be reexamined closely for anything viable they might contain. This is particularly the case with the so-called social 'utopias' (which moreover have led to very appreciable partial realizations). . . . Poets and artists in particular would be inexcusable if they tried to guard against 'utopias', when the very nature of their creation leads them to draw, at least initially, from the vague realm where utopia reigns. In some instances, this utopia might prove fruitful in reality, thereby revealing itself as having been not such a utopia after all.

(1993: 217)

6 Fourier also believed that human unhappiness was largely due to the fact that natural and spontaneous human 'passions' were continually blocked or distorted in the context of bourgeois society. Consequently, he eschewed the grand designs of other thinkers in the utopian tradition and argued that a happy and free society could result from only a few simple techniques of social organization designed to bring the passions of different human beings into harmonious alignment. For a representative sample of Fourier's writings, see Poster (1971); a good discussion of Fourier can be found in Manuel (1965), while the role played by Fourier in the development of French social thought is discussed in Gardiner (1995).

3 BAKHTIN'S PROSAIC IMAGINATION

1 Morson and Emerson's concept of prosaics in relation to the work of Bakhtin, and as a methodology for the human sciences more generally, can be found in Morson and Emerson (1989, 1990), Morson (1988, 1995), and Emerson (1995).

2 More extensive treatments of Bakhtin's life can be found in Holquist (1990), Emerson (1993), Todorov (1984), and Yaeger (1986), but the standard reference work is Clark and Holquist (1984).

3 The roots of the by now famous (or infamous) 'authorship question' can be traced to 1971, when the eminent Soviet academician V. V. Ivanov put forward the thesis that at least three key works of this Circle – Medvedev's *The Formal Method in Literary Scholarship* and Voloshinov's *Marxism and the Philosophy of Language* and *Freudianism: A Marxist Critique* – were in fact written by Bakhtin himself. Voloshinov and Medvedev, alleged Ivanov, merely edited or transcribed Bakhtin's own material. Precisely why these books were originally attributed to Voloshinov and Medvedev is unclear, especially given that Bakhtin was simultaneously publishing other works under his own name. The literature on the 'authorship question' is voluminous: Ivanov (1974) and Clark and Holquist (1984, 1986) are the principle defenders of the thesis that Bakhtin is responsible for the disputed works, while Todorov (1984) is more cautious and Titunik (1984, 1986) rejects this suggestion altogether, as do Morson and Emerson (1990).

4 At the same time, however, it must also be acknowledged that Bakhtin does not theorize the connections between language, power and social institutions in anything approaching a sociologically adequate fashion (see Gardiner 1992; Hirschkop 1986; Pechey 1989).

5 As such, Bakhtin's work cannot be easily appropriated to what Agger construes as 'establishment postmodernism', and it can be argued that Bakhtin has more in common with Habermas' vision of a 'radicalized modernity' (see Gardiner and Bell 1998; Gardiner 2000; Hirschkop 1990a; Nielsen 1995; Zalava 1988).

4 HENRI LEFEBVRE: PHILOSOPHER OF THE ORDINARY

1 Lefebvre's work is given passing treatment in Gombin (1975), Hirsch (1982) and Poster (1975). A partial exception to this relative neglect is Lefebvre's writings on urbanism and space, which have had a significant impact on a number of radical social geographers. On the latter, see Gottdiener (1985), Harvey (1983), Shields (1991) and Soja (1989).

2 See, for instance, Fukuyama (1989), who advances the thesis that with the collapse of statist communism history effectively terminates in some version of liberal capitalism.

3 Michel Maffesoli (1993, 1996), who has been influenced strongly by Lefebvre, has taken up this theme of the emergence of a body-centred culture in the context of postmodernity within numerous publications.

5 THE SITUATIONIST INTERNATIONAL: REVOLUTION AT THE SERVICE OF POETRY

1 Apart from Plant's (1992) excellent and pioneering full-length study, useful commentaries on the SI include Ball (1987), Barrot (1987), Berman, Pan and Piccone (1990–1), Bonnet (1989, 1992), Erikson (1992), Home (1988), Marcus (1989), Shipway (1987) and Wollen (1989).
2 This material includes Debord (1987, 1991a, 1991b, 1991c, 1992) and Vaneigem (1983, 1985), as well as anthologies by Blazwick (1990), Knabb (1981), Gray (1974) and Sussman (1989).
3 Debord's 1994 suicide is discussed in detail in Bracken's (1997) biography, and also in Jappe (1999).
4 There are no page numbers in *Society of the Spectacle*, only a series of numbered aphorisms of varying length organized under discrete sub-headings. When I cite this text the number will refer to the aphorism, not the page number.

6 AGNES HELLER: RATIONALITY, ETHICS AND EVERYDAY LIFE

1 For a discussion of the importance of Lukács by the most prominent members of the Budapest School, see Heller (1983). An account of the personal relationship between Heller and Lukács can be found in the last chapter of Kadarkay (1991).
2 More biographical details of Heller can be found in Gransow (1985).
3 To be more specific, Heller sees three essential 'logics' operating within modernity: capitalism, industrialization (or technology), and democracy. Each such logic is at odds with others, and vies for supremacy. Unfortunately, historically speaking, either market mechanisms (liberal capitalism) or industrialization (statist capitalism, including 'really existing socialist' societies) have tended to predominate over democracy. Heller therefore seeks to limit the power of capital and technology and to encourage the forces of democracy, which she understands as popular control of institutions as well as the conditions of everyday life (Heller and Fehér 1986a: 202).
4 The issue of human needs is one of Heller's abiding concerns. Essentially, Heller's argument is that a free and democratic society is one in which human needs, however pluralistic, are recognized as authentic, and she rejects the pervasive attempt on the left to delineate between true and false needs. On the other hand, Heller does make a

distinction between 'needs' properly understood, which are potentially universalistic and concerned with self-determination, and 'wants', which are essentially idiosyncratic desires that are fulfilled by others, and hence encourage a loss of autonomy. As such, critical social thought must be concerned with the investigation of anthropological issues pertaining to the structure of human needs and their satisfaction within determinate social contexts. This does not mean that all human needs *can* be satisfied, but that the recognition of the *validity* of such needs has to be part of a viable socialist society. See, for instance, Heller (1976, 1984b: 134–86, 1985a: 285–99; Soper 1977).

5 Although clearly influenced by Habermas, Heller does express certain reservations about his specific formulation of the ideal speech situation, which can be summarized in the following three points. (i) Whereas Habermas places a premium on the achievement of consensus as the *telos* of rational argumentation, Heller asserts that some background consensual values must already be present if dialogue is to be initiated at any level. Her point is that an acceptance of the value of rational argumentation does not in and of itself entail the achievement of consensus, particularly given the extreme multiplicity of lifeworlds in contemporary society. (ii) The ideal speech situation is conceived of by Habermas in an overly legalistic manner, and it adheres to a very narrow conception of human rationality. For Heller, ideal speech might be relevant for the adjudication of competing sociopolitical norms (justice, resource distribution, etc.), but it can tell us nothing about morals, properly understood. Furthermore, she asserts that in Habermas's theories, there is a 'lack of the sensuous experiences of hope and despair, of venture and humiliation. [The] creature-like aspects of human beings are missing' (1982a: 21, 1994; Benhabib 1987, 1990). (iii) Heller argues that although Habermas's conception of the 'ideal communication community' ostensibly aims at the dissolution of asymmetrical structures of power and authority, and of institutionalized relations of subordination and superordination, it fails to tackle this problem in a realistic or convincing fashion. Rational argumentation in and of itself cannot effectively challenge the reigning structures of power and authority, however desirable it might be as an exemplar. Elites are simply not motivated to enter into a rational discussion; as such, the power of elites must be contested by other means, *before* the goal of rational argumentation can be fully realized.

7 MICHEL DE CERTEAU: THE CUNNING OF UNREASON

1 For more information on Certeau's life and work, see Godzich (1986) and Terdiman (1992). A full-length study on Certeau in English is also now available (Ahearne 1995).

2 For a discussion of the rise of French postmodernism and the retreat of radical politics, see Callinicos (1989: 162–71). Callinicos argues that the pervasiveness of postmodernist themes in French intellectual life in the 1980s can be explained by (i) the entry of most of the May 1968 generation into managerial and administrative positions, one of the few social strata in the 1970s and 1980s with rising prosperity, combined with a general disillusionment with politics; (ii) the rise of a doctrine of 'aestheticism', which linked forms of consumerism to certain types of identity and personal worth; and (iii) a more positive assessment of liberal capitalism.

3 For Althusser (1971), the reproduction of capitalism was secured by the Ideological State Apparatuses (or ISAs for short) – that is, the assemblage of state-sponsored institutions such as schools, universities, churches and political parties. The institutions contained within the ISAs operate to 'hail' or interpellate social actors as subjects, thereby constructing or constituting their subjective identities. What this implies is that human 'agents' have no agency as such, but are simply bearers of wider structural relations. Certeau is challenging Althusser's mechanistic theories by reaffirming the possibility of agency and attacking the logic of structural determinism.

4 A valuable account of how individuals invest space with highly personal and poetical meanings, especially in the context of childhood, can be found in Bachelard (1969).

REFERENCES

Abercrombie, N., Hill, S. and Turner, B. (1980) *The Dominant Ideology Thesis*, London: George Allen and Unwin.

Adler, P. A. and Adler P. (1987) 'Everyday Life Sociology', *Annual Review of Sociology* 13: 217–35.

Adorno, T. (1973) *The Jargon of Authenticity*, K. Tarnowski and F. Will (trans.), Evanston: Northwestern University Press.

Adorno, T. (1974) *Minima Moralia: Reflections From a Damaged Life*, E. F. N. Jephcott (trans.), London: Verso.

Adorno, T. and Horkheimer, M. (1979) *Dialectic of Enlightenment*, J. Cumming (trans.), London: Verso.

Agger, B. (1992) *The Discourse of Domination: From the Frankfurt School to Postmodernism*, Evanston: Northwestern University Press.

Agger, B. (1998) *Critical Social Theories: An Introduction*, Boulder: Westview Press.

Ahearne, J. (1995) *Michel de Certeau: Interpretation and Its Other*, Cambridge: Polity Press.

Alquié, F. (1965) *The Philosophy of Surrealism*, B. Waldrop (trans.), Ann Arbor: University of Michigan Press.

Althusser, L. (1971) *Lenin and Philosophy and Other Essays*, London and New York: Monthly Review Press.

Anderson, P. (1976) *Considerations on Western Marxism*, London: Verso.

Aragon, L. (1971) *Paris Peasant*, S. W. Taylor (trans.), London: Jonathan Cape.

Arato, A. and Gebhardt, E. (1982) 'Esthetic Theory and Cultural Criticism', in A. Arato and E. Gebhardt (eds), *The Essential Frankfurt School Reader*, New York: Continuum.

Aronowitz, S. (1994) 'Literature as Social Knowledge: Mikhail Bakhtin and the Reemergence of the Human Science', in S. Aronowitz, *Dead Artists, Live Theories*, London and New York: Routledge.

Arp, H. (1971) 'Dadaland', in L. R. Lippard (ed.), *Dadas on Art*, Englewood Cliffs: Prentice-Hall, Inc.

Bachelard, G. (1969) *The Poetics of Space*, Boston: Beacon Press.

Bakhtin, M. (1981) *The Dialogic Imagination: Four Essays by M. M. Bakhtin*, M. Holquist (ed.), C. Emerson and M. Holquist (trans.), Austin: Texas University Press.

Bakhtin, M. (1984a) *Rabelais and His World*, H. Isowolsky (trans.), Cambridge MA: MIT Press.

Bakhtin, M. (1984b) *Problems of Dostoevsky's Poetics*, C. Emerson (ed. and trans.), Manchester: Manchester University Press.

Bakhtin, M. (1986) *Speech Genres and Other Late Essays*, C. Emerson and M. Holquist (eds), V. W. McGee (trans.), Austin: Texas University Press.

Bakhtin, M. (1990) *Art and Answerability: Early Philosophical Essays by M. M. Bakhtin*, M. Holquist and V. Liapunov (eds), V. Liapunov (trans. and notes), K. Brostrom (supplement trans.), Austin: Texas University Press.

Bakhtin, M. (1993) *Toward a Philosophy of the Act*, V. Liapunov (trans.), Austin: Texas University Press.

Bakhtin, M. and Medvedev, P. N. (1985) *The Formal Method in Literary Scholarship: A Critical Introduction to Sociological Poetics*, A. J. Wehrle (trans.), Cambridge MA: Harvard University Press.

Ball, E. (1987) 'The Great Sideshow of the Situationist International', *Yale French Studies* 73: 21–37.

Barrot, J. (1987) *What is Situationism?: Critique of the Situationist International*, London: Unpopular Books.

Bataille, G. (1988) *The Accursed Share Vol. 1*, R. Hurley (trans.), New York: Zone Books.

Baudrillard, J. (1981) *For a Critique of the Political Economy of the Sign,* C. Levin (trans.), St Louis: Telos Press.

Baudrillard, J. (1988) *Jean Baudrillard: Selected Writings*, Mark Poster (ed.), Cambridge: Polity Press.

Baugh, B. (1990) 'Left-Wing Elitism: Adorno on Popular Culture', *Philosophy and Literature* 14, 1: 65–78.

Bauman, Z. (1987) *Legislators and Interpreters: On Modernity, Postmodernity and Intellectuals*, Cambridge: Polity Press.

Bauman, Z. (1992) *Intimations of Postmodernity*, London and New York: Routledge.

Bauman, Z. (1994) 'Is There a Postmodern Sociology?', in S. Seidman (ed.), *The Postmodern Turn*, Cambridge: Cambridge University Press.

Beauvoir, S. de (1984) *The Second Sex*, H. M. Parshley (trans.), Harmondsworth: Penguin.

Bell, M. M. and Gardiner, M. (eds) (1998) *Bakhtin and the Human Sciences: No Last Words*, London: Sage.

Bender, C. (1998) 'Bakhtinian Perspectives on "Everyday Life" Sociology', in M. M. Bell and M. Gardiner (eds), *Bakhtin and the Human Sciences: No Last Words*, London: Sage.

Benhabib, S. (1987) 'The Generalized Other and the Concrete Other: The Kohlberg–Gilligan Controversy and Feminist Theory', in S. Benhabib and D. Cornell (eds), *Feminism and Critique*, Minneapolis: University of Minnesota Press.

Benhabib, S. (1990) 'In the Shadow of Aristotle and Hegel: Communicative Ethics and Current Controversies in Practical Philosophy', in M. Kelly (ed.), *Hermeneutics and Critical Theory*, Cambridge MA: MIT Press.

Benjamin, W. (1969) *Illuminations: Essays and Reflections*, H. Arendt (ed.), H. Zohn (trans.), New York: Schocken Books.

Benjamin, W. (1979) *One Way Street and Other Writings*, E. Jephcott and K. Shorter (trans.), London: Verso.

Benjamin, W. (1983/4) 'Theoretics of Knowledge; Theory of Progress', *The Philosophical Forum* 40, 1–2: 1–40.

Berger, P. and Luckmann, T. (1961) *The Social Construction of Reality: A Treatise on the Sociology of Knowledge*, New York: Doubleday.

Berman, R., Pan, D. and Piccone, P. (1990–1) 'The Society of the Spectacle 20 Years Later: A Discussion', *Telos* 86: 81–102.

Bernard-Donals, M. (1994) *Mikhail Bakhtin: Between Phenomenology and Marxism*, Cambridge: Cambridge University Press.

Bernard-Donals, M. (1995) 'Bakhtin and Phenomenology: A Reply to Gary Saul Morson', *South Central Review* 12, 2: 41–55.

Bernstein, M. A. (1992) *Bitter Carnival: Ressentiment and the Abject Hero*, Princeton: Princeton University Press.

Blanchot, M. (1987) 'Everyday Speech', *Yale French Studies* 73: 12–20.

Blazwick, I. (ed.) (1990) *An Endless Adventure . . . An Endless Passion . . . An Endless Banquet: A Situationist Scrapbook*, London: Verso.

Bloch, E. (1986) *The Principles of Hope, Vols I–III*, N. Plaice, S. Plaice and P. Knight (trans.), Oxford: Basil Blackwell.

Bonnet, A. (1989) 'Situationism, Geography, and Poststructuralism', *Society and Space* 7: 131– 46.

Bonnet, A. (1992) 'Art, Ideology and Everyday Space: Subversive Tendencies from Dada to Postmodernism', *Society and Space* 10: 69–86.

Bourdieu, P. (1977) *Outline of a Theory of Practice*, Cambridge: Cambridge University Press.

Bourdieu, P. (1998) *Practical Reason: On the Theory of Action*, Stanford: Stanford University Press.

Bourdieu, P., Chamboredon, J.-C. and Passerson, J.-C. (1991) 'Meanwhile, I Have Come to Know All the Diseases of Sociological Understanding: An Interview', in B. Krais (ed.), *The Craft of Sociology: Epistemological Preliminaries*, New York: Walter de Gruyer.

Bowers, R. (1994) 'Bakhtin, Self and Other: Neohumanism and Communicative Multiplicity,' *Canadian Review of Comparative Literature* 21, 4: 565–75.

Bracken, L. (1997) *Guy Debord: Revolutionary*, Venice CA: Feral House.

Brandist, C. (1996) 'The Bakhtin Circle', *The Internet Encyclopaedia of Philosophy* (http://www.utm.edu/research/iep/b/bakhtin.htm).

Breton, A. (1960) *Nadja*, R. Howard (trans.), New York: Grove Press Inc.

Breton, A. (1972) 'Second Manifesto of Surrealism', in *Manifestos of Surrealism*, R. Seaver and H. R. Lane (trans.), Ann Arbor: University of Michigan Press.

Breton, A. (1993) *Conversations: The Autobiography of Surrealism*, M. Polizzotti (trans.), New York: Paragon House.

Brown, B. (1973) *Marx, Freud and the Critique of Everyday Life: Toward a Permanent Cultural Revolution*, New York: Monthly Review Press.

Buchanan, I. (1997) 'De Certeau and Cultural Studies', *New Formations* 31: 175–88.

Burke, P. (1978) *Popular Culture in Early Modern Europe*, New York: New York University Press.

Burkitt, I. (1994) 'The Shifting Concept of the Self', *History of the Human Sciences* 7, 2: 7–28.

Burnheim, J. (ed.) (1994) *The Social Philosophy of Agnes Heller*, Amsterdam: Rodopi.

Butler, J. (1991) *Gender Trouble: Feminism and the Subversion of Identity*, London and New York: Routledge.

Callinicos, A. (1985) 'Postmodernism, Post-Structuralism, Post-Marxism?', *Theory, Culture and Society* 2, 3: 85–101.

Callinicos, A. (1989) *Against Postmodernism: A Marxist Critique*, Cambridge: Polity Press.

Campbell, M. and Manicom, A. (eds) (1995) *Experience, Knowledge and Ruling Relations: Explorations in the Social Organization of Knowledge*, Toronto: Toronto University Press.

Caws, M. A., Kuenzli, R. E. and Raaberg, G. (eds) (1991) *Surrealism and Women*, Cambridge MA: MIT Press.

Certeau, M. de (1984) *The Practice of Everyday Life*, S. Rendall (trans.), Berkeley: The University of California Press.

Certeau, M. de (1986) *Heterologies: Discourse on the Other*, B. Massumi (trans.), Minneapolis: Minnesota University Press.

Certeau, M. de (1988) *The Writing of History*, T. Conley (trans.), New York: Columbia University Press.

Certeau, M. de (1997a) *Culture in the Plural*, T. Conley (trans.), Minneapolis: The University of Minnesota Press.

Certeau, M. de (1997b) *The Capture of Speech and Other Writings*, T. Conley (trans.), Minneapolis: University of Minnesota Press.

Certeau, M. de, Girard, L. and Mayol, P. (1998) *The Practice of Everyday Life – Vol. 2: Living and Cooking*, T. J. Tomasik (trans.), Minneapolis: University of Minnesota Press.

Chtcheglov, I. (1981) 'Fomulary for a New Urbanism', in K. Knabb (ed.), *Situationist International Anthology*, Berkeley: Bureau of Public Secrets.

Chua, B.-H. (1977) 'Delineating a Marxist Interest in Ethnomethodology', *The American Sociologist* 12: 24–32.

Clark, K. and Holquist, M. (1984) *Mikhail Bakhtin*, Cambridge MA: Harvard University Press.

Clark, K. and Holquist, M. (1986) 'A Continuing Dialogue', *Slavic and Eastern European Journal* 30, 1: 96–102.

Clough, P. (1993) 'On the Brink of Deconstructing Sociology: Critical Reading of Dorothy Smith's Standpoint Epistemology', *Sociological Quarterly* 34, 1: 169–82.

Cohen, M. (1993) *Profane Illumination: Walter Benjamin and the Paris of the Surrealist Revolution*, Berkeley: University of California Press.

Cohen, S. and Taylor, L. (1976) *Escape Attempts: The Theory and Practice of Resistance to Everyday Life*, Harmondsworth: Penguin.

Collier, P. (1985) 'Surrealist City Narrative: Breton and Aragon', in E. Timms and D. Kelly (eds), *Unreal City: Urban Experience in European Literature and Art*, New York: St. Martin's Press.

Connerton, P. (1980) *The Tragedy of Enlightenment: An Essay on the Frankfurt School*, Cambridge: Cambridge University Press.

Coutts-Smith, K. (1970) *Dada*, London: Studio Vista Limited.

Crook, S. (1998) 'Minotaurs and Other Monsters: "Everyday Life" in Recent Social Theory', *Sociology* 32, 3: 523–40.

Crook, S., Pakulski, J. and Waters, M. (1992) *Postmodernization: Change in Advanced Societies*, London: Sage.

Crossley, N. (1996) *Intersubjectivity: The Fabric of Social Becoming*, London: Sage.

Davidson, A. (1992) 'Henri Lefebvre', *Thesis Eleven* 33: 152–5.

Davies, J. (1988) 'The Futures Market: Marinetti and the Fascists of Milan', in E. Timms and P. Collier (eds), *Visions and Blueprints: Avant-Garde Culture and Radical Politics in Early Twentieth-Century Europe*, Manchester: Manchester University Press.

Debord, G. (1981a) 'Report on the Construction of Situations and on the International Situationist Tendency's Conditions of Organization of Action', in K. Knabb (ed.), *Situationist International Anthology*, Berkeley: Bureau of Public Secrets.

Debord, G. (1981b) 'Critique of Separation', in K. Knabb (ed.), *Situationist International Anthology*, Berkeley: Bureau of Public Secrets.

Debord, G. (1981c) 'Situationist Theses on Traffic', in K. Knabb (ed.), *Situationist International Anthology*, Berkeley: Bureau of Public Secrets.

Debord, G. (1981d) 'Perspectives for a Conscious Alteration in Everyday Life', in K. Knabb (ed.), *Situationist International Anthology*, Berkeley: Bureau of Public Secrets.

Debord, G. (1987) *Society of the Spectacle*, London: Rebel Press.

Debord, G. (1991a) *Comments on the Society of the Spectacle*, M. Imrie (trans.), Sheffield: Pirate Press.

Debord, G. (1991b) *Panegyric*, London: Verso.

Debord, G. (1991c) *In Girum Imus Nocte Et Consumimur Igni*, L. Forsyth (trans.), London: Pelagian Press.

Debord, G. (1992) *Society of the Spectacle and Other Films*, K. Sanborn and R. Parry (trans.), London: Rebel Press.

Doran, C. (1993) 'The Everyday World is Problematic: Ideology and Recursion in Dorothy Smith's Micro-Sociology', *Canadian Journal of Sociology* 18, 1: 43–63.

Douglas, J. D. (1970) 'Understanding Everyday Life', in J. D. Douglas (ed.), *Understanding Everyday Life*, Chicago: Aldine Publishing Company.

Douglas, J. D., Adler, P. A., Adler, P., Fontana, A., Freeman, C. and Kotarba, J. (1980) *Introduction to the Sociologies of Everyday Life*, Boston: Allyn and Bacon.

Dunn, R. G. (1998) *Identity Crises: A Social Critique of Postmodernity*, Minneapolis: University of Minnesota Press.

During, S. (1993) 'Introduction', in S. During (ed.), *The Cultural Studies Reader*, London and New York: Routledge.

Eagleton, T. (1986) *Against the Grain: Selected Essays*, London: Verso.

Eagleton, R. (1991) *Ideology: An Introduction*, London: Verso.

Eksteins, M. (1989) *Rites of Spring: The Great War and the Birth of the Modern Age*, Toronto: Lester & Orpen Dennys Ltd.

Emerson, C. (1993) 'Bakhtin, Mikhail Mikhailovich', in I. R. Makaryk (ed.), *Encyclopedia of Contemporary Literary Theory: Approaches, Scholars, Terms*, Toronto: University of Toronto Press.

Emerson, C. (1995) 'Introduction: Dialogue on Every Corner, Bakhtin in Every Class', in A. Mandelker (ed.), *Bakhtin in Contexts: Across the Disciplines*, Evanston: Northwestern University Press.

Erikson, J. (1992) 'The Spectacle of the Anti-Spectacle: Happenings of the Situationist International', *Discourse* 14, 2: 36–58.

Featherstone, M. (1992) 'The Heroic Life and Everyday Life', *Theory, Culture and Society* 9: 159–82.

Fields, B. and Best, S. (1986) 'Situationist International', in R. A. Gorman (ed.), *Biographical Dictionary of Neo-Marxism*, London: Mansell Publishing Company.

Fiske, J. (1989) *Understanding Popular Culture*, Boston: Unwin Hyman.

Fiske, J. (1991) 'Popular Forces and the Culture of Everyday Life', *Southern Review* 21: 288–306.

Foucault, M. (1973) *Madness and Civilization: A History of Insanity in the Age of Reason*, R. Howard (trans.), New York: Random House.

Foucault, M. (1977) *Discipline and Punish: The Birth of the Prison*, A. M. Sheridan Smith (trans.), Harmondsworth: Penguin.

Foucault, M. (1978) *The History of Sexuality: Volume 1*, R. Hurley (trans.), Penguin: Harmondsworth.

Foucault, M. (1980) *Power/Knowledge: Selected Interviews and Writings 1972–77*, C. Gordon (ed. and trans.), New York: Pantheon Books.

Frankel, S. and Martin, D. (1973) 'The Budapest School', *Telos* 17: 122–33.

Freund, P. and Abrams, M. (1976) 'Ethnomethodology and Marxism: Their Use for Critical Theorizing', *Theory and Society* 3, 3: 377–93.

Frow, J. (1991) 'Michel de Certeau and the Practice of Representation', *Cultural Studies* 5, 1: 52–60.

Fukuyama, F. (1989) 'The End of History?', *The National Interest*, Summer: 3–18.

Gabel, J. (1975) 'Hungarian Marxism', *Telos* 25: 185–91.

Gambacorta, C. (1989) 'Experiences of Daily Life', *Current Sociology* 37, 1: 121–40.

Gardiner, M. (1992) *The Dialogics of Critique: M. M. Bakhtin and the Theory of Ideology*, London: Routledge.

Gardiner, M. (1993a) 'Bakhtin's Carnival: Utopia as Critique', in D. Shepherd (ed.), *Bakhtin: Carnival and Other Subjects*, Amsterdam: Rodopi.

Gardiner, M. (1993b) 'Ecology and Carnival: Traces of a "Green" Social Theory in the Writings of M. M. Bakhtin', *Theory and Society* 22, 6: 765–812.

Gardiner, M. (1995) 'Utopia and Everyday Life in French Social Thought', *Utopian Studies* 6, 2: 90–123.

Gardiner, M. (1996a) 'Alterity and Ethics: A Dialogical Perspective', *Theory, Culture and Society* 13, 2: 121–44.

Gardiner, M. (1996b) 'Foucault, Ethics and Dialogue', *History of the Human Sciences* 9, 3: 27– 46.

Gardiner, M. (1997) 'A Postmodern Utopia? Heller and Féher's Critique of Messianic Marxism', *Utopian Studies* 8, 1: 89–122.

Gardiner, M. (1998) '"The Incomparable Monster of Solipsism": Bakhtin and Merleau-Ponty', in M. M. Bell and M. Gardiner (eds), *Bakhtin and the Human Sciences: No Last Words*, London: Sage.

Gardiner, M. (1999) 'Bakhtin and the Metaphorics of Perception', in I. Heywood and B. Sandywell (eds), *Interpreting Visual Culture: Explorations in the Hermeneutics of Vision*, London and New York: Routledge.

Gardiner, M. (2000) '"A Very Understandable Horror of Dialectics": Bakhtin and Marxist Phenomenology', in C. Brandist and G. Tihanov (eds), *Materializing Bakhtin: The Bakhtin Circle and Social Theory*, Basingstoke: Macmillan.

Gardiner, M. and Bell, M. M. (1998) 'Bakhtin and the Human Sciences: A Brief Introduction', in M. M. Bell and M. Gardiner (eds), *Bakhtin and the Human Sciences: No Last Words*, London: Sage.

Geuss, R. (1981) *The Idea of a Critical Theory*, Cambridge: Cambridge University Press.

Giddens, A. (1984) *The Constitution of Society*, Berkeley: University of California Press.

Giddens, A. (1987) 'Structuralism, Post-Structuralism and the Production of Culture', in A. Giddens and J. Turner (eds), *Social Theory Today*, Stanford: Stanford University Press.

Godzich, W. (1986) 'Foreword: The Further Possibility of Knowledge', in M. de Certeau, *Heterologies: Discourse on the Other*, B. Massumi (trans.), Minneapolis: University of Minnesota Press.

Godzich, W. (1991) 'Correcting Kant: Bakhtin and Intercultural Interactions', *Boundary 2* 18, 2: 5–17.

Gombin, R. (1975) *The Origins of Modern Leftism*, Harmondsworth: Penguin.

Gooding, M. (ed.) (1991) *Surrealist Games*, London: Redstone Press.

Gorz, A. (1993) 'Political Ecology: Expertocracy vs. Self-Limitation', *New Left Review* 202: 55– 68.

Gottdiener, M. (1985) *The Social Production of Space*, Austin: Texas University Press.

Gottdiener, M. (1996) 'Alienation, Everyday Life, and Postmodernism as Critical Theory', in F. Geyer (ed.), *Alienation, Ethnicity, and Postmodernism*, Westport CT and London: Greenwood Press.

Gouldner, A. (1975) 'Sociology and the Everyday Life', in L. A. Coser (ed.), *The Idea of Social Structure: Papers in Honor of Robert K. Merton*, New York: Harcourt Brace Jovanovich.

Gouldner, A. (1976) *The Dialectic of Ideology and Technology*, Oxford: Oxford University Press.

Gramsci, A. (1971) *Selections from the Prison Notebooks*, Q. Hoare and G. Nowell-Smith (eds), New York: International Publishers.

Gransow, V. (1985) 'Agnes Heller', in R. A. Gorman (ed.), *Biographical Dictionary of Neo-Marxism*, London: Mansell Publishing Limited.

Gray, C. (ed.) (1974) *Leaving the Twentieth Century: Incomplete Works of the Situationist International*, London: Free Fall Press.

Grumley, J. (1993) 'Dissatisfied Society', *New German Critique* 58: 253–78.

Habermas, J. (1976) *Legitimation Crisis*, London: Heinemann.

Habermas, J. (1983, 1987) *The Theory of Communicative Action*, 2 vols, Boston: Beacon Press.

Haraway, D. (1995) 'Situated Knowledges: The Science Question in Feminism and the Privilege of Partial Perspective', in A. Feenberg and A. Hannay (eds), *Technology and the Politics of Knowledge*, Bloomington: Indiana University Press.

Harding, S. (1986) *The Science Question in Feminism*, Ithaca: Cornell University Press.

Harding, S. (1990) 'Feminism, Science, and the Anti-Enlightenment Critiques', in L. J. Nicholson (ed.), *Feminism/Postmodernism,* London: Routledge.

Harvey, D. (1983) *The Limits of Capital*, London: Macmillan.

Haug, W. F. (1986) *Critique of Commodity Aesthetics: Appearance, Sexuality and Advertising in Capitalist Society*, R. Bock (trans.), Cambridge: Polity Press.

Haug, W. F. (1987) *Commodity Aesthetics, Ideology and Culture*, New York: International General.

Heidegger, M. (1962) *Being and Time*, J. Macquarrie and E. Robinson (trans.), New York: Harper & Row.

Heidegger, M. (1977) 'The Question Concerning Technology', in D. F. Krell (ed.), *Heidegger: Basic Writings*, San Francisco: HarperCollins Publishers.

Hekman, S. (1997) 'Truth and Method: Standpoint Theory Revisited', *Signs* 22, 2: 341–65.

Heller, A. (1975) 'Towards a Sociology of Knowledge of Everyday Life', *Cultural Hermeneutics* 3: 7–18.

Heller, A. (1976) *The Theory of Need in Marx*, London: Alison and Busby.

Heller, A. (1977) 'On the New Adventures of the Dialectic', *Telos* 31: 134–42.

Heller, A. (1978) *Renaissance Man*, London: Routledge & Kegan Paul.

Heller, A. (1979) *A Theory of Feelings*, Assen: Van Gorcum.

Heller, A. (1982a) 'Habermas and Marxism', in J. Thompson and D. Held (eds), *Habermas: Critical Debates*, Cambridge MA: MIT Press.

Heller, A. (1982b) *A Theory of History*, London, Routledge & Kegan Paul.

Heller, A (ed.) (1983) *Lukács Revalued*, Oxford: Basil Blackwell.

Heller, A. (1984a) *Everyday Life*, London: Routledge & Kegan Paul.

Heller, A. (1984b) *A Radical Philosophy*, J. Wickham (trans.), Oxford: Basil Blackwell.

Heller, A. (1985a) *The Power of Shame: A Rational Perspective*, London: Routledge & Kegan Paul.

Heller, A. (1985b) 'Interview With Agnes Heller', *New Socialist*, 10, 3: 38–9.

Heller, A. (1986) 'The Sociology of Everyday Life', in U. Himmelstrand (ed.), *The Social Reproduction of Organization and Culture*, London: Sage.

Heller, A. (1987) 'Can Everyday Life Be Endangered?', *Philosophy and Social Criticism* 13, 2: 297–313.

Heller, A. (1988) 'What Is and What Is Not Practical Reason', *Philosophy and Social Criticism* 14, 3/4: 391–410.

Heller, A. (1990a) 'The Contingent Person and the Existential Choice', in M. Kelly (ed.), *Hermeneutics and Critical Theory in Ethics and Politics*, Cambridge MA: MIT Press.

Heller, A. (1990b) *Can Modernity Survive?*, Cambridge: Polity Press.

Heller, A. (1991) 'The Role of Interpretation in Modern Ethical Theory', *Philosophy and Social Criticism* 17, 2: 83–102.

Heller, A. (1993) *A Philosophy of History in Fragments*, Oxford: Basil Blackwell.

Heller, A. (1994) 'The Discourse Ethics of Habermas: Critique and Appraisal', in J. Bernstein (ed.), *The Frankfurt School: Critical Assessments Vol. IV*, London and New York: Routledge.

Heller, A. (1996) *An Ethics of Personality*, Oxford: Basil Blackwell.

Heller, A. and Fehér, F. (1986a) *Eastern Left, Western Left: Totalitarianism, Freedom and Democracy*, Cambridge: Polity Press.

Heller, A. and Fehér, F. (1986b) 'The Necessity and the Irreformability of Aesthetics', in A. Heller and F. Fehér (eds), *Reconstructing Aesthetics: Writings of the Budapest School*, Oxford: Basil Blackwell.

Heller, A. and Fehér, F. (1988) *The Post-Modern Political Condition*, New York: Columbia University Press.

Heller, A. and Fehér, F. (eds) (1991) *The Grandeur and Twilight of Radical Universalism*, New Brunswick: Transaction Publishers.

Hirsch, A. (1982) *The French Left: A History and Overview*, Montréal: Black Rose Books.

Hirschkop, K. (1986) 'Bakhtin, Discourse and Democracy', *New Left Review* 160: 92–113.

Hirschkop, K. (1990a) 'Heteroglossia and Civil Society: Bakhtin's Public Square and the Politics of Modernity', *Studies in the Literary Imagination* 2, 1: 65–75.

Hirschkop, K. (1990b) 'On Value and Responsibility', *Critical Studies* 2, 1/2: 13–27.

Holquist, M. (1990) *Dialogism: Bakhtin and His World*, London and New York: Routledge.

Holquist, M. (1993) 'Forward', in M. Bakhtin, *Toward a Philosophy of the Act*, Austin: University of Texas Press.

Home, S. (1988) *The Assault on Culture: Utopian Currents from Lettrisme to Class War*, London: Aporia and Unpopular Books.

Home, S. (ed.) (1996) *What is Situationism? A Reader*, Edinburgh: AK Press.

Hudson, W. (1982) *The Marxist Philosophy of Ernst Bloch*, London: Macmillan.

Huelsenbeck, R. (1970) 'Dada Manifesto of 1918', in K. Coutts-Smith (ed.), *Dada*, London: Studio Vista.

Huelsenbeck, R. (1971) 'Dada Forward', in L. R. Lippard (ed.), *Dadas on Art*, Englewood Cliffs: Prentice-Hall, Inc.

Ivanov, V. V. (1974) 'The Significance of M. M. Bakhtin's Ideas on Sign, Utterance, and Dialogue for Modern Semiotics', in H. Baran (ed.), *Semiotics and Structuralism: Readings from the Soviet Union*, White Plains: International Arts and Sciences Press, Inc.

Jacoby, R. (1981) *Dialectic of Defeat: Contours of Western Marxism*, Cambridge: Cambridge University Press.

Jameson, F. (1971) *Marxism and Form: Twentieth-Century Dialectical Theories of Literature*, Princeton: Princeton University Press.

Jameson, F. (ed.) (1977) *Aesthetics and Politics*, London: Verso.

Jappe, A. (1999) *Guy Debord*, Berkeley: University of California Press.

Jay, M. (1984) *Marxism and Totality: Adventures of a Concept*, Berkeley: University of California Press.

Jay, M. (1993) *Downcast Eyes: The Denigration of Vision in Twentieth-Century French Thought*, Berkeley: University of California Press.

Johnson, R. (1986/7) 'What is Cultural Studies Anyway?', *Social Text* 16: 38–80.

Kadarkay, A. (1991) *Georg Lukács: Life, Thought and Politics*, Oxford: Basil Blackwell.

Kaplan, A. and Ross, K. (1987) 'Introduction', *Yale French Studies* 73: 1–4.

Karp, D. and Yoels, W. (1986) *Sociology and Everyday Life*, Itasca IL: Peacock.

Katsiaficas, G. (1997) *The Subversion of Politics: European Autonomous Social Movements and the Decolonization of Everyday Life*, Atlantic Highlands: Humanities Press, Inc.

Keller, E. F. (1985) *Reflections on Gender and Science*, New Haven: Yale University Press.

Khayati, M. (1981) 'Captive Words: Preface to a Situationist Dictionary', in K. Knabb (ed.), *Situationist International Anthology,* Berkeley: Bureau of Public Secrets.

Kinser, S. (1992) 'Everyday Ordinary', *Diacritics* 22, 2: 70–82.

Knabb, K. (ed.) (1981) *Situationist International Anthology*, Berkeley: Bureau of Public Secrets.

Kofman, E. and Lebas, E. (1996) 'Lost in Transposition – Time, Space and the City', in L. Lefebvre, *Writings on Cities*, E. Kofman and E. Lebas (eds and trans.), Oxford: Blackwell.

Kosík, K. (1976) *Dialectics of the Concrete: A Study on Problems of Man and World*, Boston and Dordrecht: D. Reidel Publishing Company.

Kotányi, A. and Vaneigem, R. (1981) 'Elementary Program for the Bureau of Unitary Urbanism', in K. Knabb (ed.), *Situationist International Anthology*, Berkeley: Bureau of Public Secrets.

Kurzweil, E. (1980) *The Age of Structuralism: Lévi-Strauss to Foucault*, New York: Columbia University Press.

Lachmann, R. (1989) 'Bakhtin and Carnival: Culture as Counter-Culture', *Cultural Critique* 11: 115–52.

Lalli, P. (1989) 'The Imaginative Dimension of Everyday Life: Towards a Hermeneutic Reading', *Current Sociology* 37, 1: 103–14.

Langbauer, L. (1992) 'Cultural Studies and the Politics of the Everyday', *Diacritics* 22, 1: 47–65.

Larrain, J. (1983) *Marxism and Ideology*, London: Macmillan.

Lash, S. (1990) *Sociology of Postmodernism*, London and New York: Routledge.

Lee, M. J. (1993) *Consumer Culture Reborn: The Cultural Politics of Consumption*, London and New York: Routledge.

Lefebvre, H. (1955) *Rabelais*, Paris: Les Editeurs françois réunis.

Lefebvre, H. (1965) *Métaphilosophie*, Paris: Editions de Minuit.

Lefebvre, H. (1968a) *Dialectical Materialism*, J. Sturrock (trans.), London: Jonathan Cape Ltd.

Lefebvre, H. (1968b) *The Sociology of Marx*, New York: Vintage Books.

Lefebvre, H. (1969) *The Explosion: Marxism and the French Revolution*, A. Ehrenfeld (trans.), New York and London: Monthly Review Press.

Lefebvre, H. (1976) *The Survival of Capitalism: Reproduction of Relations of Production*, F. Bryant (trans.), London: Allison and Busby.

Lefebvre, H. (1984) *Everyday Life in the Modern World*, S. Rabinovitch (trans.), New Brunswick: Transaction Publishers.

Lefebvre, H. (1987) 'The Everyday and Everydayness', *Yale French Studies* 73: 7–11.

Lefebvre, H. (1988) 'Toward a Leftist Cultural Politics: Remarks Occasioned by the Centenary of Marx's Death', in C. Nelson and L. Grossberg (eds), *Marxism and the Interpretation of Culture*, London: Macmillan.

Lefebvre, H. (1991a) *Critique of Everyday Life: Volume I, Introduction*, J. Moore (trans.), London: Verso.

Lefebvre, H. (1991b) *The Production of Space*, D. Nicholson-Smith (trans.), Oxford: Basil Blackwell.

Lefebvre, H. (1995) *Introduction to Modernity*, J. Moore (trans.), London: Verso.

Lefebvre, H. (1996) *Writings on Cities*, E. Kofman and E. Lebas (eds and trans.), Oxford: Blackwell.

Leiss, W. (1972) *The Domination of Nature*, Boston: Beacon Press.

Leiss, W. (1978) *The Limits to Satisfaction: An Essay on the Problem of Needs and Commodities*, Toronto: University of Toronto Press.

Levin, D. M. (ed.) (1995) *Modernity and the Hegemony of Vision*, Berkeley: University of California Press.

Levinas, E. (1994) *Outside the Subject*, Stanford: Stanford University Press.

Levitas, R. (1993) 'The Future of Thinking About the Future', in J. Bird *et al.* (eds), *Mapping Futures*, London and New York: Routledge.

Levitas, R. (1997) 'Educated Hope: Ernst Bloch on Abstract and Concrete Utopia', in J. O. Daniel and T. Moylan (eds), *Not Yet: Reconsidering Ernst Bloch*, London: Verso.

Lewis, H. (1990) *Dada Turns Red: The Politics of Surrealism*, Edinburgh: Edinburgh University Press.

Longino, H. E. (1993) 'Feminist Standpoint Theory and the Problems of Knowledge', *Signs* 19, 1: 201–12.

Lukács, G. (1971) *History and Class Consciousness: Studies in Marxist Dialectics*, R. Livingstone (trans.), Cambridge MA: MIT Press.

Lunn, E. (1982) *Marxism and Modernism: An Historical Study of Lukács, Brecht, Benjamin, and Adorno*, Berkeley: University of California Press.

Lyotard, J. F. (1984) *The Postmodern Condition: A Report on Knowledge*, G. Bennington and B. Massumi (trans.), Minneapolis: University of Minnesota Press.

McChesney, R.W. (1996) 'Is There Any Hope For Cultural Studies?', *Monthly Review* 47, 10: 1– 18.

McRobbie, A. (1991) 'Moving Cultural Studies On: Post-Marxism and Beyond', *Magazine of Cultural Studies* 4: 18–21.

Maffesoli, M. (1989) 'The Sociology of Everyday Life (Epistemological Elements)', *Current Sociology* 37, 1: 1–16.

Maffesoli, M. (1990) 'Post-Modern Sociality', *Telos* 85: 89–92.

Maffesoli, M. (1993) *The Shadow of Dionysus: A Contribution to the Sociology of the Orgy*, Albany: State University of New York Press.

Maffesoli, M. (1996) *The Time of the Tribes: The Decline of Individualism in Mass Society*, London: Sage.

Mandelker, A. (ed.) (1995) *Bakhtin in Contexts: Across the Disciplines*, Evanston: Northwestern University Press.

Manuel, F. E. (1965) *The Prophets of Paris*, New York: Harper Torchbooks.

Marcus, G. (1989) *Lipstick Traces: A Secret History of the Twentieth Century*, London: Secker and Warburg.

Marcuse, H. (1955) *Eros and Civilization: A Philosophical Inquiry into Freud*, Boston: Beacon Press.

Marcuse, H. (1964) *One-Dimensional Man: Studies in the Ideology of Advanced Industrial Society*, Boston: Beacon Press.

Marcuse, H. (1965) 'Repressive Tolerance', in H. Marcuse, R. P. Wolff and B. Moore, Jr., *A Critique of Pure Tolerance*, Boston: Beacon Press.

Marcuse, H. (1968) *Negations: Essays in Critical Theory*, J. Shapiro (trans.), Harmondsworth: Penguin.

Márkus, G. (1978) *Marxism and Anthropology*, Assen: Van Gorcum.

Mathy, J-P. (1993) *Extrême-Occident: French Intellectuals and America*, Chicago: Chicago University Press.

May, T. (1996) *Situating Social Theory*, Buckingham: Open University Press.

Melucci, A. (1989) *Nomads of the Present: Social Movements and Individual Needs in Contemporary Society*, London: Hutchinson Ltd.

Morris, M. (1988) 'Banality in Cultural Studies', *Discourse* 10, 2: 3–29.

Morson, G. S. (1988) 'Prosaics: An Approach to the Humanities', *American Scholar* Autumn: 515–28.

Morson, G. S. (1995) 'Prosaic Bakhtin: *Landmarks*, Anti-Intelligentsialism, and the Russian Countertradition', in A. Mandelker (ed.), *Bakhtin in Contexts: Across the Disciplines*, Evanston: Northwestern University Press.

Morson, G. S. and Emerson, C. (1989) 'Introduction: Rethinking Bakhtin', in G. S. Morson and C. Emerson (eds), *Rethinking Bakhtin: Extensions and Challenges*, Evanston: Northwestern University Press.

Morson, G. S. and Emerson, C. (1990) *Mikhail Bakhtin: Creation of a Prosaics*, Stanford: Stanford University Press.

Nadeau, M. (1973) *History of Surrealism*, R. Howard (trans.), Harmondsworth: Penguin.

Nemas, A. (1985) *Nietzsche: Life as Literature*, Cambridge MA: Harvard University Press.

Nielsen, G. (1995) 'Bakhtin and Habermas: Towards a Transcultural Ethics', *Theory and Society* 24, 6: 803–35.

Norris, C. (1990) *What's Wrong With Postmodernism: Critical Theory and the Ends of Philosophy*, Baltimore: Johns Hopkins University Press.

Norris, C. (1992) *Uncritical Theory: Postmodernism, Intellectuals and the Gulf War*, Amherst: University of Massachusetts Press.

O'Brien, M. (1989) *Reproducing the World*, San Francisco and London: Westview Press.

O'Neill, J. (1995) *The Poverty of Postmodernity,* London and New York: Routledge.

Oakley, A. (1981) *Subject Women*, Oxford: M. Robinson.

Outhwaite, W. (1975) *Understanding Social Life: The Method Called Verstehen*, London: George Allen and Unwin

Pêcheux, M. (1982) *Language, Semantics and Ideology: Stating the Obvious*, H. Nagpal (trans.), London: Macmillan.

Pechey, G. (1989) 'On the Borders of Bakhtin: Dialogisation, Decolonization', in K. Hirschkop and D. Shepherd (eds), *Bakhtin and Cultural Theory*, Manchester: Manchester University Press.

Pechey, G. (1993) 'Eternity and Modernity: Bakhtin and the Epistemological Sublime', *Theoria* 81, 82: 61–85.

Pierre, J. (ed.) (1992) *Investigating Sex: Surrealist Discussions 1928–1932*, M. Imre (trans.), London: Verso.

Plant, S. (1990) 'The Situationist International: A Case of Spectacular Neglect', *Radical Philosophy* 55: 3–10.

Plant, S. (1992) *The Most Radical Gesture: The Situationist International in the Postmodern Age*, London and New York: Routledge.

Polan, D. (1989) 'Bakhtin, Benjamin, Sartre: Toward a Typology of the Intellectual Critic', in C. Kelly, M. Makin, and D. Shepherd (eds), *Discontinuous Discourses in Modern Russian Literature*, London: Macmillan.

Pollner, M. (1991) 'Left of Ethnomethodology: The Rise and Fall of Radical Reflexivity', *American Sociological Review* 56: 370–80.

Poster, M. (ed.) (1971) *Harmonian Man: Selected Writings of Charles Fourier*, Garden City: Doubleday and Company, Inc.

Poster, M. (1975) *Existential Marxism in Postwar France: From Sartre to Althusser*, Princeton: Princeton University Press.

Poster, M. (1992) 'The Question of Agency: Michel de Certeau and the History of Consumerism', *Diacritics* 22, 2: 94–107.

Queroz, J. M. de (1989) 'The Sociology of Everyday Life as a Perspective', *Current Sociology* 37, 1: 31–9.

Richter, H. (1965) *Dada: Art and Anti-Art*, London: Thames and Hudson.

Ricoeur, P. (1981) *Hermeneutics and the Human Sciences*, J. B. Thompson (ed. and trans.), Cambridge: Cambridge University Press.

Ricoeur, P. (1985) 'The Text as Dynamic Entity', in M. Valdes and O. Miller (eds), *Identity of the Literary Text*, Toronto: University of Toronto Press.

Rigby, B. (1991) *Popular Culture in Modern France: A Study of Cultural Discourse*, London and New York: Routledge.

Rose, H. (1983) 'Hand, Brain and Heart: A Feminist Epistemology for the Natural Sciences', *Signs* 9, 1: 73–90.

Sacks, O. (1987) *The Man Who Mistook His Wife For a Hat and Other Clinical Tales*, New York: HarperCollins Publishers.

Sayre, R. and Löwy, M. (1984) 'Figures of Romantic Anti-Capitalism', *New German Critique* 32: 42–92.

Schirato, T. (1993) 'My Space or Yours?: De Certeau, Frow and the Meanings of Popular Culture', *Cultural Studies* 7, 2: 282–91.

Schütz, A. (1967) *The Phenomenology of the Social World*, G. Walsh and F. Lehnert (trans.), Evanston: Northwestern University Press.

Schmidt, A. (1972) 'Henri Lefebvre and Contemporary Interpretations of Marx', in D. Howard and K. E. Klare (eds), *The Unknown Dimension: European Marxism Since Lenin*, New York and London: Basic Books, Inc.

Scott, J. C. (1990) *Domination and the Arts of Resistance: Hidden Transcripts*, New Haven and London: Yale University Press.

Seidman, S. (1983) *Liberalism and the Origins of Modern Social Theory*, Berkeley: University of California Press.

Seidman, S. (1994) *Contested Knowledge: Social Theory in the Postmodern Era*, Oxford: Basil Blackwell.

Sheppard, R. W. (1979) 'Dada and Politics', *Journal of European Studies* 9: 39–74.

Shields, R. (1991) *Places on the Margin: Alternative Geographies of Modernity*, London and New York: Routledge.

Shields, R. (ed.) (1992) *Lifestyle Shopping: The Subject of Consumption*, London and New York: Routledge.

Shields, R. (1999) *Lefebvre, Love and Struggle: Spatial Dialectics*, London and New York: Routledge.

Shipway, M. (1987) 'Situationism', in M. Rubel and J. Crump (eds), *Non-Market Socialism in the Nineteenth and Twentieth Centuries*, London: Macmillan.

Short, R. S. (1966) 'The Politics of Surrealism, 1920–36', in W. Laqueur and G. L. Mosse (eds), *Left-Wing Intellectuals Between the Wars: 1919–1939*, New York: Harper Torchbooks.

Short, R. S. (1979) 'Paris Dada and Surrealism', *Journal of European Studies* 9: 75–98.

Simpson, L. C. (1995) *Technology, Time and the Conversations of Modernity*, London and New York: Routledge.

Situationist International (1981a) 'The Bad Days Will End', in K. Knabb (ed.), *Situationist International Anthology*, Berkeley: Bureau of Public Secrets.

Situationist International (1981b) 'Questionnaire', in K. Knabb (ed.), *Situationist International Anthology*, Berkeley: Bureau of Public Secrets.

Situationist International (1981c) 'Definitions', in K. Knabb (ed.), *Situationist International Anthology*, Berkeley: Bureau of Public Secrets.

Situationist International (1981d) 'Theory of the Dérive', in K. Knabb (ed.), *Situationist International Anthology*, Berkeley: Bureau of Public Secrets.

Situationist International (1981e) 'Instructions for Taking Up Arms', in K. Knabb (ed.), *Situationist International Anthology*, Berkeley: Bureau of Public Secrets.

Situationist International (1981f) 'The Decline and Fall of the Spectacle-Commodity Economy', in K. Knabb (ed.), *Situationist International Anthology*, Berkeley: Bureau of Public Secrets.

Sloterdijk, P. (1984) 'Cynicism: The Twilight of False Consciousness', *New German Critique* 33: 190–206.

Smith, D. E. (1974) 'The Ideological Practices of Sociology', *Catalyst* 8: 39–54.

Smith, D. E. (1979) 'A Sociology For Women', in J. A. Sherman and E. T. Beck (eds), *The Prism of Sex: Essays in the Sociology of Knowledge*, Madison: University of Wisconsin Press.

Smith, D. E. (1981) 'On Sociological Description: A Method from Marx', *Human Studies* 4: 313–37.

Smith, D. E. (1987) *The Everyday World as Problematic*, Milton Keynes: Open University Press.

Smith, D. E. (1989) 'Feminist Reflections on Political Economy', *Studies in Political Economy* 30: 37–59.

Smith, D. E. (1990a) *Texts, Facts, and Femininity: Exploring the Relations of Ruling*, London and New York: Routledge.

Smith, D. E. (1990b) *The Conceptual Practices of Power: A Feminist Sociology of Knowledge*, Toronto: University of Toronto Press.

Smith, D. E. (1992) 'Remaking a Life, Remaking Sociology: Reflections of a Feminist', in W. K. Carroll, L. Christiansen-Ruffman, R. F. Currie and D. Harrison (eds), *Fragile Truths: Twenty-Five Years of Sociology and Anthropology in Canada*, Ottawa: Carleton University Press.

Smith, D. E. (1993) 'High Noon in Textland: A Critique of Clough', *Sociological Quarterly* 34, 1: 183–92.

Smith, D. E. (1994) 'A Berkeley Education', in K. P. Meadows-Orlans and R. A. Wallace (eds), *Gender and the Academic Experience: Berkeley Women 1952–1972*, Lincoln: University of Nebraska Press.

Smith, D. E. (1996a) Personal e-mail correspondence.

Smith, D. E. (1996b) 'Telling the Truth After Postmodernism', *Symbolic Interaction* 19, 3: 171– 202.

Smith, D. E. (1997) 'Comment on Hekman's "Truth and Method: Standpoint Feminism Revisited"', *Signs* 22, 2: 392–402.

Smith, D. E. (1998) 'Bakhtin and the Dialogic of Sociology: An Investigation', in M. M. Bell and M. Gardiner (eds), *Bakhtin and the Human Sciences: No Last Words*, London: Sage.

Smith, D. E. (1999) *Writing the Social: Critique, Theory and Investigations*, Toronto: University of Toronto Press.

Sohn-Rethel, A. (1978) *Intellectual and Manual Labour: A Critique of Epistemology*, M. Sohn-Rethel (trans.), London: Macmillan.

Soja, E. W. (1989) *Postmodern Geographies: The Reassertion of Space in Social Theory*, London: Verso.

Soper, K. (1977) 'The Needs of Marxism', *Radical Philosophy* 15: 37–42.

Spivak, G. (1988) 'Can the Subaltern Speak?', in C. Nelson and L. Grossberg (eds), *Marxism and the Interpretation of Culture*, London: Macmillan.

Stallybrass, P. and White, A. (1986) *The Politics and Poetics of Transgression*, London: Methuen.

Stam, R. (1989) *Subversive Pleasures: Bakhtin, Cultural Criticism and Film*, Baltimore: Johns Hopkins University Press.

Sussman, E. (ed.) (1989) *On the Passage of a Few People Through a Rather Brief Moment in Time: The Situationist International 1957–1972*, Cambridge MA: MIT Press.

Swingewood, A. (1977) *The Myth of Mass Culture*, London: Macmillan.

Swingewood, A. (1991) *A Short History of Sociological Thought*, 2nd edn, London: Macmillan.

Terdiman, R. (1992) 'The Response of the Other', *Diacritics* 22, 2: 2–10.

Thompson, J. B. (1984) *Studies in the Theory of Ideology*, Cambridge: Polity Press.

Thornton, W. H. (1994) 'Cultural Prosaics as Counterdiscourse: A Direction for Cultural Studies After Bakhtin', *Prose Studies* 17, 2: 74–93.

Titunik, I. R. (1984) 'Bakhtin &/or Voloshinov &/or Medvedev: Dialogue &/or Doubletalk?', in B. Stolz *et al.* (eds), *Language and Literary Theory*, Ann Arbor: Michigan Slavic Publications.

Titunik, I. R. (1986) 'The Baxtin Problem: Concerning Katerina Clark and Michael Holquist's *Mikhail Bakhtin*', *Slavic and East European Journal* 30, 1: 91–5.

Todorov, T. (1984) *Mikhail Bakhtin: The Dialogical Principle*, Minneapolis: Minnesota University Press.

Toulmin, S. (1990) *Cosmopolis: The Hidden Agenda of Modernity*, Chicago: Chicago University Press.

Trebitsch, M. (1991a) 'Preface', in H. Lefebvre, *Critique of Everyday Life*, J. Moore (trans.), London: Verso.

Trebitsch, M. (1991b) 'Philosophy and Marxism in the 1930s: Henri Lefebvre's Marxist Critique', *Annals of Scholarship* 8, 1: 9–32.

Tzara, T. (1971) 'Dada Manifesto 1919', in L. R. Lippard (ed.), *Dadas on Art*, Englewood Cliffs: Prentice-Hall, Inc.

Vaneigem, R. (1981a) 'Basic Banalities II', in K. Knabb (ed.), *Situationist International Anthology*, Berkeley: Bureau of Public Secrets.

Vaneigem, R. (1981b) 'Basic Banalities', in K. Knabb (ed.), *Situationist International Anthology*, Berkeley: Bureau of Public Secrets.

Vaneigem, R. (1981c) 'All the King's Men', in K. Knabb (ed.), *Situationist International Anthology*, Berkeley: Bureau of Public Secrets.

Vaneigem, R. (1983) *The Revolution of Everyday Life*, D. Nicholson-Smith (trans.), no place: Left Bank Books and Rebel Press.

Vaneigem, R. (1985) *The Book of Pleasures*, J. Fullerton (trans.), London: Pending Press.

Viénet, R. (1992) *Enragés and Situationists in the Occupations Movement, France, May '68*, London and New York: Autonomedia and Rebel Press.

Voloshinov, V. N. (1973) *Marxism and the Philosophy of Language*, L. Matejka and I. R. Titunik (trans.), Cambridge MA: Harvard University Press.

Voloshinov, V. N. (1976) *Freudianism: A Marxist Critique*, N. Bruss and I. R. Tikunik (eds), I. R. Tikunik (trans.), New York and London: Academic Press.

Watier, P. (1989) 'Understanding and Everyday Life', *Current Sociology* 37, 1: 71–81.

Wall, A. and Thomson, C. (1993) 'Cleaning up Bakhtin's Carnival Act', *Diacritics* 23, 2: 47–70.

Warf, B. (1986) 'Ideology, Everyday Life and Emancipatory Phenomenology', *Antipode* 18, 3: 268–83.

Weber, M. (1976) *The Protestant Ethic and the Spirit of Capitalism*, London: Allen & Unwin.

Williams, R. (1977) *Marxism and Literature*, Oxford: Oxford University Press.

Williams, R. (1989) 'Culture is Ordinary', in R. Williams, *Resources of Hope*, London: Verso.

Wittgenstein, L. (1963) *Philosophical Investigations*, G. E. M. Anscombe (trans.), Oxford: Basil Blackwell.

Wolin, R. (1987) 'Agnes Heller on Everyday Life', *Theory and Society* 16: 295–304.

Wollen, P. (1989) 'The Situationist International', *New Left Review* 174: 67–95.

Yaeger, P. (1986) 'Emancipatory Discourse', *Contemporary Literature* 27, 2: 246–56.

Young, A. (1981) *Dada and After: Extremist Modernism and English Literature*, Manchester: Manchester University Press.

Zalava, I. R. (1988) 'Bakhtin Versus the Postmodern', *Sociocriticism* 4.2, 8: 51–69.

Zijderveld, A. (1982) *Reality in a Looking-Glass: Rationality Through an Analysis of Traditional Folly*, London: Routledge & Kegan Paul.

INDEX

Name Index

Adorno, T. 14, 77, 146, 214n
Adorno, T. and Horkheimer, M. 86, 89, 159–61, 167, 168
Agger, B. 15, 210n, 215n
Ahearne, J. 161
Althusser, L. 170, 210n, 218n
Appollinaire, G. 33
Aragon, L. 35, 38–9
Aronowitz, S. 63
Aristotle, 139, 148
Alquié, F. 34, 38, 39
Arp, H. 29, 31

Bachelard, G. 217
Bacon, F. 131
Bakhtin, M. 10, 20, 21, 22, 43–70, 92, 130, 175, 205
Barthes, R. 63
Bataille, G. 24, 159
Baudrillard, J. 84, 160, 169, 171
Bauman, Z. 94, 129–30, 179, 183, 184
Beauvoir, S. de 193
Beerbohm, M. 154
Benjamin, W. 35, 77, 160
Bentham, J. 165
Bergson, H. 36, 47
Bernard-Donals, M. 59–60, 64–5
Bernstein, M. A. 13
Blanchot, M. 1, 211n
Bloch, E. 19, 20, 145, 212n, 213n
Bourdieu, P. 7, 12, 89, 169–70, 193
Bowers, R. 58
Brecht, B. 156
Breton, A. 32–42, 82, 106, 214n
Buber, M. 43
Buffet, G. 29
Burke, P. 68–9

Burkitt, I. 202
Butler, J. 195

Callinicos, A. 9, 218n
Castoriadis, C. 106, 153
Certeau, M. de. 12, 16, 20, 21, 22, 157–79, 195, 210n, 217n, 218n
Chtcheglov, I. 104
Clark, K, and Holquist, M. 65
Crossley, N. 53

Debord, G. 22, 74, 104, 105, 106, 107, 108–14, 115, 116, 119, 121, 122, 123
Descartes, R. 48, 75, 123
Douglas, J. D. 210n
Durkheim, E. 143

Eco, U. 171
Elliot, T. S. 10

Featherstone, M. 10, 210n
Fehér, F. 128
Feuerbach, L. 110, 194
Fiske, J. 85
Foucault, M. 10, 11, 16, 42, 95, 115, 158, 165–8, 173–4, 179, 183, 185, 195, 212n
Fourier, C. 40, 81, 214n
Freud, S. 33, 35, 209n
Fukuyama, F. 215n

Gambacorta, C. 14, 15–16
Garfinkel, H. 4
Giddens, A. 5, 174
Godzich, W. 12, 52
Goethe, J. W. von 49

237

Subject Index